Robert S. McGee & Dale W. McCleskey

with Pat Springle and Susan Joiner

CONQUERING CHEMICAL DEPENDENCY

A CHRIST-CENTERED 12-STEP PROCESS

Learning Activities by Dale W. McCleskey

Robert S. McGee
Publishing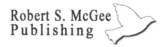

ACKNOWLEDGEMENTS

Overcoming Chemical Dependency: A Christ-Centered 12-Step Process was originally co-published by Word, Inc. and Rapha Resources, Inc. and is available in its original version in Christian bookstores. We want to thank Rapha Hospital Treatment Centers for making this book available to the LifeWay Press for its use.

Rapha is a manager of inpatient psychiatric care and substance-abuse treatment from a distinctively Christian perspective in hospitals located nationwide. For information about Rapha you may contact Rapha at 1-800-383-HOPE or write to Rapha, 12700 Featherwood, Houston, Texas 77034.

Conquering Chemical Dependency: A Christ-Centered 12-Step Process
Copyright © 1994 by Rapha Publishing
Fifth Printing August 2003

ISBN 0-8054-9983-0   Dewey Decimal Number 616.89
Subject Heading: Drug Addiction / / Drug Addicts – Rehabilitation

Sources for definitions in *Conquering Chemical Dependency: A Christ-Centered 12-Step Process:* By permission. From Merriam-*Webster's Collegiate Dictionary, Tenth Edition* ©1993 by Merriam-Webster Inc., publisher of the Merriam-Webster® dictionaries; *Vine's Expository Dictionary of Old and New Testament Words* (Fleming H. Revell Company, 1981); Craig Naaken, *The Addictive Personality: Understanding the Compulsion in Our Lives,* (Center City, MN: Hazelden Foundation, 1988).

Unless otherwise indicated, biblical quotations are from the *New American Standard Bible.* © The Lockman Foundation, 1960, 1962, 1963, 1968, 1971, 1972, 1973, 1975, 1977. Used by permission. Other versions used: From the Holy Bible, *New International Version,* copyright © 1973, 1978, 1984 by International Bible Society (NIV); the *King James Version* (KJV).

Printed in the United States of America

Robert S. McGee
Publishing

mcgeepublishing.com
800.460.4673

Table of Contents

The Journey Begins

INTRODUCTION

GOD CHANGED MY LIFE!

Today, Sheri experiences a freedom she once believed never would occur. She credits this freedom to Jesus Christ and the 12-Step recovery program. She feels freed because drugs no longer control her.

For years, Sheri struggled with depression. She discovered that when she was depressed, under stress, or feeling any strong emotion, alcohol and other drugs helped her to cope. At first the drugs seemed to help, but then Sheri began to lose control of her drug use. When she began to use, she could not stop. She felt shame about her loss of control, and the shame increased her "need" to use.

After being arrested for driving under the influence, Sheri attended a 12-Step group as part of her sentence. There she found people with stories just like her own. They told about the same feelings of defeat and shame, but they also told about something more. They said that by applying the teachings of Jesus Christ through the 12 Steps, they were overcoming their addictions. Jesus Christ was doing for them what they could not do for themselves. They assured Sheri that if she would honestly work the program, God would change her life.

Today, Sheri has a new life. God gave her this new life through His Son Jesus as she worked through the 12-Step program. She remains clean and sober one day at a time through the program, but she says avoiding these patterns is only a small part of her recovery. She says, "The important part is that working the program has taught me how to live. It has helped me to get to know and love God. Jesus Christ changed my life through the 12 Steps!"

What is chemical dependency? What causes it? In *Conquering Chemical Dependency: A Christ-Centered 12-Step Process* you will learn more about addiction to mood-altering substances about the causes of and the solution to chemical dependency.

If you suffer from addiction to one or more chemicals, the important issue is recovery—how to overcome the compulsion to drink or use. You can overcome through the power of God. A Christ-centered 12-Step program can help you to achieve a healthy and Christ-honoring life-style. In this process, you will discover the resources you need to experience these positive changes.

Wrong choices contribute to our addictions, but the complexity of chemical dependency demonstrates a fact for you to reinforce in your mind. You do not have an addiction because you are weak or because you are bad. Many of the most determined people in the world—people with enormous amounts of willpower—are chemically dependent. People who deeply love God and desire to live for Him struggle with addictions. Shame makes us feel that we are evil, wrong, or defective in a unique way—that we are worse than others. You cannot shame yourself into recovery. You are a person of infinite worth because God created you and because He loves you. You are not bad because you have an addiction. What you are is human.

In a 12-Step meeting you may hear someone say, "I am a grateful recovering _____ (alcoholic, addict, etc.)." At first you may be confused by that statement, or you may misunderstand. You may think the person is saying, "I am grateful because I am recovering and am no longer a _____." In time, however, you may understand that some of these individuals are saying, "I am grateful that I have this problem, because the problem has led me to this relationship with God."

What are the 12 Steps?

You will conquer your problem as you work the Christ-centered 12 Steps. The 12 Steps show us a means for effective living. Many of us are familiar with a booklet called *The Four Spiritual Laws*. The booklet is an effective means by which we can share Jesus Christ with people. The booklet helps us to understand key facts so we can begin a relationship with Christ. *The Four Spiritual Laws* booklet, by Bill Bright, presents basic theology. It organizes the information in the Bible in a practical way, so we can apply it to our lives. In a similar way the 12 Steps give us an organized plan to live life effectively. *The Four Spiritual Laws* is designed to introduce us to Jesus Christ, while the 12 Steps are designed to guide us in successful living through Jesus Christ.

Twelve-Step programs began with the establishment in the 1930s of the first program, Alcoholics Anonymous. Alcoholics Anonymous was adapted from a Christian revival organization known as the Oxford Group. The Twelve Steps were written in the laboratory of human experience as people sought God's solution for alcoholism, but they can apply to everyone.

Those of us who have come to know Jesus through *The Four Spiritual Laws* have a special respect for the little booklet. Those of us who have experienced deliverance from life-crushing problems through the 12 Steps have a similar respect for the 12-Step program. We respect the program because the Steps have led us, through Jesus Christ, to know, love, and obey God. As a reference you'll find the Twelve Steps of Alcoholics Anonymous on page 223 and our adaptation of them—the Christ-Centered 12 Steps—on page 224.

The purpose of this book is to help you begin and work the 12-Step process in your life. You will find *Conquering Chemical Dependency: A Christ-Centered 12-Step Process* is true to the proved 12-Step recovery tradition. Without apology we identify Jesus Christ as our Higher Power.

Definitions

If you are new to the 12-Step process, you will encounter some unfamiliar terms in this book. They are expressions people frequently use in 12-Step groups. Below we have given you an overview of some of these terms.

• **Recovery**—The entire process of healing from the painful effects of dysfunctional behavior is called recovery. In a larger sense everything in Christian ministry is recovery. You may think of it this way: God created us with a glorious purpose. Sin warped and twisted that purpose. Recovery is the process of restoring what sin has taken away.

Recovery is for everyone. For some of us it is specialized. For the chemically dependent person, recovery includes restoration of sobriety, but it goes

The Program:

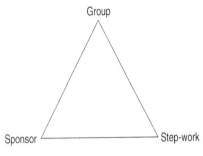

beyond abstinence from drinking or using. By sheer determination some people stop using. They become hard and brittle from the strain. The goal of recovery is to live a life of joyful obedience—to maintain abstinence because we want to, not because we have to. Recovery means developing the Christ-honoring lifestyle that meets the needs we tried to satisfy with chemicals.

- **The Program**—The term refers to the process of restoration that comes through working the 12 Steps. The program includes attending meetings, the sponsoring model of personal accountability and discipleship, and doing the written and verbal work to apply the Steps to our lives. The program applies the classical disciplines of the Christian faith to practical life situations.

- **Sponsor**—The 12-Step program uses the ancient biblical practice of apprenticeship for spiritual growth. Each person is encouraged to enlist a sponsor—someone who has progressed in the recovery process. The sponsor does not take care of, rescue, or fix the person he or she sponsors. The sponsor makes assignments and guides the newcomer to work the Steps.

- **Working the Steps** (or **"Step-work"**)—The goal of the program is to glorify God as we develop healthy, Christ-honoring behavior. God makes these changes in our lives as we work this discipleship program called the 12 Steps. Working the Steps is the entire process of learning and growing. The key parts of working the Steps include the relationship with a sponsor, attendance and sharing at meetings, and completing certain written work. *Conquering Chemical Dependency* is a workbook to help you work the Steps.

Distinctives

Conquering Chemical Dependency: A Christ-Centered 12-Step Process is distinct in at least three ways. It is Christ-centered. It is based on the biblical 12-Step process for life change. It is written in an interactive style we call "writing for life change." The information in this workbook is Christ-centered. We recognize that the life-threatening problem of addiction is, in part, the result of damaged relationships. The ultimate solution includes relationships. We need healthy relationships with God and with each other. Only in Jesus Christ do we find the forgiveness and grace to achieve those healing relationships. As you study *Conquering Chemical Dependency: A Christ-Centered 12-Step Process* and as you participate in a 12-Step support group, you will have opportunities to establish and deepen your relationship with God and with others.

The purpose of this book is to help you begin and work the 12-Step process in your life. The writers have many years' experience in recovery and with the 12 Steps. You will find *Conquering Chemical Dependency: A Christ-Centered 12-Step Process* is true to the proved 12-Step recovery tradition. Without apology we identify Jesus Christ as our Higher Power. *Conquering Chemical Dependency: A Christ-Centered 12-Step Process* is not merely designed for you to understand concepts. The purpose of this material is life change through Jesus Christ.

Conquering Chemical Dependency is an integrated course of study. To achieve the full benefit of the educational design, complete your written work in the book, share it with your sponsor, and participate in the group sessions. This is not a course which you will study and then forget. It represents an opportunity to understand and change basic areas which have generated pain in your life.

Study Tips. This book is written as a tutorial text. Study it as if Robert S. McGee or Dale W. McCleskey is sitting at your side helping you learn. When the book asks you a question or gives you an assignment, you will benefit most by writing your response. Each assignment is indented and appears in **boldface type**. When you are to respond in writing, a pencil appears beside the assignment. For example, an assignment will look like this:

✎ **Read Psalm 139:13. Write what the verse tells about God's care for you.**

Of course, in an actual activity, a line would appear below each assignment or in the margin beside the assignment. You would write your response as indicated. Then, when we ask you to respond in a non-written fashion—for example, by thinking about or praying about a matter—a ➤ appears beside the assignment. This type of assignment will look like this:

➤ **Pause now to pray and thank God for accepting you unconditionally.**

In most cases your "personal tutor" will give you some feedback about your response—for example, you may see a suggestion about what you might have written. This process is designed to help you learn the material and apply the concepts more effectively. Do not deny yourself valuable learning by skipping the learning activities.

Set a definite time and select a quiet place where you can study with little interruption. Keep a Bible handy for times in which the material asks you to look up Scripture. Memorizing Scripture is an important part of your work. Set aside a portion of your study period for memory work. Make notes of problems, questions, or concerns that arise as you study. You will discuss many of these with your sponsor or during your 12-Step meetings. Write these matters in the margins of this textbook so you can find them easily.

Your 12-Step support group will add a needed dimension to your learning. If you have started a study of *Conquering Chemical Dependency* and you are not involved in a group, try to enlist some friends or associates who will work through this material with you. Approach your church leaders about beginning such a group. *Conquering Chemical Dependency: A Christ-Centered 12-Step Process Facilitator's Guide* provides guidance in how to begin a Christ-centered 12-Step group. It is available for free download at www.lifeway.com/discipleplus/download.htm.

A key decision

Conquering Chemical Dependency: A Christ-Centered 12-Step Process is written with the assumption that you already have received Jesus Christ as your Savior and Lord and that you have Him guiding you in the healing process. If you have not yet made the important decision to receive Christ, you will find guidance for how to do so in Step 3. You will benefit far more from *Conquering Chemical Dependency: A Christ-Centered 12-Step Process* if you have Jesus working in your life and guiding you in the process.

STEP 1

We admit powerlessness.

Admitting My Powerlessness

A ROMANCE BEGINS

As Al entered the eighth grade, others would have described him as a reasonably successful and well-adjusted young man. He was an A student with a few B's, and he was a second-string athlete with an average number of friends. On the inside was a different story. Al was afraid of girls, though they probably never would have guessed. His self-esteem was completely based on performance, and he felt that his performance was dreadful. He tried to keep up a tough-guy front, but inside was a lonely, scared little boy who didn't know how to ask for help or know who to ask even if he had known how.

Al had heard the boasts of his friends. Some of them stole beer from their parents, camped out to drink it, and bragged about their actions. Al's best friend had an older brother who bought liquor for minors. One September evening this friend produced a bottle of vodka. Al arranged to spend the night at the friend's house. The friend's mother was a prescription drug-addict. She would be stoned, so the boys could do anything they wanted.

As they spent the evening drinking that bottle of liquor, something amazing happened. The loneliness ceased to matter. Al's inferiority melted away. He actually phoned a girl he liked. For the first time Al felt that he belonged in the world. From that night he knew that his newfound romance would be something special. It wasn't a romance with a person, however; it was a romance with alcohol. (Read more about Al's story on page 10.)

Step 1   *We admit that by ourselves we are powerless over chemical substances—that our lives have become unmanageable.*

Memory verse   *There is a way that seems right to a man, but its end is the way of death.*
                                                –Proverbs 14:12

Overview for Step 1

Lesson 1: Where Did It Begin?
         Goal: You will learn about the addiction process and begin to evaluate the effects of addiction in your life.

Lesson 2: Stages of Addiction
         Goal: You will identify the progress of chemical dependency in your life.

Lesson 3: Powerlessness
         Goal: You will describe your chemical use.

Lesson 4: Unmanageability
         Goal: You will examine your life for signs of unmanageability.

Lesson 5: Reality
         Goal: You will describe a process for confronting denial and for accepting realty.

Where Did It Begin?

We admit that by ourselves we are powerless over chemical substances—that our lives have become unmanageable.

There is a way that seems right to a man, but its end is the way of death.
Proverbs 14:12

Key Concept:
Addiction is cunning, baffling, and powerful.

mood altering–adj. chemical substances that give a "high" include inhalants, stimulants, depressants (including alcohol) and hallucinogens. Some drugs like marijuana share characteristics of stimulants, depressants, and/or hallucinogens.

Other drugs such as caffeine and nicotine are extremely addictive, but they are only mildly mood altering—they do not produce the effects of intoxication. This study primarily concerns the mood-altering substances which produce intoxication.

No one, in charting the course of his or her future, makes plans to become chemically dependent. Addiction usually is the last thing on the person's mind when he or she takes that first drink or experiences a first high. Instead people are thinking about having peers accept them or about the glamour and excitement they believe the drinking or using will bring.

> Note: This guide to the 12 Steps is concerned with all **mood-altering** chemicals, the most common of which is alcohol. Since alcohol is a drug and to avoid repetition, we use the terms *drug* or *using* to refer either to using alcohol or any other drug.

Read the following paragraph which describes the progress of addiction. Circle each word or phrase that describes something you have experienced or that describes a reason you continue using.

When we become hooked, the benefits we gained from our early drug use begin to fade as the years pass. Even though the early rewards are gone, our drug of choice becomes a reward for diligent work, a remedy for anger, a means of controlling other people, a boost for our energy level, an escape from pain—even when it is the cause of the pain, a substitute for companionship, a self-prescribed treatment for depression. The habit becomes a need. As the need grows, our lives begin to crumble. The drug of choice no longer will bring a sense of freedom. Instead a sense of bondage, isolation, anxiety, fear, and shame grows. We may experience broken relationships, the loss of a job, financial failure, declining health, and deteriorating self-esteem. Sadly, we may be the last to see our addiction. Without help we probably will die.

Did you circle a word or two? Three or four? Did you identify with several actions and feelings?

More of Al's story

As you began this unit, you read about Al. To continue with his story, we find him in the gas station where he works. Someone has left a pamphlet in the gas station office. In the pamphlet was a checklist. Al casually read the list and checked the appropriate boxes.

Check the box beside each statement which describes your experience.

My drug use doesn't make me feel as good as it used to.
When I have been working dilligently, I reward myself with my drug.
I sometimes use because I am angry.
I sometimes use to cope with difficult people.
I sometimes use as a "pick-me-up"—to boost my energy level.

I sometimes use to escape pain.
I sometimes use because I am lonely.
I sometimes use because I am depressed.
I sometimes experience blackouts—periods of memory loss.
I sometimes feel that I need to use.
I sometimes feel that my life is crumbling.
I feel guilty for using.
I have broken relationships because of my drug use.
I think my self-esteem is lower now than it was when I began to use.
My using has contributed to my loss of a job.
My using is affecting my health negatively.
I have tried to quit and then began using again.
I sometimes feel shame because I can't quit.
It takes more of the substance to give me a high than it used to.
It takes less of the substance to "wipe me out" than it used to.

How many of the items did you check?_____

The checklist Al completed looked a lot like the exercise you just worked. He checked 13 of 20 items. When he got to the bottom of the pamphlet, he read, "If you checked two or more, you probably have a problem." Then the pamphlet said that if a person checked four or more of the statements, he or she probably is an alcoholic. Reading that simple checklist started the process of breaking down Al's **denial**.

denial–n. all the false beliefs and excuses our addictions hide behind. Like a living thing an addiction will fight to stay alive. Its first line of defense is to remain hidden, so it constructs powerful arguments for why we are not really addicted.

Evaluating the Checklist

Don't assume that you do not have a problem if you left blank several or most of the items in the checklist. Some of the statements indicate that a person is in a very late stage of addiction. Since various chemicals have different effects on the central nervous system, not all the items on the checklist can apply to any one person. In fact, if you checked several of them, you are in extreme danger. If you checked even a couple of boxes, we would urge you to consider your situation. You may need at least to investigate the option of professional help. Many facilities and counselors will assist you with a free evaluation.

The last two statements on the checklist are particularly important. As addiction progresses, we develop tissue tolerance. That means we require more of the substance to get us drunk or high.

Can you drink or use more without showing the effect of it than you originally could?   Yes   No

Then as the addiction damages the organs of our bodies, the process reverses. We require less of the substance to get us high than what we required earlier in our using history.

Do you get high on less of the substance than you once did?
Yes   No

If you answered no to both of these questions, this does not mean you don't have a problem. Remember that various substances or combinations of substances differently affect the body. If, however, you answered yes to either, especially the last question, your condition is very, very serious. Dr. E.M.

If you are reading this book out of concern for someone you care about who has a drug problem, we suggest you also consider studying *Conquering Codependency: A Christ-Centered 12-Step Process* (see description on page 219)

Jellinek, a pioneer in addiction studies, described the progress of alcoholism. The following chart shows how the addictive process grows and changes.[1]

Read and examine carefully the following chart. Draw a line on the curve to show how far your addiction has progressed.

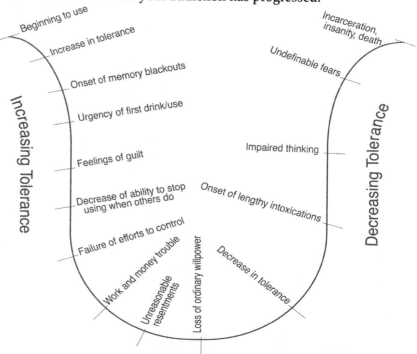

The chart shows the progressive nature of addiction. The addiction moves on toward loss of our finances, family, health, and dignity. If we do not stop the process, it results in loss of everything we hold dear, and finally it results in death. Beware, however, of one thing. Chemical substances can kill at any spot on the chart. The chart shows the progress toward a certain, painful, and degrading death. But sports stars—in excellent health—have died suddenly due to drug overdose. Healthy college students have died of alcohol toxicity—they simply were poisoned by consuming too much alcohol in too short a time. Friends have died in accidents. All these remind us that drug use can bring death anywhere on the curve.

The Progressive Nature of Addiction

The chart implies that once we have developed a problem with our pattern of drinking or using, we cannot return to being a "social user." The progression of the addiction is in part a matter of damage to the organs of the body. The body has normal restorative powers. However, the psychological effects and some of the physiological effects of drug use may not be reversible. This means that once substance use has become an addiction, we never can go back to using normally or drinking socially. In fact the very opposite is true. The body continues to age so with the passage of time—even time without drug use—we become less able to tolerate the chemical.

A story in the "Big Book," *Alcoholics Anonymous*, illustrates this principle. "A man of 30 was doing a great deal of spree drinking. He was very nervous in the morning after these bouts and quieted himself with more liquor. He was ambitious to succeed in business but saw that he would get nowhere if he

Once substance use has become an addiction, we never can go back to using normally or drinking socially.

drank at all. Once he started, he had no control whatever. He made up his mind that until he had been successful in business and had retired, he would not touch another drop. An exceptional man, he remained bone dry for 25 years and retired at the age of 55, after a successful and happy career. Then he fell victim to a belief which practically every alcoholic has—that his long period of sobriety and self-discipline had qualified him to drink as other men. Out came his carpet slippers and a bottle. In two months he was in a hospital, puzzled and humiliated." This man, with all his willpower, was dead within four years.[2]

Write a statement of the what the story you just read means to you.

_____

_____

You may have written something like the following. This man had stopped drinking for 25 years. In those 25 years his pancreas, liver, and other bodily organs continued to age. Thus when he began to drink again, he had not returned to an earlier stage on the chart. His body had aged so that he was more susceptible to the damaging effects of alcohol. This story has helped many of us to avoid the first drink on more than a single occasion. It reminds us that though we may have been sober for many years, our bodies would react even more strongly to the substance than they did when we last drank or used.

> ### Key Concept for Lesson 1
> Addiction is cunning, baffling, and powerful.

Pray and ask God how this concept can apply in your life. Now please review this lesson. What has God shown you that can help you?

_____

_____

Write Proverbs 14:12, this Step's memory verse, three times in the margin. Begin to memorize it.

<table>
<tr><td>

LESSON
2

Key Concept:
Addiction progressively takes over my life.

</td><td>

The Stages of Addiction

We admit that by ourselves we are powerless over chemical substances—that our lives have become unmanageable.

For that which I am doing, I do not understand; for I am not practicing what I would like to do, but I am doing the very thing I hate.

Why do people become chemically dependent? No one really is sure. What we know is that besides a complex interaction of cultural, environmental, and biological factors, the body of an addict cannot process alcohol or drugs

</td></tr>
</table>

normally. Some drugs like crack are 100 percent addictive. The presence of the chemical substance alters the cells of the nervous system. This results in a craving for the substance and withdrawal symptoms when it is taken away.[3]

Researchers estimate that one in every 10 persons becomes chemically dependent and that these people cannot stop drinking or using by themselves. While it does occur, it generally is a myth that the addict will have enough insight to see his or her condition and seek treatment for the problem.[4] The idea that addiction favors those on skid row also is a myth. In actuality, only five percent of those who are chemically dependent live on skid row.[5]

Addiction is very commonplace in society and can happen to people just like us, regardless of our reputation, social standing, or religious beliefs.

If you are chemically dependent, you are not alone. Some of the world's strongest leaders—in their country, community, or business—have been where you are now. Their problems weren't solved in a day, a week, or even a year. They have made great progress in their lives because they've had an opportunity to work a 12-Step program. Our work in recovery is not just deliverance from alcohol or drugs. Our work is deliverance from unhealthy patterns of behavior we learned both before and after we started drinking or using.

Reread the last sentence and compare it to the slogan printed in the margin. Write below what you think the slogan in the margin means.

A slogan overheard at a meeting: "I don't have a drinking problem; I have a living problem."

_____

_____

The challenge in living clean and sober is not just to stop using. The challenge is to live life effectively. The 12 Steps do not just help us stop using. Following the principles in the Steps can make life worthwhile. We can arrive at the place that we are glad to be who we are—glad to be alive. *Conquering Chemical Dependency: A Christ-Centered 12-Step Process* is designed to help you to change life patterns and to complement the original 12 Steps of Alcoholics Anonymous, which were derived from a Christian organization called the Oxford Group. The questions and studies will help you understand why we think and act as we do. Based on our experience with others, we are convinced that a deep application of biblical truth over a period of time can bring profound and lasting change to your life. For this reason, we refer to the 12 Steps as steps of progress. Progress—not perfection—is our goal in recovery.

Feelings and Addiction

Our feelings or moods play a part in the way addiction develops. Everyone has a range of emotions. Sometimes we feel up. Sometimes we feel depressed. But seldom do we feel wildly, deliriously happy or terribly, suicidally depressed. We can picture our normal range of mood as follows[6]:

We all have a range of mood that constitutes our normal. Our feelings vary within that normal range. One person normally may feel good—happy about life, with positive feelings of self-worth. Another person may feel generally unhappy, possibly with feelings of low self-esteem. These two individuals have different "normals," as the drawing below shows.

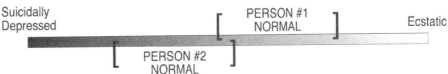

If both people drink or use, something very different may happen. The mood-altering chemical changes the brain chemistry of the user. As the chemical takes effect, people who feel good actually may dislike the feeling. They begin to feel "out of control." The feeling is uncomfortable for them, and they say things like, "No thanks, I've had enough." They may choose not to drink or use again. On the other hand, people who feel depressed experience a different reaction. As the chemical takes effect, they feel a relief from the depression. They may describe the feeling as "wonderful." Their reaction looks like this:

Depression and addiction

If our normal range of mood tends toward depression, we have an added risk for addiction.

> **On the line below draw brackets indicating your "normal" range of emotion before you began to use chemicals.**

> **Which of the following better describes your first experience or few experiences with chemicals?**
>
> I'm most like the person described above who normally felt positive, who tried chemicals and disliked the feeling of losing control.
> I'm most like the person who normally felt lonely or inadequate and for whom drug use produced a feeling of relief—a "high."

All addictive substances create a problem for those of us who experience relief from depression. We get "high" and feel better or even euphoric, but then our mood swings back, past our starting point—toward depression. The result looks like this.

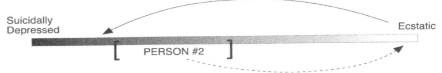

The increased depression that the drug use causes strongly motivates us to return to the chemical.

If we discontinue using chemicals, our mood returns to normal after a period of time. However, having experienced the mood enhancement, we often continue the activity. The increased depression that the drug use causes, combined with our memories of how good we felt while high, strongly motivates us to return to the chemical.

insidious adj. harmful but enticing, awaiting a chance to entrap (Webster's)

Chemicals are—
cunning
baffling
powerful

With time and increased drug use our mood swings increase, with an added **insidious** factor. Our normal moves to the left—toward depression. We gradually become more depressed until we find ourselves drinking or using in an attempt to feel as good as we once felt on a bad day. The picture now looks like this.

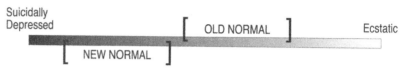

Our using no longer makes us feel great as it once did. Now we use to relieve the depression and to feel normal.

On the scale below draw the change in your normal mood brought about by chemicals. Draw brackets representing your old normal. Then draw brackets representing your normal now or when you actively were using.

Suicidally
Depressed   Ecstatic

The picture you just drew may help you see the progress of your addiction. Al wrote of his alcoholism, "At first I drank to feel good. Then I drank to keep from feeling bad. Then I drank to feel as good as I used to feel when I felt bad. This is crazy!"

The Stages of Addiction

addiction–n. a pathological love and trust relationship with an object or event (*Naaken*)

In his book *The Addictive Personality*, author Craig Naaken defined **addiction** in terms of a relationship. An addiction is like a romance. His definition appears in the margin. Consider the fact that an addiction is a relationship.[1]

More of Al's story

When Al used alcohol that first time, it did something for him that seemed wonderful. From the very first time that he used, he was developing a love and trust relationship with a chemical substance. He had begun an addiction—in the form of a relationship with a clear, liquid drug.

Relationships go through predictable stages. In the same way, addictions follow a predictable cycle which generally includes four stages. The stages are experimenting and learning, seeking, obsessing, and consuming.

Read the descriptions that follow of the four stages of addiction. As you read, check each circumstance that you have experienced in your drinking or using career.

Stage One: Experimenting and Learning
At this stage the user—

    receives encouragement from peers, counselor, dental, or medical practitioner to try alcohol or other drugs.

    personally desires to be accepted and/or to escape, modify, or avoid pain—emotional and/or physical pain.

    typically uses "light stuff" (alcohol or marijuana), though occasionally may use hard drugs.

euphoric-adj. describes a feeling of well-being or elation (Webster's). We often try to recapture the original feeling which our drug of choice gave us.

OLD CHINESE

PROVERB—

THE MAN TAKES

A DRINK,

THE DRINK TAKES

A DRINK,

THE DRINK TAKES

THE MAN

distortion of attention–n. just as people in love cannot keep their minds from returning to their loved one, as our affair with our drug of choice progresses we find ourselves thinking about using even when we are not using.

ritualization–n. pattern of use becomes like a ceremony, or a religious ritual.

experiences **euphoric** effects of alcohol or other drugs and usually suffers few consequences for using or drinking behavior.
learns to trust the chemical substance and its effects and learns that the amount of intake controls those effects.

How many of these circumstances have you experienced?_____

First-stage users have begun the romance with the substance, learned that the effects are desirable, and learned to control the effects to achieve desired results.

Stage Two: Seeking
Having learned that chemicals will produce "good" feelings, the user—
uses socially.
establishes limits for using ("Two drinks are my limit." "I only take my medication as directed." "I never take a drink until after my kids are in bed and the day's responsibilities are over.")
may use to excess occasionally and may experience hangovers, blackouts, or other physical manifestations of overdoing.
usually can continue to control the amount he or she uses.
may experience disruption in regular work or school activities as a result of using.
generally feels no emotional pain when choosing to drink or use.

How many of these circumstances have you experienced?_____

Stage Three: Obsessing
Alcohol or other drugs become important. In this stage, the user—
becomes preoccupied with getting "high." This is called **distortion of attention**.
begins to experience periodic loss of control over use.
breaks self-imposed rules about substance use established in stage two and increases times and quantities of use.
loses sense of self-worth and instead begins to feel guilt and shame for behaviors when high.
projects self-hatred onto others as using adversely affects health, emotional stability, relationships, and fellowship with God.
develops **ritualization**—a compulsive approach to using.
begins to rationalize, to justify, or to minimize negative feelings about himself or herself.

How many of these circumstances have you experienced?_____

Describe how you have experienced one or more of these results. For example, you might write, "I would make promises that I would use only on the weekend. Then I would find myself on Tuesday searching for a source to buy something."

_____

_____

_____

Stage Four: Consuming

The substance "has" the user, and now he or she—

must use just to feel "normal."

believes other people and circumstances—never self—are the root of his or her problems.

may entertain thoughts of additional escape possibilities such as suicide, leaving his or her family, or moving to another town (some people call this a geographic cure).

experiences deteriorating physical as well as mental, spiritual, and emotional health.

feels guilt, shame, remorse, anxiety, paranoia.

experiences withdrawal symptoms.

How many of these events have you experienced?_____

Patti had been clean and sober for four months when she heard her pastor say, "Sin will take you further than you want to go, keep you longer than you want to stay, and cost you more than you want to pay." *Wow!* she thought, *I don't know all about sin, but that is exactly what my addiction has done. I hardly can believe that I did some of the things I said I never would do.*

Review your answers to the checklist. Below write a paragraph describing how your using has taken you further than you wanted to go, kept you longer than you wanted to stay, and cost you more than you wanted to pay.

_____

_____

_____

_____

_____

Key Concept for Lesson 2

Addiction progressively takes over my life.

Pray and ask God how this concept can apply in your life. Now please review this lesson. What has God shown you that can help you?

_____

_____

Below write this Step's memory verse. Refer to page 9 to verify the verse.

_____

_____

Powerlessness

We admit that by ourselves we are powerless over chemical substances—that our lives have become unmanageable.

Blessed are the poor in Spirit, for theirs is the kingdom of heaven.

Matthew 5:3

Key Concept:
Drug use makes me feel powerful and in control while it makes me powerless.

Addiction wears many faces; it has no respect for a person's age, race, sex, social standing, profession, or religious belief. Some people seem to be genetically susceptible to chemical addiction and are "hooked" with the first drink, puff, or pill. Others may abuse chemical substances for a number of years before they cross the line to dependency.

The first great obstacle to recovery is denial. In the next three paragraphs circle each factor which contributes to denial.

Powerlessness is the distinguishing mark of addiction. We have difficulty seeing our powerlessness because the feeling we gain from using is a feeling of control. We feel that our drug of choice gives us more power and puts us in control. We *think* we are in control when we are drinking or using. We likely feel out of control only when our drug of choice has been taken away, and we begin to feel discomfort. In reality, the sense of control we gain from using is false.

The sense of control we gain from using is false.

Two types of addicts exist. Some addicts know they are powerless over chemicals but cannot stop drinking or using. Others cannot yet see their powerlessness. The nature of drugs themselves is one reason these addicts cannot see the truth. Mood-altering chemicals act on the central nervous system to produce feelings of euphoria, a lack of inhibitions, and a sense of well-being. Some of these substances accurately are labeled "pain-killers." They not only deaden physical pain—they deaden emotional pain as well. More often than not, the person suffering from addiction also is suffering from emotional pain.

Part of the emotional pain results from our drug use. Because of our using, our lives become unmanageable. In an effort to block pain and maintain the illusion that we are in control, we build defense mechanisms that hide the truth from us. Denial combines with the numbing effects of the drug and makes it very difficult to see reality as it is.

You may have circled these statements: The drug makes us feel powerful and in control; We feel euphoric, a lack of inhibitions, and a sense of well-being; Drugs deaden pain; We build defense mechanisms.

Jim's euphoric recall

Jim attended the *Narcotics Anonymous* meeting only because his parole officer insisted. He had no intention of listening, but the words the speaker used caught his attention. The speaker said, "If you can remember your first joint, drink, or high, you're probably an addict." He went on to explain that addicts often had a first or early experience that felt very good. That experience made them feel so good—euphoric—that they kept using. They always tried to recapture that early feeling. "The result of my drug use was to make me feel progressively worse," he said. "But I kept right on using, because that memory led me on. I was like my grandfather talking about the 'good old days.' I don't think his good old days were nearly as good as he remembered, and I know my good old days weren't as good as I remembered them."

Euphoric recall, Jim muttered to himself. *So there's a name for it and I'm not the only one who kept hoping to recapture that feeling. Maybe there is more to this than I have been willing to admit.*

By the time we begin to seek help, we usually aren't able or willing to recognize that drug use is the reason for our pain. Instead we blame the boss or our parents, our spouse or the children, our circumstances or God. When our lives start to fall apart, we usually think that if we can get these other people or circumstances to straighten out, life again will be comfortable, and we can continue drinking or using happily ever after.

Before you can hope to make any progress or feel better, examine your life for signs of powerlessness and unmanageability. Looking backward usually precedes moving forward; before we adequately can deal with the present, we must examine our past.

Powerlessness

Answer the following questions as accurately and completely as possible. The questions are entirely for your own benefit. Your answers will help you to see the truth about your relationship with chemical substances. Use additional sheets of paper if you need to do so.

What kinds of drugs—including alcohol—have you used in your lifetime?

_____

_____

When did you first begin using alcohol? _____

Other drugs? _____

On the time line that appears in the margin, write a brief summary of your history of using. For example, "began to sniff glue at age eight," or "first drank alcohol at age 13."

What reasons can you identify that led you to begin to use?

_____

_____

What reasons can you identify that led you to continue to use?

_____

_____

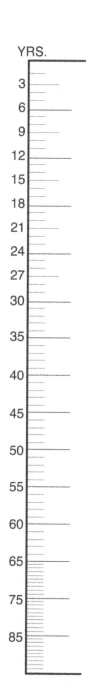

YRS.

3
6
9
12
15
18
21
24
27
30
35
40
45
50
55
60
65
75
85

"So I'm not the only one who kept hoping to recapture that feeling."

How often have you used drugs/alcohol?

_____

_____

In what amounts have you used drugs/alcohol?

_____

_____

Do you think your answers to the above questions indicate "normal" usage—like the rest of society?   Yes   No

Sherry's drinking pattern

Sherry always thought she drank the same amount as anyone else. Then she heard a speaker explain in different terms about alcohol consumption. He said that if all the alcohol consumed in this country was represented by 10 cans of beer, here is how it is consumed: Half of the people don't drink at all. Thirty percent of all people are moderate drinkers. They drink the equivalent of two of the cans. That leaves 20 percent of all people—the alcoholics and "problem" drinkers—who drink 80 percent of all the alcohol consumed.

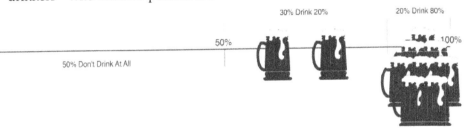

Sherry began to wonder, *In which group do I belong?* The speaker explained more about how little "social" drinkers drink. The statement that really struck Sherry was, "Social drinkers drink a little bit, and when they begin to feel the effects, they don't like it, and they say, 'No thanks, I've had enough.' Social drinkers don't drink for the effects of the alcohol."

Sherry never could remember having had enough.

Sherry was badly shaken. She drank specifically because she wanted the effect of the drug, and though she often stopped short of drunkenness, she never could remember having enough.

Do you have anything in common with Sherry? Do you use for the effect the chemical gives you?   Yes   No   Explain your answer.

_____

_____

Have you ever experienced loss of memory, dulled vision, or loss of consciousness as a result of using or drinking?   Yes   No

If you have used different types of drugs, how have they affected you?

_____

_____

**I realize my powerless-
ness because—**

_____

_____

_____

_____

_____

_____

_____

_____

_____

_____

Have you ever tried to control your consumption of chemicals or alcohol?
Yes   No If so, why?

_____

_____

Were you able to stop or control your use easily?   Yes   No

Estimate how often you usually think about using chemicals or alcohol.

_____

How much of your time usually was spent on some aspect of drinking or using before you entered treatment or began recovery—for example, planning to use, obtaining, using, or recuperating from use of drugs?

_____

Review your answers in this lesson. In the margin box describe how you have come to see your powerlessness over your drug of choice.

Key Concept for Lesson 3
Drug use makes me feel powerful and in control while it makes me powerless.

Pray and ask God how this concept can apply in your life. Now please review this lesson. What has God shown you that can help you?

_____

_____

Write this Step's memory verse in the margin. Refer to page 9 to check your work.

LESSON 4

Key Concept:
Addiction makes my life unmanageable.

Unmanageable

We admit that by ourselves we are powerless over chemical substances—that our lives have become unmanageable.

For I know that nothing good dwells in me, that is, in my flesh; for the wishing is present in me, but the doing of the good is not.

Romans 7:18

"Why don't they just leave me alone?" Susan's parents always were nagging her. Now her boss was complaining and threatening, too. They said her getting high was the problem, but Susan knew better. If only they would get off her back . . . .

Life out of control

Ray awoke with his mouth tasting like the floor of a taxi and his head throbbing like a jackhammer. He had no idea where he was or what he had been doing. Mornings like this were becoming more and more common for Ray. Then he saw the bars of the jail cell. His life had just become more unmanageable.

Judy knew that using was dangerous for her unborn baby. She felt guilty every time she looked down at her swelling body, but she couldn't sleep at night without her pills, and her hands shook when she had not had an "eye opener."

Richard always had planned to move away from home and start his own business. Ten years and two marriages later, here he was, still working for his dad—still stealing from petty cash to buy marijuana. He knew his smoking was a part of why he never accomplished his goals. He hated the TV commercial that said,"Marijuana can make nothing happen for you, too." Richard hated his lack of motivation. The trouble was that he didn't seem able to *do* anything about the problem.

Susan, Ray, Judy and Richard are very different people. Their circumstances and personalities are different, but they share a common issue. Their drug usage has made their lives unmanageable.

Describe what you consider an unmanageable life.

_____

_____

Going nowhere

Unmanageability means different things to different people. Manageable means capable of being directed. It means that one's life is going in a direction. Whatever the specific example, unmanageability means life out of control—going nowhere.

Is your use of chemical substances controlling your life?   Yes   No

What is your current physical condition? (ulcers, blood pressure, stamina, ability to sleep well, heart, liver, kidneys, chronic diarrhea, etc.)

_____

Could your physical problems, if any, stem from using?   Yes   No

What symptoms have you tried to change or ignore through drinking/using?

_____

Describe any mood swings or unpredictable behaviors you have experienced from using alcohol or other drugs.

_____

_____

Forced to use

Have you ever experienced negative physical or emotional symptoms as a result of *not* drinking or using? These might include nausea, vomiting, feeling especially weak, being prone to illness, having an elevated blood pressure, unexplained sweating, depressed mood, anxiety, irritability, headaches, hallucinations, insomnia. Below describe any of these feelings.

_____

_____

_____

Has has your use of chemicals been destructive to you?   Yes   No

How has it been destructive to others? (For example, you may list accidents, dangerous situations, physical or verbal abuse, etc.)

_____

_____

_____

I said "I'd never"

Name five ways chemicals and/or alcohol have led you to compromise your values. (For example, you might describe what chemicals have led you to do that you once thought you never would do or that you now feel guilty for doing.)

1. _____

2. _____

3. _____

4. _____

5. _____

Name five ways chemicals and or alcohol have contributed to financial, occupational, or legal problems in your life.

1. _____

2. _____

3. _____

4. _____

5. _____

What crises have resulted in your life from using chemicals or alcohol?

_____

_____

What crisis has brought you to consider getting help at this time in your life? Describe it in detail.

_____

_____

_____

_____

_____

Symptoms of Chemical Dependency

The questions appearing on the past several pages have given you an opportunity to reflect on your behavior as it relates to your previous experiences with alcohol and other drugs. Now we'll examine symptoms common to chemical dependency.

chemical dependency–n. the compulsion—forceful urge—to use a chemical substance to achieve a desired effect, despite the experience of negative consequences.

By definition **chemical dependency** is the compulsion to use a mood-altering chemical to achieve a desired effect, despite the experience of negative consequences. Codependency is the condition occurring when a person's God-given needs for love and security have been blocked in a relationship with a dysfunctional—dependent—person. Codependents often help people continue their addictive behavior by rescuing the dependent person from the consequences of his or her behavior.

Many people exhibit both codependent and chemical dependent behavior. People who have three of the following symptoms for a month's duration, or repeatedly over a longer period of time, typically are classified as chemically dependent.[7]

In the list of symptoms below, check those you have experienced.

Using a substance in larger amounts over a longer period of time than originally intended.

Demonstrating an inability to reduce or control substance use, despite one's desire to stop or cut back.

Large amounts of time

Spending large amounts of time in activities revolving around substance use. These activities can include planning, obtaining, using, and recuperating from the effects of use.

Being intoxicated or suffering from withdrawal when you are expected to fulfill obligations at work, school, or home, or using in situations when substance use is hazardous to oneself and or others, such as driving, piloting, operating machinery.

Giving up or avoiding important social, occupational, or recreational activities to drink or use.

Continuing to drink or use after recognizing that substance use is contributing to one's physical, psychological, relational, financial, occupational, or legal problems.

Requiring increasingly larger amounts of the substance to achieve the desired effect.

Experiencing withdrawal

Experiencing withdrawal symptoms when you stop taking the substance or when you reduce your intake of it.

Resuming or increasing substance use to relieve or avoid withdrawal symptoms—"eye openers."

Look back at the inventory you have just taken. Does it indicate that you are addicted to one or more chemicals?   Yes   No

From the work you have done this far, would you describe your life as unmanageable?   Yes   No

A sponsor in Narcotics Anonymous once asked, "You are a pretty intelligent guy, aren't you?" His friend responded, "Yes, I think I am." Then the sponsor wisely said, "Look back over the years of your life and your using career. Where has all your intelligence gotten you?"

How would you answer that question? Does the evidence in your life indicate that you can run your own life and control both your life and your drug use?

_____

_____

You may be very successful externally. Remember that 95 percent of chemical dependents *look* successful—only 5 percent are on "skid row." On the scale below, indicate where you picture yourself.

Meaning and Purpose!   **Going Nowhere** F A S T

Are you now ready to take the first Step and admit your powerlessness—that your life has become unmanageable?   Yes   No

> ## Key Concept for Lesson 4
> Addiction makes my life unmanageable.

Pray and ask God how this concept can apply in your life. Now please review this lesson. What has God shown you that can help you?

_____

_____

Write this Step's memory verse. Refer to page 9 to check your work.

_____

_____

_____

LESSON 5

Reality

We admit that by ourselves we are powerless over chemical substances—that our lives have become unmanageable.

> *You shall know the truth, and the truth shall make you free.*
>
> John 8:32

Key Concept
Being real is more difficult but much better than is living in denial and unreality.

Pamela now tells how she came to the first Step. "When I first heard the first Step, I thought it meant giving up something. I thought that if I surrendered and took the Step, I would be giving up control of my life—that I would become pitiful and weak. Imagine my surprise when my sponsor explained that Step 1 simply was living life on life's terms. She told me to make a list of things I couldn't do. She said for me to begin with 'I can't do brain surgery or fly the space shuttle.' By the time I had added a few things to the list, I began to see her point. The choice was not whether or not I was powerless. The choice was, 'Do I want to live in reality or in insanity?'"

From the following list, check the best moral to Pamela's story.
1. Admitting powerlessness is a sign of weakness.
2. Admitting powerlessness is something that only addicts have to do.
3. Everybody is powerless over many things.
4. Admitting powerlessness is my choice to see things as they really are.
5. Admitting powerlessness is giving up my rights.

Taking Step 1 is not giving up my rights.

By now you see that taking Step 1 is not giving up rights but choosing to see things the way they really are. It is choosing to live in reality. The choice is not between power or powerlessness. The choice is between reality and insanity. Answers 3 and 4 both are true. Answer 4 best expresses the moral of the story.

Steps Toward Acceptance

A strange fact is true about addiction. Remember that addictions are romances. Even though we may have hated some parts of the addiction, we had—and to some degree may always have—a passionate love affair with our drug of choice. We thought about it. We planned to be with it. We savored it, and we felt pain when separated from it. When we finally accept the fact that this lover is no good for us, a grief process begins.

The grief is just as real and powerful as if our closest human friend or lover died or rejected us. Despite the negative consequences, we likely will experience profound feelings of loss as we begin sobriety. The feelings eventually will decline in frequency and intensity, but they may last from several weeks to several years.

The grief process includes the following five stages.[5] These stages are not a straight-line process from one to another, but you probably will find yourself in each of the stages at times.

Denial	Bargaining	Anger	Grief	Acceptance

Denial

Most chemically dependent persons are unable or unwilling to acknowledge—to themselves or others—their addiction. The addiction protects itself with denial even though both the addict and his or her loved ones are suffering as a result of it.

David was a dentist with a 15-year addiction to demerol and codeine. When he lost his house, he blamed his wife. When his wife left him, he blamed his practice. When he lost his license, he blamed God "who's had it out for me since the beginning." Several times people confronted David about his drug problem. "Problem? What problem? I've just had a rough go of things," he said. Sadly, David remained unconvinced of his dependency. He drifted from state to state and job to job hiding his identity as a dentist to avoid the shame of being found out.

Bargaining

Bargaining usually marks the beginning of the dependent person's recognition of his or her addiction and is an attempt to postpone quitting. Bargaining can occur with oneself: "I need to kick this, but I'm just too restless right now. What's one more Valium? I'll quit later." Or, it can be a response to others: "Of course I'm still serious about quitting, and I will—right after this project at work blows over." Or, it can be a plea to God: "God, help me stop—tomorrow."

In the margin box, describe some of the bargaining statements you have made to yourself, God, or others.

Anger

When we no longer can escape the facts pointing to our addiction and/or when we finally enter treatment, we become angry. We direct our anger at God, family members, or close friends, all of whom—we think—contributed to our addiction or entry into treatment. We also direct our anger toward others who are drinking or using, toward the circumstances of needing to enter recovery, or anger toward ourselves for allowing this to happen.

On the list below rank your anger by putting a number 1 by the object of your greatest anger, a 2 by the second, etc. We often have great difficulty admitting—even to ourselves—that all of us who have become addicted have a great deal of anger. Rate at least your top five objects of anger.

_____ boss	_____ sister
_____ mother	_____ grandparent
_____ father	_____ church
_____ God	_____ military
_____ myself	_____ school
_____ a co-worker	_____ spouse
_____ my drug of choice	_____ ex-spouse
_____ brother	_____ other_____

When Brenda's sponsor insisted that she make a list of the objects of her anger, Brenda replied, "I'm not angry." After becoming both more honest and more in touch with her feelings, she said, "I was angry at everything. I was angry at my parents, at those who had abandoned me, at those I *thought* had

---

My bargaining statements—

_____

_____

_____

_____

_____

_____

_____

_____

_____

_____

Angry at everything

abandoned me, at those I thought *might* abandon me. I was especially angry at God. When I was able to work through my anger by working the Steps, I found I could love and enjoy. I found a new life."

Grief

We have become experts at avoiding painful emotions. The experience of deep distress or grief during recovery comes as an unwelcome surprise. Feelings of grief are a normal response to the loss of anything we consider important to our well-being. Our drug of choice did things for us. It calmed our nerves, blocked feelings of pain, hid feelings of failure or disappointment. Our drug of choice gave us a sense of security, a feeling of euphoria, courage, power, and control. It became our primary means of support. When this support is taken away, we feel as though we have lost our only friend. Grieving over such a loss is a normal, healthy aspect of recovery—even though it hurts. We grieve properly when we give ourselves the freedom to feel the loss whenever something reminds us of the loss.

We feel as though we have lost our only friend.

This is a painful exercise. Go back to the last paragraph and underline everything your drug of choice did for you. As you do so, permit yourself to feel and express the loss you feel when you realize that you cannot continue to use.

Al's story again

Al says, "My drug of choice did something for me nothing else was ever able to do. It took all the problems away. It took all the fear, all the responsibility, all the feeling of inadequacy—all away. I still get angry sometimes that I can't have that simple solution for life, but I can't. That simple solution is death for me. What I can do is feel the grief, express the anger, and move on to a life that is much more difficult—but a life that is real."

Acceptance

Over time as we continue in recovery, we are able to accept our addiction and our need for recovery. Gradually we are able to accept with serenity, and eventually with joy, our life apart from drugs.

These stages often overlap in actual experience. You may be experiencing more than one stage at the same time. Which one(s) are you in now? Describe your present feelings.

_____

_____

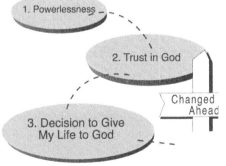

You will find the course map on the inside back cover of this book. The course map pictures the 12 Steps. On the portion of the course map that appears in the margin, write your own restatement of Step 1.

Just like becoming addicted, recovery is a process. It is not like taking a pill or having a drink and then suddenly feeling better. Recovery actually is far more satisfying, and it leads to a contentment and peace within that is lasting. Along the way you may discover that your addiction is a combination of different problems, but you also will have the satisfaction of seeing many of the problems that developed as a result of chemical use subside. Again, this will take time. Be patient with yourself. Be patient with those around you who may not be accustomed to your new patterns of behavior. But above all, continue to work the program. It really is worth it, and it works if you work it!

In recovery meetings you probably will hear people introduce themselves with statements like, "Hi, I'm Ann, I'm a grateful recovering addict." When you first hear those words, you may think, *This person is crazy. How could you be grateful to be an addict?* You will find the phrase has meaning two ways. Early in recovery you may say, "I'm grateful because I'm recovering." You may mean *I am grateful because I no longer am destroying myself and causing myself and others pain.* Later, with maturity you may come genuinely to feel and say, "I am grateful that I am a recovering addict because the pain of addiction led me to a new life. I have gained so much that I even am glad for all the pain. Without the pain I never might have found this life and these relationships with God and with others."

Key Concept for Lesson 5
Being real is more difficult but much better than is living in denial and unreality.

Pray and ask God how this concept can apply in your life. Now please review this lesson. What has God shown you that can help you?

_____

_____

Below write this Step's memory verse. Refer to page 9 to verify your work.

_____

_____

Notes

[1]Reprinted with permission from *The Disease Concept of Alcoholism*, by E.M. Jellinek. Copyright 1960 by Alcohol Research Documentation, Inc., Rutgers Center of Alcohol Studies, New Brunswick, NJ 08903.

[2]Reprinted from pages 32-33 of *Alcoholics Anonymous* with permission. AA is a program of recovery from alcoholism only and is not affiliated with other self-help programs.

[3]Hart, Larry, "Confronting Chemical Dependency in Your Church," *Mission Journal*, Feb., 1987, 4.

[4]Johnson, Vernon E., *I'll Quit Tomorrow* (San Francisco, CA: Harper & Row, 1980), 1.

[5]Spickard, Anderson, M.D., and Barbara R. Thompson, *Dying for a Drink: What You Should Know About Alcoholism* (Waco, TX: Word Books, 1985), 17.

[6]Adapted from the work of Johnson, *I'll Quit Tomorrow*, 16-26.

[7]The American Psychiatric Association, Diagnostic and Statistical Manual of Mental Disorders, 3rd Edition, Revised (Washington, DC: The American Psychiatric Association, 1987), adapted from pp. 166-167.

[8]Adapted from the work of Elizabeth Kubler-Ross in her book *On Death and Dying* (New York: MacMillan Publishing, 1969).

STEP 2

We come to believe in Him.

Coming to Believe

FIRE GOD?

Jen had been attending meetings for several weeks. During that time, she had been able to remain drug free except for one slip. For the first time she genuinely had taken Step 1. With no more bargaining she admitted that she was powerless over alcohol.

Jen had admitted and gradually was recognizing that she cannot drink like a "normy," but she was having a terrible time trying to work Step 2. One night the meeting was small. The group members sat around a table sharing their problems and progress in applying the Steps. Jen shared her struggle to believe that God cared anything about her. "After all I've done, all the times I've failed, I just can't believe God cares any more. He's given up on me."

Jen was shocked when her sponsor spoke up and said, "Jen, what I think you need to do is fire that god of yours."

"What?" Jen replied.

"Fire that god of yours. He's no good. In fact, I don't believe he even exists except in your keen alcoholic mind. Fire him and replace him with my God. My God has a Son named Jesus who loves you so much that He died for you and He promised He'd never leave you or forsake you. You fire yours and take my God. He is faithful and consistent." (Read more about Jen on page 32).

Step 2   *We come to believe that God, through Jesus Christ, can restore us to sanity.*

Memory verse   *For it is God who is at work in you, both to will and to work for His good pleasure.*
–Philippians 2:13

Overview for Step 2

Lesson 1: Restore Us to Sanity
    Goal: You will identify attitudes and actions characteristic of distorted thinking.
Lesson 2: The Origin of Our Concept of God
    Goal: You will describe the effects on your life of guilt and blame.
Lesson 3: Your Parents and You
    Goal: You will analyze past relationships with your parents.
Lesson 4: Your Relationship with God
    Goal: You will describe the impact of your past relationships on your view of God.
Lesson 5: Believing the Truth about God
    Goal: You will act to correct elements of your faulty concept of God.
Lesson 6: Believing the Truth about You
    Goal: You will act to correct elements of your faulty self-concept.

31

<table>
<tr><td>

LESSON

1

</td></tr>
</table>

Restore Us to Sanity

We come to believe that God, through Jesus Christ, can restore us to sanity.

The wise woman builds her house, But the foolish tears it down with her own hands.

–Proverbs 14:1

Key Concept:
Addictive logic is insane thinking.

Jen is learning to distinguish between the God who really exists and the god in her head. One is the Creator of the universe while the other is the product of her imagination and her experiences—many of them distorted by alcohol and a dysfunctional family system.

Two things make Step 2 difficult. The first is the matter of God. Our experiences both before we became addicted and since we have been using have alienated us from God. As a result, when we began recovery most of us felt nothing but anger, abandonment, and criticism from the god in our heads. The second obstacle to the Step is the matter of sanity. Nobody wants to be considered insane. We will consider the second obstacle—the matter of insanity—in this lesson.

Sanity

While it is true that prolonged use of chemical substances can lead to personality changes and mental illness, sanity in this Step has the meaning used in *Webster's New World Dictionary*: "soundness of judgment." Using our drug of choice, in spite of the damage it is doing in our lives, is not using sound judgment. Here are some examples of insanity—unsound judgment or "stinking thinking"—that are typical outcomes of our addiction.

> **Write the number of the following examples of insanity on the line next to the matching story that follows. We have done the first one as an example.**
>
> 1. Drinking or using despite warnings of deteriorating health
> 2. Drinking or using despite the pain it causes others
> 3. Drinking or using in retaliation against someone who has offended us or made us angry—"I'll show you, I'll kill myself."
> 4. Drinking or using to prove we can "handle it," despite our experience that we can't
>
> **_3_** Jodi's boss was a jerk. He kept putting more and more pressure on her at work. She thought, *It's no wonder I have to drink to put up with him.*
>
> _____ Ron really did love Sally. He felt guilty when she begged him to quit his cocaine habit.
>
> _____ *So what*, Cheryl thought. Sure she got drunk the last time she drank, but this time she would have only a couple of drinks.
>
> _____ The doctor looked angry this time. He repeatedly told Terry to quit. This time he said, "You're just going to have to find another doctor. I refuse to treat you if you insist on killing yourself."

I am a lot of things but crazy
isn't one of them.

When John first heard the second Step, he violently rejected the suggestion that either he or his behavior was insane. "I certainly don't need to be 'restored' to sanity," he said. "I am a lot of things but crazy isn't one of them." Later John said, "I traded my self-respect, my health, my family, my job, and my reputation for a high. Now, that was crazy." The first set of answers were : 3, 2, 4, and 1.

With the next four examples of "unsound judgment," write your own story of a situation or statement about yourself or someone else that illustrates the example. We have done the first one for you.

5. Getting close to success in any area of life, then "blowing it" with a binge

> I got a promotion; my job was going well, but I got scared, got high, cursed at my boss, and quit my job.

6. Changing or cancelling appointments or commitments to make time for using

_____

_____

7. Blaming other people for both our behavior and our inability to control our use of chemical substances

_____

_____

Somehow "different"

8. Insisting that we are somehow "different" from other people who are addicted to chemical substances

_____

_____

Below you will find the final three examples of insanity. Many of us identify with these statements. Check each example that you have used or said.

9. Drinking or using despite threats of loss—job, home, spouse—if we continue
10. Cutting ourselves off from friends, family members, or anyone else who attempts to interfere with our using
11. Drinking or using despite our earnest desire to stop

Look back over the 11 examples of insanity. With how many of them do you identify? Write in the margin your own statement or definition of the insanity of chemical dependency.

The insanity of chemical dependency is that we continue to experience the consequences of our actions—at an accelerated rate as our addiction progresses—and yet, for a long time, no price is so high that it makes us willing to stop.

The wise woman builds her house, But the foolish tears it down with her own hands.
—Proverbs 14:1

Proverbs 14:1, the Scripture verse for this lesson, appears in the margin. The verse points out an example of the insanity of sin. Imagine a person pulling the walls of her home down around her. Yet, with use of chemicals, that is exactly what many of us have done. Our sick love and trust relationship with the substance leads us to give up everything of real value in our lives for an experience that, in the long run, makes us feel worse rather than better.

Using the examples in this lesson as a guide, list five occasions when you have acted in such a way that an objective observer, who knows you and your circumstances, might say, "That's insane!"

1. _____

2. _____

3. _____

4. _____

5. _____

Key Concept for Lesson 1
Addictive logic is insane thinking.

Pray and ask God how this concept can apply in your life. Now please review this lesson. What has God shown you that can help you?

_____

_____

Write this Step's memory verse in the margin. Begin to memorize it.

LESSON 2

The Origin of Our Concept of God

We come to believe that God, through Jesus Christ, can restore us to sanity.

For God did not send the Son into the world to judge the world; but that the world should be saved through Him.
—John 3:17

God created the world, and He created people so that He could love us and we could love Him. He has a plan for how we grow into that relationship. His intention begins with the way He created us. It includes the family, the church, and our personal experience.

Key Concept:
Our relationships with parents shape our concept of God.

His plan begins with His creation. He created us with an awareness of God and with an inborn desire and need to have loving relationships. He intended that we grow up in families with parents who would love us and model the character of God for us. We get our earliest understanding of who God is from our parents or caretakers. Then He intended that we would get to know Him personally through His Son and our Savior, Jesus Christ. Finally, He intended that our experiences—based on wise choices—would reinforce and build our knowledge of and relation with Him.

> **Use the information in the paragraph you just read to put in order the following stages in the development of our intended relationship with God. Place a 1 by the first stage, a 2 by the second, and so on.**
>
> _____ a. Our experiences build and reinforce our relationship.
> _____ b. Parents model character of God.
> _____ c. We learn facts about God and Jesus.
> _____ d. We are born with awareness of and desire for God.
> _____ e. We meet God personally through Jesus Christ and the Holy Spirit.

Unfortunately, we live in a fallen world. Sin touches and damages everything in this world in one way or another. We begin life with a desire to come to know God but also with an inclination to selfishness. Our parents were less than the perfect models of the character and nature of God—sometimes less than perfect in the extreme. So our relationship with God already is far off the track. We have a warped concept of who God is and how to please Him. Some of us have experienced abuse which greatly confused and distorted our situation. Then we complicate the problem further with wrong choices. When we have used mood-altering chemicals extensively, we inevitably have made many wrong choices. The resulting guilt and shame drives us further away from God.

One possible order for the stages above is: a. 5, b. 2, c. 3, d. 1, e. 4.

> **Use the information in the paragraph you just read to put in order the following stages of how our warped and distant relationship with God develops.**
>
> _____ a. We make wrong choices that result in increased guilt and shame.
> _____ b. We are born with a tendency to sin.
> _____ c. We feel angry and alienated from God.
> _____ d. Our parents gave us a distorted image of the character of God.

If talking about God makes you feel uncomfortable, that is perfectly understandable. By the time we become willing to admit that we are addicted, our concept of God is usually fairly negative. One possible order for the activity is a. 3, b. 1, c. 4, d. 2.

> **In the margin write whatever insights you have gained from the preceding activities. How have your family experiences and your choices affected your relationship with God?**

In this lesson you will explore how guilt and blame distort one's concept of God. Then in the next lesson you will explore the impact of your parents on your concept of God.

My family experiences and choices have . . .

_____
_____
_____
_____
_____
_____
_____
_____
_____
_____
_____

Guilt

Guilt crushes and drives us. Sometimes we feel guilty for our drug use. More often we feel guilty for what we have done while drinking or using.

[With our values gone, we make bad choices.]

Chemical substances work on the central nervous system. They release our inhibitions and cause feelings of euphoria. When substances release our inhibitions, our values often go with them, and we make bad choices. A man or woman who would not otherwise be unfaithful to his or her spouse might, under the influence of chemicals, crawl into bed with a perfect stranger. Or, to protect himself and his chemical supply, the dependent person may resort to stealing or lying. The result is actual guilt because of our bad behavior and the feeling of guilt because we have violated our standards of right and wrong.

How would you describe feelings of guilt? How does any type of guilt feel?

_____

How do you deal with guilt? Do you feel the guilt? Do you block the pain of guilt by denying that you've done anything wrong? Or, do you both feel and deny guilt? Explain.

_____

_____

_____

Describe how guilt has affected—

your self-esteem: _____

_____

your relationship with your family: _____

_____

your relationships with others: _____

_____

your relationship with God: _____

_____

Blame

Still another obstacle in our relationship with God is blame. As our addictions progress, we become increasingly preoccupied with the "habit." We always wonder when we will be able to drink or use again and how we'll feel if we do or if we don't get high. As a result, our focus is continually turned inward, toward ourselves, and protecting ourselves becomes our greatest priority.

Low self-esteem may add to this self-protective behavior. We may have suffered from a poor self-image prior to using. For many of us, low sense of self-worth led us to escape through chemicals in the first place. Add to this our burden of guilt and shame for what we've done either to get high or while we were high, and the result is deep self-hatred.

We project our self-hatred onto other people by blaming them either instead of or in addition to blaming ourselves. We blame others because we truly believe that they—and we—should get what they deserve. We blame others because our success may depend on their work, and when they fail, it makes us look bad. Putting someone else down may make us feel better temporarily.

Putting someone else down may make us feel better about ourselves.

Blame is often the result of unmet expectations. By blaming someone who fails, we often feel superior. In fact, the higher the position of one who fails— such as a parent, pastor, or boss—the further they fall, and the better we feel. What higher authority can we blame than God?

Describe how you feel when you fail. What names do you call yourself?

_____

_____

_____

How do you respond to others when they fail?

_____

_____

_____

Ways we condemn others—

- gossip
- feeling superior
- slander
- angry actions
  the silent treatment
- sarcastic remarks
- ridicule
- shaming remarks
  avoidance
  others _____

_____

_____

_____

The margin box contains a list of ways we condemn others. Check those methods you use, and add any other ways you use to condemn others.

Do you blame God? If so, describe how and why. _____

_____

_____

_____

Do you feel that God is condemning of you? If so, describe how and why.

_____

_____

_____

1. Powerlessness

2. Trust in God

3. Decision to Give My Life to God

In the margin the first three Steps in the course map appear. The map pictures the journey to an effective, meaningful, Christ-honoring life. Draw a roadblock between Step 1 and Step 3.

Below describe how the habit of applying guilt and blame form a roadblock that keeps many people from completing the journey.

_____

_____

_____

We deal with God in the same ways we deal with ourselves and others, so it comes as no surprise that guilt and blame block our attempts to trust God. You may have explained that we fear guilt and blame. We expect God to treat us the same way that we have treated ourselves and others and the same way that others have treated us. The fear of blame and the misperception of God forms a roadblock that keeps many people from trusting God. Since in order to recover we need to replace our sick relationship with chemicals with a healthy relationship with God and others, we must overcome the roadblock. We overcome the roadblock by working Step 2.

Come to Believe . . .

Note that Step 2 says that we "come to believe." Because of the issues you have described in this lesson and because of other complications in our personal relationship with God, coming to believe is a process. Spiritual giants are not born that way. It takes time, understanding, and experience before our faith in God actually begins to take root and grow.

Whether you believe any of the above obstacles are true of you or not, know that no one plans to force Him on you. Rather, our intent is to present you with an opportunity to examine your perceptions of God and correct any that you may find faulty. In the lessons ahead you will explore more about your view of God, about the origin of your feelings about God, and how you may make the changes you choose.

Key Concept for Lesson 1
Our relationships with parents shape our concept of God.

Pray and ask God how this concept can apply in your life. Now please review this lesson. What has God shown you that can help you?

_____

_____

Below write this Step's memory verse to help you memorize it.

_____

_____

_____

LESSON 3

Your Parents and You

We come to believe that God, through Jesus Christ, can restore us to sanity.

for the Son of Man did not come to destroy men's lives, but to save them.
                                                            –Luke 9:56

Key Concept:
A distorted concept of God makes trusting Him difficult.

Jen (from the unit story) said, "I wanted to please God. I pushed myself to the limits of my people-pleasing abilities by thinking that 'just a little more' would do the trick, but I never felt accepted and loved by God. After I failed Him again and again, I began to believe that I just wasn't able to please Him. I decided that I didn't have enough faith—and I gave up on ever having His approval, His love, or His acceptance."

If you feel distant from God, you may do so partly because of a faulty relationship with one or both of your parents. A complex set of factors shapes your views about God, your self-concept, and your ability to relate to others. Perhaps the most powerful of these factors is your relationship with your parents or those who reared you. If your parents were loving and supportive, you probably believe that God is loving and strong. If, however, your parents were harsh and demanding, you may feel that God is impossible to please. Either way, the foundation of your emotional, social, and spiritual health usually is formed by observing your parents' model. The results can be wonderful or tragic.

To gain a better understanding of this "shaping" process, you can look at some personal characteristics of your parents and how they related to you. The following exercise will help you evaluate your relationships with your mother and your father as you were growing up.

Think back to how your parents related to you when you were young and place an *F* (for Father) and an *M* (for Mother) in the appropriate boxes after each characteristic. If someone other than your birth parents reared you, relate the characteristics to your primary caretakers. You will find it most helpful if you complete the checklist for one parent at a time.

To help you get an accurate reflection of your relationships with your parents, turn each characteristic into a question. For example, ask, "How often did (or do) I feel that my father/mother was gentle . . . stern, etc.?" Leave room for up to three letters per box. Below is an example.

Characteristics	Always	Very Often	Some-times	Hardly Ever	Never	Don't Know
Gentle		M	F			
Stern	F			M		
Loving			F		M	
Disapproving		F,M				
Distant			F		M	

Carefully fill in the chart below. Do this first for one parent then the other. [1]

Characteristics	Always	Very Often	Some-times	Hardly Ever	Never	Don't Know
Gentle	M		F			
Stern	F			M		
Loving	M F					
Disapproving			M F			
Distant					M	
Close, intimate	M	F				
Kind	M	F				
Angry			F	M		
Caring	M	F				
Demanding			M F			
Harsh			F		M	
Trustworthy	M F					
Joyful	M		F			
Forgiving		M F				
Good	M F					
Cherished me	M F					
Impatient			F	M		
Unreasonable				M F		
Strong	F			M		
Protective	M	F				
Passive	M			F		
Encouraging	M F					
Sensitive	M	F				
Unpredictable					M F	

Evaluating Your Relationship with Your Father

What does this inventory tell you about your relationship with your father?

_____

_____

What were his strengths? _____

_____

Give two examples of a time when he related to you in a positive way.

1. _____

2. _____

What were his weaknesses? _____

_____

Give two examples of a time when he related to you in a negative way.

1. _____

2. _____

If you were an outside observer of the type of relationship you have just described, how would you feel toward the father?

Angry   Sad   Sympathetic   Happy
No feeling   Afraid   Other _____

Write a letter to your father. Tell him your feelings this exercise revealed about some of the issues from your past. (Note: Whether or not your father is living, you will benefit from completing this exercise. The benefit is in the reflecting and writing. We do not require you to send the letter. Consult your sponsor or counselor, pray, and wait before you even consider sending the letter.)

Evaluating Your Relationship with Your Mother

What does this inventory tell you about your relationship with your mother?

_____

_____

What were her strengths? _____

_____

Give two examples of times when she related to you in a positive way.

1. _____

2. _____

What were her weaknesses? _____

_____

Give two examples of times when she related to you in a negative way.

1. _____

2. _____

If you were an outside observer of the type of relationship you have just described, how would you feel toward the mother?

Angry   Sad   Sympathetic   Happy
No feeling   Afraid   Other _____

Write a letter to your mother. Tell her your feelings this exercise revealed about some of the issues from your past. (Note: Whether or not your mother is living, you will benefit from completing this exercise. The benefit is in the reflecting and writing. Again, we do not require you to send the letter. Consult your sponsor or counselor, pray, and wait before you even consider sending the letter.)

If you have a strained relationship with a parent, how do you think that relationship might impact your substance addiction?

_____

_____

_____

_____

_____

People respond in a variety of ways to feeling unloved. Several responses can cause or support an addiction. Some of us use chemicals to numb emotional pain, or to gain control back from an overpowering parent.

Key Concept for Lesson 3
A distorted concept of God makes trusting Him difficult.

Memorize this Step's memory verse, Philippians 2:13.

LESSON 4

Your Relationship with God

We come to believe that God, through Jesus Christ, can restore us to sanity.

I speak the things which I have seen with My Father; therefore you also do the things which you heard from your father.

–John 8:38

Key Concept:
My concept of God comes primarily from my parents.

Evaluating Your Relationship with God

In the previous lesson you examined your relationship with your parents. Now look at your relationship with God. By first evaluating your present relationship with Him and then comparing it with your past relationship to your parents, you can begin to see how your relationship with your parents has influenced your view of God. The following inventory will help you determine some of your feelings toward God. Because it is subjective, no right or wrong answers exist. To make sure that the test shows your actual feelings, please follow the instructions carefully.

- Go back to the inventory you completed in the last lesson and take it again. This time evaluate your relationship with God.

- Turn each characteristic into a question. For example: "To what degree do I really feel that God loves me?" or "To what degree do I really feel that God understands me?"

- Place a *G* in the appropriate column to the right of the characteristic for your answer. Your answers may or may not match those for your parents' characteristics. Mark these answers without thinking about the previous ones.

- Answer openly and honestly. Don't give answers from your knowledge of theology or church doctrine but from personal experience, especially as you reflect on your feelings.

- Don't describe what the relationship *ought* to be, or what you *hope* it will be, but what it *is* right now.

- Some people feel God might be angry if they give a negative answer. Nothing is further from the truth. God is pleased with our honesty. He wants us to know we can trust His love enough to share our deepest feelings with Him. Openness and honesty form the foundation of growth.

Complete the inventory on page 40.

Now look at your responses. What does this inventory tell you about your relationship with God?

_____

_____

If you were an outside observer of the relationship you have just described, what would you think of the God who was described? Check all that apply. God seems to be—

Loving	Caring	Understanding
Harsh	Critical	Other _____
Angry	Sympathetic	_____

Write a letter to God. Express whatever feelings this exercise has brought to your awareness about Him. Be honest with Him. He can tolerate your anger, grief, doubt, and fear. You may be like the little girl who was angry because her father had refused a request. She wrote him a note that read, "Dear Dad, I hate you. Love, Jodi." Express your feelings—including confusion—as they are.

Your Parents' Influence on Your Relationship with God

You examined your present relationship with God. Now look at how your relationship with your parents has influenced your view of your Heavenly Father.

To make the comparison, do the following:

- Turn back to the chart on page 40. For each characteristic, circle each response where you placed a *G* in the same box with an *F* or an *M*. Below is an example:

Characteristics	Always	Very Often	Some-times	Hardly Ever	Never	Don't Know
Gentle		M	F,G			
Stern	F			M,G		
Loving				F	M	G
Disapproving		F,M				
Distant			F,G		M	

If few or none of your responses were in the exact same boxes, circle the responses which were close to the same.

List the characteristics which are the same (or similar) of your parents and of God.

Of your father and of God: _____

_____

Of your mother and of God: _____

_____

List the characteristics which are quite different (two or more boxes away from each other):

Of your father and of God: _____

_____

Of your mother and of God: _____

_____

What patterns (if any) do you see? _____

_____

_____

Write a summary paragraph about how your relationship with your father has shaped your view of God.

_____

_____

_____

Write another paragraph telling how your relationship with your mother has shaped your view of God.

_____

_____

_____

_____

Key Concept for Lesson 4
My concept of God comes primarily from my parents.

Thank you for taking time to evaluate honestly your relationships with your father, mother, and God.

Memorize this Step's memory verse, Philippians 2:13.

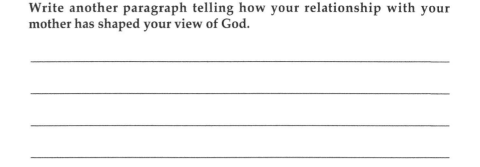

LESSON 5

Believing the Truth About God

We come to believe that God, through Jesus Christ, can restore us to sanity.

> *And Jesus said to him, "'If You can!' All things are possible to him who believes."*
>
> –Mark 9:23

Key Concept:
Correcting my faulty concept of God is an important recovery task.

When we do the work in the past two lessons, many of us discover an amazing fact. We discover that our concept of God—the God we had been trying to serve or trying to avoid—originated more from our own life experiences and dysfunctional families than from reality.

Check the statement below that most nearly expresses the meaning of the paragraph above.

1. The god in your head may not be similar to the real God.
2. We derive our concept of God primarily from our parents.
3. We need to get to know God rather than just our concept of God.
4. Just as we can have a wrong impression of a person, we may have a wrong impression of God.
5. God is just as we imagine Him to be.

Every person's greatest task is to know God. Often a faulty concept of God stands in the way. All the statements except number 5 reflect ideas from the paragraph, but number 1 most clearly summarizes the meaning of the passage.

Knowing God from Psalm 139

Some passages in Scripture teach God's nature and character. Psalm 139 is one of the greatest passages for this purpose. Studying this psalm can help you understand how God knows you so completely and loves you so thoroughly. You may want to read the entire psalm from your Bible before you examine it more carefully in the following activities.

God Knows Me Thoroughly

O LORD, you have searched me and you know me. You know when I sit and when I rise; you perceive my thoughts from afar. You discern my going out and my lying down; you are familiar with all my ways. Before a word is on my tongue you know it completely, O LORD.

       –Psalm 139: 1-4, NIV

Read verses 1-4 in the margin. Answer the questions below.

God always knows everything about you. You can keep no secrets from Him, yet He loves you unconditionally! How does this make you feel?

afraid	excited	condemned
hopeful	sad	grateful
glad	accepted	_____

In what ways does God's powerful knowledge give you courage and strength?

_____

_____

_____

He Protects Me

You hem me in– behind and before; you have laid your hand upon me. Such knowledge is too wonderful for me, too lofty for me to attain.

       –Psalm 139:5-6, NIV

Read verses 5-6. Answer the questions below.

God's perfect knowledge about you makes Him able to protect you (to hem you in). From what do you need His protection?

_____

_____

_____

Is it difficult for you to understand the Lord's complete knowledge that this passage mentions? Why or why not?

_____

_____

_____

_____

He Always Is Present

Where can I go from your Spirit? Where can I flee from your presence? If I go up to the heavens, you are there; if I make my bed in the depths, you are there. If I rise on the wings of the dawn, if I settle on the far side of the sea, even there your hand will guide me, your right hand will hold me fast. If I say, "Surely the darkness will hide me and the light become night around me," even the darkness will not be dark to you; the night will shine like the day, for darkness is as light to you.

–Psalm 139:7-12, NIV

Read verses 7-12. Answer the questions below.

The most important promise to one who has strayed is that he is not lost! How close is God to you?

_____

How close does He seem to be? _____

_____

How far can you get from Him? _____

_____

Some of us have looked with a distorted view at God's nearness. We have heard, "Where can I go from Thy Spirit?" as if God were pursuing us to do us harm. The entire passage speaks of God's great love and care. His love will follow us—no matter where we go.

He Is a Sovereign Creator

For you created my inmost being; you knit me together in my mother's womb. I praise you because I am fearfully and wonderfully made; your works are wonderful, I know that full well. My frame was not hidden from you when I was made in the secret place. When I was woven together in the depths of the earth, your eyes saw my unformed body.

–Psalm 139:13-16a, NIV

Read verses 13-16a. Answer the questions below.

What is God's opinion of you and of your body? _____

_____

The psalmist said he was a marvelous creation of God. He said all of God's works—including you—are wonderful. God made you, and He did it well.

The psalmist felt awe at the realization that God created his body. Describe what you think it would be like to feel totally accepting of your own body.

_____

_____

Do you think (or worry) about what other people think of your appearance? Why or why not?

_____

_____

How could this psalm help free you from the fear of what others think of you?

_____

_____

God Has a Plan for You

All the days ordained for me were written in your book before one of them came to be.
–Psalm 139:16b, NIV

Read verse 16b. Answer the questions below.

Describe any comfort you gain from knowing that God has a plan for your life.

_____

_____

Here are some examples of God's plans for you:

- He wants to strengthen you (Isaiah 40:29).
- He wants to provide for your welfare and give you a future and a hope (Jeremiah 29:11).
- He wants to give you things that will be good for you (Matthew 7:7-11).
- He wants you to spend eternity with Him (John 14:1-3).
- He wants you to have a love relationship with Him through His Son, Jesus Christ (John 3:16-18).
- He wants to give you a full and abundant life (John 10:10).

God Is Constant and Consistent

How precious to me are your thoughts, O God! How vast is the sum of them! Were I to count them, they would outnumber the grains of sand. When I awake, I am still with you.
–Psalm 139:17-18, NIV

Read verses 17-18. The Lord is infinite (never ending), and He is thinking about you all the time! How does that fact comfort and encourage you?

_____

_____

Your Response

Search me, O God, and know my heart; test me and know my anxious thoughts. See if there is any offensive way in me, and lead me in the way everlasting.
–Psalm 139:23-24, NIV

Read verses 23-24. Are you open to God's correction and guidance? Why or why not?

_____

_____

Openness to God's correction and guidance is the way the psalmist responds to the secure position he has with God. You also can have a secure position with God, through Jesus Christ, who died to pay for your sins and who rose from the dead to give you new life.

Your Sponsor

Being open to God's correction and guidance often involves dealing with input and feedback from persons who have developed some maturity, both in their relationship with God and in a life apart from compulsive-addictive behavior. A mature sponsor can be a tremendous help to your recovery.

Preferably this person is someone who also is in recovery from chemical dependency and who is working through a 12-Step format like yours. This person has at least one year's time (preferably more) in recovery and can supervise your Step work and be available to you in emergencies. A trusted friend or minister will do, although your best bet is with a sponsor in recovery or a Christian counselor who specializes in chemical dependency.

A sponsor should be someone who has maturity and wisdom about recovery issues and who is willing to set up proper boundaries with you. This means having an ability to help without trying to "save" you when what is best for your growth and development is responsibly facing problems, making choices, and living with the consequences. A good sponsor teaches and helps but leaves you free to make your own decisions.

> **Key Concept for Lesson 5**
> Correcting my faulty concept of God is an important recovery task.

Memorize this Step's memory verse: Philippians 2:13.

LESSON 6

Key Concept:
Correcting one's faulty concept of self is an important recovery task.

He (Jesus) said, "It is not those who are healthy who need a physician, but those who are sick. But go and learn what this means, 'I desire compassion, and not sacrifice,' for I did not come to call the righteous, but sinners."

–Matthew 9:12-13

Believing the Truth About You

We come to believe that God, through Jesus Christ, can restore us to sanity.

> *As far as the east is from the west, so far has He removed our transgressions from us.*
>
> –Psalm 103:12

Read Matthew 9:12-13. For whom did Jesus show the greatest concern?

_____

_____

From the statement "I desire compassion and not sacrifice," which of the following pleases God? He is pleased for you to be—

1. a perfect person who never makes mistakes.
2. a righteous person who obeys all the laws.
3. a caring person who has experienced failure.

Jesus' concern always has been for hurting people. He showed concern for two groups of people—those who were ill and those who saw themselves as sinners.

Do you believe that God, through Jesus Christ, can restore you to "sanity"—a life free from chemicals?   Yes   No

Describe how you think it would feel really to *believe* that Jesus wants to restore you.

_____

_____

Mark 9:16-28 tells about a father whose demon-possessed son was desperately ill. The father asked Jesus to help his son. Jesus said, "All things are possible to him who believes."

In the margin read this father's response to Jesus. If you do not believe that God can restore you to "sanity," how can you follow the father's example to "come to believe"?

_____

You can ask God to help you overcome your unbelief just as the boy's father asked. Are you willing to ask God to help you in your unbelief?

If you are willing to have God help you to overcome unbelief, will you write a prayer asking Him to give you faith in Him? If you are not yet willing, write the prayer honestly expressing your feelings.

_____

_____

_____

_____

Belief Systems

In the last two lessons you have described both your perception of God and what the Bible reveals of His nature and character. Understanding the truth of God's Word is the beginning of our restoration. Jesus repeatedly emphasized the importance of believing Him, because our actions usually are based on what we believe.

Jesus repeatedly emphasized the importance of believing Him.

The Search for Significance (www.searchlife.org) identifies four false beliefs which distort our perceptions of God and ourselves.[1] All of these lies are based on the primary belief that our self-worth equals our performance plus others' opinions. In other words we suffer from a misconception that what we do and what others think of us determines our significance, or worth.

Each of these four false beliefs results in a specific fear:

False Belief: *I must meet certain standards to feel good about myself. If I fail to meet these standards, I cannot really feel good about myself.* This belief results in the fear of failure.

False Belief: *I must be approved (accepted) by certain people to accept myself. If I do not have the approval of these people, I cannot accept myself.* This belief results in the fear of rejection.

False Belief: *Those who fail are unworthy of love and deserve to be blamed and condemned.* This belief leads to the fear of punishment and the tendency to punish others.

False Belief: *I am what I am. I cannot change. I am hopeless.* This means I am simply a total of all my past performances, both good and bad. I am what I have done. This belief leads to a sense of shame.

Each of these false beliefs has a corresponding truth from God's Word, the Scriptures:[2]

False Beliefs	Painful Emotions	God's Truths
The Performance Trap: *I must meet certain standards to feel good about myself.*	**The fear of failure**	I am completely forgiven by and fully pleasing to God. I no longer have to fear failure (Romans 5:1).
Approval Addict: *I must have the approval of certain others to feel good about myself.*	**The fear of rejection**	I am totally accepted by God. I no longer have to fear rejection (Colossians 1:21-22).
The Blame Game: *Those who fail (including myself) are unworthy of love and deserve to be punished.*	Guilt	I am deeply loved by God. I no longer have to fear punishment or punish others (1 John 2:2).
Shame: *I am what I am. I cannot change. I am hopeless.*	**Feelings of shame**	I have been made brand-new, complete in Christ. I no longer need to experience the pain of shame (2 Corinthians 5:17).

Rich and rewarding

Renewing your perception of God, others, and yourself by changing your belief systems will take time, study, and experience. You have taken years to develop patterns of behavior that reflect a false belief system. You will need time to change. Throughout this workbook we will continue to examine these beliefs. The process of learning to apply God's truths to our lives may be painful at times, but it also is rich, rewarding, and exciting!

Summary

Step 2 is a means for examining your overall belief system. Remember that the Steps are helps you will use for the rest of your life. The process of examining your concept of God and growing in your belief will continue as you recover.

You are now ready for Step 3, in which we will deal with another aspect of your believing. Step 3 is the most important aspect of faith. As you increasingly admit reality in Step 1 and grow in the ability to trust God in Step

2, you will become more capable of making life's key decision—the decision to turn your life and will over to Jesus Christ.

Relapse

relapse–n. returning to an addictive behavior (such as an addiction to chemicals) after a period of abstinence

Before moving to Step 3, you need to learn something about **relapse**. Relapse is returning to an addictive behavior after a period of abstinence. Relapse is possible for anyone in recovery, regardless of how long he or she has abstained from a particular behavior. Be alert to signs pointing toward relapse.

Warning Signals

Relapse is a process rather than an event. A group of behaviors, attitudes, feelings, and thoughts develop first. Then these lead to an action—acting out the addiction. One may fall into a relapse over a period of hours, days, weeks, or even months. Warning signals to alert you to a possible relapse include:

Signs of relapse

- Feeling uneasy, afraid, and anxious about staying clean and sober. This begins to increase as "serenity" decreases.
- Ignoring feelings of fear and anxiety and refusing to talk about them with others.
- Having a low tolerance for frustration.
- Becoming defiant, so that rebelliousness begins to replace what has been love and acceptance. Anger becomes one's ruling emotion.
- The "ISM" (I-Self-Me) attitude grows. Self-centered behavior begins to rule one's attitudes and feelings.
- Increasing dishonesty, whereby small lies begin to surface as deceptive thinking again takes over.
- Increased isolation and withdrawal characterized by missing group meetings and withdrawing from friends, family, and other support.
- Exhibiting a critical, judgmental attitude—a behavior which often is a process of projection as the person in recovery feels shame and guilt for his or her negative behaviors.
- Lack of self-confidence shown by putting down oneself, overwhelming feelings of failure, a tendency to set up oneself for failure.
- Overconfidence demonstrated by statements such as, "I'll never do that again," or by simply believing that one is the "exception" to all rules about recovery.

Special Stressors

In addition to these warning signals, be alert to certain times which can make a person more vulnerable to relapse. Some of these include:

- Completing the first week of sobriety.
- Completing the first 21 days of sobriety and any anniversaries thereafter, specifically: 90 days, six months, nine months, one year.
- Holidays.
- Personal anniversaries, birthdays, or other special days.
- Experiencing "high" moods of exuberance, perhaps after receiving a raise, getting a job, or becoming engaged or getting married. (Many people fail to realize that "high" moods are as stressful as low moods.)

- Becoming overly hungry, angry, lonely, or tired. Using the acronym, HALT, (Hungry, Angry, Lonely, Tired) can help avoid a potential relapse.

Resisting Urges

The urge to drink or use again is a normal part of recovery. The intensity and frequency of these urges depends on the severity of one's addiction and differs with each person. Be alert to those things which might trigger a compelling urge to drink or use again.

Things you once did or associate with using may be triggers to relapse. Eating certain foods, spending time in certain restaurants or bars, listening to some types of music or particular songs, being involved in certain types of festivities, such as outdoor lake parties or barbecues all may trigger the urge to drink or use. You may simply see someone drinking a beer, and suddenly you feel a strong urge to have a drink.

The above are outer triggers for drinking or using; however, we also need to be alert about what we're feeling inside that may prompt us to drink or use. Some examples might be feeling angry, distressed, overwhelmed, pressured to meet a deadline, or jealous of others who seem able to drink or use.

Being alert to what we feel

Think of times when you have experienced a strong desire to drink or use. Describe one of those situations as best you can recall it.

_____

_____

What outer triggers prompted your urge to use? _____

_____

_____

What inner feelings were you experiencing at the time? _____

_____

_____

What were some of your attitudes about recovery, about yourself, and about others at the time?

_____

_____

What steps did you take to overcome your desire to drink or use? _____

_____

_____

Try to think of five actions you can take in the future when you feel a strong urge to use. Write them in the spaces below.

_____

_____

_____

_____

_____

Key Concept for Lesson 6
Correcting my faulty concept of self is an important recovery task.

Write this Step's memory verse.

_____

_____

Step Review

Step 2 says: *We come to believe that God, through Jesus Christ, can restore us to sanity.* **Write in your own words what Step 2 means.**

_____

_____

_____

Describe how you will daily apply Step 2 to your life and recovery.

_____

_____

_____

Notes
[1]These charts adapted from Jim Craddock, Scope Ministries International, and appear in *Your Parents and You* (Houston: Rapha Publishing, 1990).
[2]Robert S. McGee, *Search for Significance* LIFE Support Edition (Houston: Rapha Publishing, 1992), 11.
[3]Ibid.

STEP 3

3. Decision to Give My Life to God

We turn our lives over to Him.

Turning It Over

A SURPRISING SURRENDER

Richard's motto was simple: "I don't need anybody." He came to the recovery group only as a condition of parole. *I don't need these people*, he grumbled to himself.

Richard was puzzled by the people he met at the meeting. He always had suspected that Christians were mindless individuals, with a list of sins to tell them what not to do and a heavenly-cop God—just waiting to make an arrest. The people at the meeting didn't fit Richard's expectations at all. They were thoughtful people with a variety of opinions and viewpoints. Most surprising, they knew how to have more fun than anyone Richard had known. The meetings included tears of grief and tears of joy. By the time he began seriously to work the Steps, Richard's motto was crumbling. Maybe he did need somebody after all.

In Step 1 Richard honestly faced his powerlessness. For the first time he admitted that his self-sufficiency was an illusion. He was a puppet on a string. A chemical jerked him here and there.

In Step 2 Richard began to identify the flaws in his concept of God. How strange it was to realize that the god for whom he had held all this anger was just a creation of Richard's experience and addiction.

Now came the really hard-to-believe part. Richard—Mr. I Don't Need Anybody—seriously was thinking about deciding to trust and surrender his life to God. (Read more about Richard on page 56)

Step 3 *We make a decision to turn our will and our lives over to God through Jesus Christ.*

Memory verse *I urge you therefore, brethren, by the mercies of God, to present your bodies a living and holy sacrifice, acceptable to God, which is your spiritual service of worship.*
—Romans 12:1

Overview for Step 3 Lesson 1: Why Step 3?
 Goal: You will describe the twofold nature of Step 3.
Lesson 2: A Change of Mind
 Goal: You will describe the biblical concept of repentance.
Lesson 3: Your Position in Christ
 Goal: You will identify the complete forgiveness Christ gives.
Lesson 4: Working the Step, Part One
 Goal: You will have an opportunity to express personal faith in Christ.
Lesson 5: Working the Step, Part Two
 Goal: You will describe the ongoing process of applying Step 3 to practical problems.

Why Step 3?

We make a decision to turn our will and our lives over to God through Jesus Christ.

> *Hence, also, He is able to save forever those who draw near to God through Him, since He always lives to make intercession for them.*
> –Hebrews 7:25

Key Concept:
I must make a decision.

Do you see the beauty and simplicity of the Steps beginning to emerge? We have lived in self-deception. We have attempted to control our moods and emotions with the result that we have become more depressed and guilt ridden. We have attempted to control everything, and in the process our lives have become more and more chaotic and painful—unmanageable. Now the Steps teach us to—

(Step 1) admit honestly that we are human beings—powerless to control many things. We especially cannot control chemical substances, which by their very nature alter our thoughts and emotions;

(Step 2) begin to believe that God cares and that if we will trust Him, He can bring order to our lives;

(Step 3) make the only possible sane decision—to stop trying to control our lives and circumstances—to let God be God. We can let Him begin to give us wisdom and strength to deal with our circumstances.

More about Richard

Romans 6:16 made a big impact on Richard. The verse says people become slaves to whatever they "present themselves." As he worked to apply Step 1 and Step 2, Richard only connected the verse to his drug of choice. He said, "Did I ever present myself to marijuana! I gave it my money, my body, and most of all my time. I can't believe how the years got away, stolen by pot."

As Richard began to work Step 3, he saw a deeper application of the verse. One night in a meeting he announced, "The problem isn't with the drug. The problem is me. Sure, if I surrender myself to the drug, it takes over. But I'm just beginning to realize that when I try to manage my life for myself, selfishness takes over. It's as if I have this thing inside that wants to control me, and either I commit myself to follow God or I will become a slave to my compulsions."

✎ **Compare Romans 6:16 that appears in the margin to Richard's statement above. Below describe how you see the principle in the verse applying to your life.**

> Do you not know that when you present yourselves to someone as slaves for obedience, you are slaves of the one whom you obey, either of sin resulting in death, or of obedience resulting in righteousness?
> –Romans 6:16

_____

_____

_____

You may have written something like this: "I cannot control and manage my life alone. Either I will become the slave of my selfishness, habits, and addictions, or I will allow God to be my master."

Why Step 3 Is Necessary

The Old Testament describes in detail the origin of sin and the fall of humanity. Adam and Eve were perfect in body, mind, and spirit, and they were free to enjoy all that was within their perfect environment—with one exception. A single tree was forbidden. God gave humanity an opportunity to choose obedience or disobedience. The verse in the margin describes the choice God offered. Adam and Eve followed Satan's suggestion and disobeyed God.

And the LORD God commanded the man, saying, "From any tree of the garden you may eat freely; but from the tree of the knowledge of good and evil you shall not eat, for in the day that you eat from it you shall surely die."
–Genesis 2:16-17

 Go back and read Romans 6:16 that appears in the margin of page 56. As long as Adam and Eve chose to obey God, they lived in the freedom of paradise. What happened when instead they chose to be their own boss and run their own lives?

_____

_____

As a result of their decision they became slaves. The slavery appears in many forms. They lost the glory God had intended for all humans, and they forfeited fellowship with God—effects all people since have felt. Adam's and Eve's deliberate rebellion also aided Satan's purpose. It gave Satan power and authority on earth. From that moment on, all of history would lead to a single hill outside of Jerusalem, where God appointed a Savior to pay the penalty for humanity's sin and rebellion. The payment would be valid not only for Adam's and Eve's acts of rebellion but for the sins of all people.

The Twofold Nature of Step 3

Step 3 works in two distinct ways. One is a once-in-a-lifetime decision. The other is a moment-by-moment decision. A woman in a group compared the Step to marriage. She said, "I was married on a specific day and time, but each day I have to live out that decision. I decide to act married."

 Read the following paragraph. Identify the two different expressions of Step 3 you find there. Underline the descriptions of the once-for-all decision and draw a circle around the descriptions of the decision which we must repeat.

submission–n. yielding to the authority or control of another

Placing your trust in Christ alone for your salvation is a one-time event through which you forever are saved from your sins and brought into an eternal relationship with God. However, living in **submission** to Him is a daily (sometimes hourly!) choice. Probably few people like the concept of being submissive in a relationship, but God's Word says you will become slaves of that which you obey (Romans 6:16).

Did you underline such phrases as "placing your trust in Christ alone," "salvation," and "brought into a relationship with God"? Did you circle such phrases as "daily submission"?

"Working" Step 3 has both meanings. Some people have made the decision to accept Jesus as their Savior, but they aren't making the decision to turn their will over to Him daily. Others seek to surrender to God their daily issues—

such as their chemical dependency—but they never have received Jesus Christ as their Savior. The way of joy and of effective living comes through working Step 3 in both ways—the Bible calls it having Jesus as Savior and Lord.

Key Concept for Lesson 1
I must make a decision.

 Pray and ask God how this concept can apply in your life. Now please review this lesson. What has God shown you that can help you?

_____

_____

➔ **Take five minutes to begin to memorize this Step's memory verse:**

I urge you therefore, brethren, by the mercies of God, to present your bodies a living and holy sacrifice, acceptable to God, which is your spiritual service of worship.

–Romans 12:1

<table>
<tr><td>

LESSON

2

</td><td>

A Change of Mind

We make a decision to turn our will and our lives over to God through Jesus Christ.

to the praise of the glory of His grace, which He freely bestowed on us in the Beloved.

–Ephesians 1:6

</td></tr>
</table>

Key Concept:
I must decide to turn over my will.

Your iniquities have made a separation between you and your God, and your sins have hidden His face from you, so that He does not hear.
–Isaiah 59:2

Our problem is self-will. Individually and collectively we have chosen to be our own bosses and run our own lives. Step 3 is the decision to reverse that self-will. As a result of Step 1—realizing that I am incapable of being God and of managing my own life—and as a result of Step 2—coming to realize that God loves me and is willing and able to save me from sin and from myself—Step 3 is a decision to turn control over to God.

 Circle the words *you* and *your* each time they appear in the passage in the margin.

Describe how your self-will has damaged your life in the following areas:

in my relationship with others _____

_____

_____

in my health _____

_____

in my finances _____

_____

in my relationship with God _____

_____

Human selfishness began when Adam rebelled against God. He brought on all people both the burden and the penalty of sin. As a result, we by nature rebel against God. We are separated from Him and deserve His righteous judgment, but God still loves us. He desires to have a loving relationship with us. We enter that love relationship through Step 3.

repentance–n. to change one's mind or purpose (Vine's)

The decision to turn our will over to God is part of what the Bible calls **repentance**. The word means a changed mind. Repentance means we turn from our sin, much like a soldier who makes an about face and marches in the opposite direction from which he was traveling before. It also means to change your mind and thoughts about something.

Repentance is not something people do completely on their own. The change includes a miracle that God works in a person's life. The decision in Step 3 could be called the door to repentance. The entire 12 Steps represent a path to repentance. The reason to work the Steps is to have a changed mind and as a result, a changed life. Humanity's problem originates from the fact that we all have attempted to take control of our will and lives. The solution begins with the decision to turn that control back to God.

✎ **Have you ever made a promise to change your life and then failed to carry out that resolution?** ❑ Yes ❑ No

In the above two paragraphs about repentance, what clue can you find that might explain why we try and fail to change our lives? Write your conclusion below.

_____

_____

You may have written that since repentance includes a miracle God works in a person's life, we cannot make some life-changes without His help. Our resolutions fail because we need God's power and wisdom.

The book *Alcoholics Anonymous* contains the story of an American business man who went to the famous psychiatrist Carl Jung. After many attempts at sobriety and much therapy, the psychiatrist declared the man a hopeless alcoholic. He said the only hope was a "vital spiritual experience" that would completely change the man's ideas and motives.[1] *Alcoholics Anonymous* defines spiritual experience or spiritual awakening as "the personality change sufficient to bring about recovery from alcoholism."[2] The 12 Steps are a practical guide for how to cooperate with God so that He will change our lives—restructure our desires, thought patterns, and motivations.

✎ Below check the best description of the "change of mind" called repentance.

❏ 1. I repent by being sorry for my wrong behavior and determining to do better in the future.
❏ 2. Since changing a life is an act of God, nothing I do can bring about repentance.
❏ 3. By practicing the principles in the 12 Steps I can cooperate with God as He changes the way I think, feel, and act.

The change called repentance is deeper than the remorse or resolutions in answer 1. God does not simply make the personality change Dr. Jung described apart from our cooperation as answer 2 suggests. The 12 Steps are a means to cooperate as God rebuilds our lives. Answer 3 is correct.

➡ Stop for a moment to pray. Thank God for loving you and desiring the best for you. Thank Him for His power, wisdom, and strength—characteristics He wants to develop in your life.

> ### Key Concept for Lesson 2
> I must decide to turn over my will.

✎ Pray and ask God how this concept can apply in your life. Now please review this lesson. What has God shown you that can help you?

_____

_____

_____

➡ Take five minutes to continue to memorize Romans 12:1.

LESSON 3

Your Position in Christ

We make a decision to turn our will and our lives over to God through Jesus Christ.

> _being justified as a gift by His grace through the redemption which is in Christ Jesus._
>
> –Romans 3:24

Key Concept:
In Christ I am unconditionally forgiven and totally accepted by God.

God's Provision for Your Sin

Having created you for fellowship with Him, God also created a way by which you can be united with Him. He sent His Son to die in your place, and through Christ's death, to pay the price for your sins. As a result you can have fellowship with God.

For Christ also died for sins once for all, the just (_____) for the unjust (_____), in order that He might bring us to God.

–1 Peter 3:18

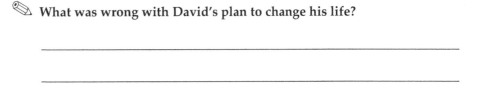 **In the verse on the left "just" means righteous—without sin. In the appropriate blanks in the verse in the margin write the name "Jesus" and your name. According to the verse, what is the result of Christ's dying for you?**

_____

_____

In the verse Jesus is the just, and we are the unjust. God's open acceptance and forgiveness is the result of Christ's death—to "bring us to God." He has paid for all sin. When we come to Him, He promises He will receive us and as the verse on the left promises, He will not cast us out. In Christ, God loves us just as if we never had sinned.

All that the Father gives Me shall come to Me, and the one who comes to Me I will certainly not cast out.

–John 6:37

Don is an 18-year-old recovering addict. These past weeks in a Christ-centered 12-Step program had changed Don's life. He realized many areas of powerlessness in his life. He was growing in the ability to trust God to take care of things he previously had sought to manage on his own. He decided to turn his will and life over to God as the only sane course of action. With so many positive changes in his life, Don determined to share his story with David, his friend and employer. David had an obvious drinking problem.

When Don shared his story, he was unprepared for David's reply. "I want to be right with God," David said. "As soon as I get this drinking problem under control, I'm going to get right with God, but He would never accept me as I am now."

 What was wrong with David's plan to change his life?

_____

_____

David thought he had to please God by his own efforts. He somehow got the idea that God would not accept him unless he was *good enough*. He could not understand and accept God's grace—because grace is the opposite of performance-based acceptance. David was unable to have what he wanted—a position of acceptance with God—precisely because what he wanted to earn is a gift that cannot be earned.

Jen was excited to share her story with her friend Lisa. She hoped Lisa would attend the group and begin to experience recovery. Jen was surprised by Lisa's response. "I have done too many things wrong," Lisa said. "God never could forgive me."

By this the love of God was manifested in us, that God has sent His only begotten Son into the world so that we might live through Him. In this is love, not that we loved God, but that He loved us and sent His Son to be the propitiation for our sins.

–1 John 4:9-10

Neither David nor Lisa understand a vitally important truth about God. The Bible expresses this truth in many ways.

1 John 4:9-10 expresses the truth that Lisa needs in her life. Read the verse and circle the second big, unfamiliar word.

The first big word—*manifested*—simply means "showed" or "demonstrated." God demonstrated His love in Jesus. But did you catch the second big word? The definition of the word **propitiation** appears in the margin of page 62.

propitiation–n. describes what happened when Christ, through His death, became the means by which God's wrath was satisfied and God's mercy was granted to the sinner who believes on Christ.

Here is some background to help you appreciate the meaning of propitiation. Have you ever watched an old movie in which one character challenged another to a duel? The character may have said something like, "You have offended my honor, and I demand satisfaction!" The idea behind "satisfaction" was that someone must pay for the insult to one's honor or reputation. The biblical idea of propitiation comes from a similar background. Our sin has offended God. He is holy and righteous, and He simply cannot overlook our offense. He would cease to be righteous if He ignored sin. His holiness must be satisfied. Payment must be made. In the Old Testament system that payment would be called the propitiation. The propitiation had to be a perfect sacrifice which was offered to pay for the person's sin.

✎ **Read again 1 John 4:9-10. Describe how the propitiation was made for our sin.**

_____

Did you see it in the verse? God "sent" Jesus to be the propitiation for our sin. Jesus' death on the cross made the payment. He became the satisfaction for all of humanity's sin.

✎ **The passage said God's wrath—His righteous anger—was satisfied. How much of His wrath was satisfied?**

❑ 1. Only God's wrath about the sins of other people.
❑ 2. Only God's wrath about sins committed in ignorance.
❑ 3. Only God's wrath for my sins before I became a Christian.
❑ 4. God's wrath about every single sin I've ever committed or ever will commit.

Jesus is the absolutely perfect sacrifice. His payment was complete. He did not satisfy some of God's wrath. He satisfied it all. Lisa, in the previous story, would benefit by understanding, believing, and applying this truth to her life. The answer is number 4.

For God so loved the world, that He gave His only begotten Son, that whoever believes in Him should not perish, but have eternal life. For God did not send the Son into the world to judge the world, but that the world should be saved through Him. He who believes in Him is not judged; he who does not believe has been judged already, because he has not believed in the name of the only begotten Son of God.

–John 3:16-18

✎ **Read the passage on the left. Jesus' death was for all people. He loves everyone. But the payment does not automatically apply to all people. Describe what you must do for Jesus' payment for sin to be effective in your life.**

_____

God loved the world so much He gave His only Son to die for us, yet only those who believe in Christ can experience God's unconditional love. Believers in Jesus will not perish—experience God's wrath—but will have eternal life instead. They will not be judged for their sins since they have accepted Christ's judgment on the cross on their behalf. Unbelievers will die without eternal life and will be judged for their own sins since they rejected Christ's payment for them.

✎ **Write your name in each of the blanks below.**

For God so loved _____, that He gave His only begotten Son,

that if _____ believes in Him, _____ should not

perish, but have eternal life. For God did not send the Son into the world to judge ______________, but so that ______________ should be saved through Him. If ______________ believes in Him ______________ is not judged.

➜ **Stop and thank God for sending His only Son, Jesus, to the world specifically for you.**

You Are Completely Forgiven by God

Christ's death not only prevented the wrath of God from falling on all of us who believe in Him, but He fully paid our debt of sin so that we are completely forgiven.

When you were dead in your sins . . . God made you alive with Christ. He forgave us all our sins, having canceled the written code, with its regulations, that was against us and that stood opposed to us; he took it away, nailing it to the cross.
–Colossians 2:13-14, NIV

➜ **Read the passage in the margin. The words "the written code" refer to the Old Testament law. The law points out our sin so that we will come to Christ for forgiveness. Pray as you read Colossians 2:13-14 and the paragraph below. Picture Jesus taking your sin and nailing it to His cross. Express to Him your thanks, love, fear, doubt, and any other emotion you feel.**

All the sins you've ever committed, all the lies you've ever told, all the evil thoughts you've ever had, all the missed opportunities for doing good—all of these and more make up your indebtedness to God. But in one eternally sufficient act through Christ's death, He covered your guilt, buried your sin, and completely forgave you of every wrong you ever committed or ever will commit.

You cannot be too bad or "too far gone" to be deeply loved and totally forgiven by God.

➜ **Ask God to forgive you for the sins in your life that have built barriers between you and Him. Thank Him for His forgiveness and for His love, even though you do not deserve it, and you cannot earn it.**

You Are Totally Accepted by God

Christ's payment for your sins removed the barrier between Him and you; you can be His beloved child and friend. Just before Jesus went to die on the cross for our sins, He spoke the words that appear in the margin.

No longer do I call you slaves, for the slave does not know what his master is doing; but I have called you friends, for all things that I have heard from My Father I have made known to you.
–John 15:15

✎ **Describe how you think it would feel to believe that Jesus considers you His valued and trusted friend.**

____

____

____

Please pray and ask God how this concept can apply in your life. Now please review this lesson. What has God shown you that can help you?

_____

_____

➜ Memorize this Step's memory verse, Romans 12:1.

LESSON
4

Key Concept:
I can begin a new relationship with God.

Working the Step, Part One

We make a decision to turn our will and our lives over to God through Jesus Christ.

> _Yet to all who receive him, to those who believed in his name, he gave the right to become children of God._
>
> –John 1:12, NIV

As you learn to apply the Steps, you will discover these principles apply to many different areas of your life. On page 57 you learned about two ways to apply Step 3. In this lesson you will explore Step 3 and your relationship with God. In the next lesson you will explore Step 3 and your relationship with recovery from chemical dependency.

Trusting in Christ

God desires to have an intimate relationship with you. He has provided you with continual access to Himself through His Son, Jesus Christ.

Are you trusting in your own abilities to earn acceptance with God?

Are you trusting in your own abilities to earn acceptance with God, or are you trusting in the death of Christ to pay for your sins? Are you trusting in what you can accomplish, or are you trusting in the resurrection of Christ to give you new life?

 Take a moment to reflect on this question. On a scale of 0 to 100 percent, how sure are you that you would spend eternity with God if you died today? Circle your response.

Unsure										Sure
0	10	20	30	40	50	60	70	80	90	100

An answer of less than 100 percent may indicate that you are trusting, at least in part, in yourself. You may be thinking, _Isn't it arrogant to say that I am 100 percent sure?_ Indeed, it would be arrogant if you were trusting in yourself—

If you were to die today and stand before God, and He were to ask you, "Why should I let you into heaven?" What would you tell Him?

your abilities, your actions, and good deeds—to earn your salvation. However, if you no longer trust in your own efforts but in the all-sufficient payment of Christ, then 100-percent certainty is a response of humility and thankfulness, not arrogance.

➜ **Reflect on the question to the left. Would you mention your abilities, church attendance, kindness to others, Christian service, abstinence from a particular sin, or some other good deed?**

Paul wrote to Titus:

But when the kindness of God our Savior and His love for mankind appeared, He saved us, not on the basis of deeds which we have done in righteousness, but according to His mercy.

–Titus 3:4-5

And to the Ephesians he wrote:

For by grace you have been saved through faith; and that not of yourselves, it is the gift of God; not as a result of works, that no one should boast.

–Ephesians 2:8-9

✎ **From these two passages, which of the things listed below are necessary in order to be saved? (Check all that apply.)**

- ❏ God's grace
- ❏ good deeds
- ❏ a positive attitude
- ❏ attempts to reform
- ❏ self-punishment
- ❏ help from others
- ❏ willpower
- ❏ faith in God

Only the first and last items in the list—God's grace and faith in God—are essential to salvation. The others actually may block the way because of a false sense of pride in your own efforts. Give up your own efforts to achieve righteousness. Instead, trust Christ's death and resurrection alone to pay for your sin and separation from God.

In Acts 16:31, Luke wrote, "Believe in the Lord Jesus, and you shall be saved."

If you have not done so already, you can receive Jesus Christ right now by invitation. Read the promise of John 1:12 appearing in the margin.

Yet to all who received him, to those who believed in his name, he gave the right to become children of God.
–John 1:12, NIV

If you are not 100 percent sure that you would spend eternity with God if you died today, and if you are willing to trust Christ and accept His payment for your sins, tell this to God in prayer right now. You may use this sample prayer to express your faith.

Lord Jesus, I need You. I want You to be my Savior and my Lord. I accept Your death on the cross as payment for my sins, and I now entrust my life to Your care. Thank You for forgiving me and for giving me a new life. Please help me grow in my understanding of Your love and power so that my life will bring glory and honor to You. Amen.

_____ (signature) _____ (date)

If you have placed your trust in Jesus Christ before you read this, consider reaffirming your faith and commitment to serve Him. You may do so by using this prayer:

Lord Jesus, I need You and thank You that I am Yours. I confess that I have sinned against You, and I ask You to "create in me a clean heart, and renew a steadfast spirit within me" (Psalm 51:10). I renew my commitment to serve You. Thank You for loving me and forgiving me. Please give me Your strength and wisdom to continue growing in You so that my life can bring glory and honor to You. Amen.

_____ (signature) _____ (date)

Trusting in Christ does not guarantee that you will be delivered instantly from chemical dependency or from any other problem in life. It means that you are forgiven; that you are restored to a relationship with Him that will last throughout eternity; and that you will receive His unconditional love and acceptance, as well as His strength, power, and wisdom, as you continue to grow in recovery.

Baptism

Identifying with Christ

Water baptism is the biblical way of showing on the outside what Christ has done for you on the inside. The act of baptism symbolizes being dead, buried, and raised with Christ. Through baptism we identify ourselves publicly with Christ and with His people. I encourage you to go to a Bible-believing church, make a public profession of your faith in Christ, and demonstrate that faith through water baptism.

> **Key Concept for Lesson 4**
> I can begin a new relationship with God.

➡ **Say aloud five times this Step's memory verse, Romans 12:1.**

LESSON 5

Key Concept:
A new relationship with God can help me overcome my addiction.

Working the Step, Part Two

We make a decision to turn our will and our lives over to God through Jesus Christ.

> *He who has found his life shall lose it, and he who has lost his life for My sake shall find it.*
> —Matthew 10:39

In the last lesson you had an opportunity to express your decision to turn your will and life over to God or to renew your previous decision. That decision applies Step 3 to your relationship with God. The Bible compares that decision to a spiritual birth. Just as physical birth is a once-in-a-lifetime experience, spiritual birth is permanent. When you are born into the Father's family, you never will be rejected again. You never will be able to commit a sin for which Jesus has not paid. Your relationship with God is absolutely secure in Jesus.

The wonderful truth in the last paragraph does not mean that your problems all are solved. Now you are ready to begin applying Step 3 in a second way. God wants to help you grow and learn to trust Him in all areas of your life.

Colossians 2:6 is a wonderful verse that describes the two ways we work Step 3: *As you therefore have received Christ Jesus the Lord, so walk in Him.*

 In the margin box describe how you received Christ. Then describe how Colossians 2:6 says you are to continue to follow Him.

Someone paraphrased Colossians 2:6 this way, "The way you get in is the way you go on." Did you note that you received Christ entirely by faith and not by any act of your own? You may have used the words of the Step. Those words said that you made a decision to turn your will and life over to Jesus Christ. Therefore, the only workable solution to living problems is to make the same decision in practical matters every day.

Making the responsible choice to trust God moment by moment, day by day, begins your new life of healing, growth, and renewal. When troubles arise, your response can be the same—to turn your life over to God through Jesus Christ. When circumstances threaten to overwhelm you and your drug of choice calls to you—turn your life over to God through Jesus Christ. When you need to make an important personal decision—turn your life over to God through Jesus Christ. When anxiety and fear threaten to overtake you, when you experience trouble and hardship—your decision can be the same. Turn your life over to God through Jesus Christ.

The Promise of Hope

The Bible word *hope* means the confidence or certainty that comes from God. He is completely dependable so we can have hope—confidence—that what He says He will do.

 Four verses about our hope in Christ appear in the margin. Match the passages to the following statements. Next to the statement which best reflects the meaning write the reference of the Scripture. We have done the first one as an example.

Ephesians 2:12   1. Before I received Christ, I had no hope.

_____ 2. My hope is assured by Jesus' victory over death.

_____ 3. God will use all the events in my life to bring about His glory and my good.

_____ 4. My hope comes from the fact that Jesus Christ lives in me.

_____ 5. My hope comes not from my performance but from God's mercy.

How I received Christ—

_____

_____

_____

_____

How I am to continue—

_____

_____

_____

_____

And we know that God causes all things to work together for good to those who love God, to those who are called according to His purpose.
–Romans 8:28

remember that you were at that time separate from Christ, excluded from the common-wealth of Israel, and strangers to the covenants of promise, having no hope and without God in the world.
–Ephesians 2:12

Christ in you, the hope of glory.
–Colossians 1:27

Blessed be the God and Father of our Lord Jesus Christ, who according to His great mercy has caused us to be born again to a living hope through the resurrection of Jesus Christ from the dead.
–1 Peter 1:3

The verses reveal that we have hope because of Christ. His love, forgiveness, and power give hope for a new life. We can be confident in knowing that absolutely nothing happens to the believer that God doesn't use to his or her betterment. The answers were: 1. Ephesians 2:12; 2. 1 Peter 1:3; 3. Romans 8:28; 4. Colossians 1:27; 5. 1 Peter 1:3.

In the Bible,
Hope = confidence
in God's power

This hope—confidence in God's power—is key to conquering your chemical dependency. Complete the following statement and memorize it.

> By the authority and power of the Son of God, I have hope that I
>
> will conquer _____

The Promise of Faithfulness

God's faithfulness is His very nature. Christ always is faithful to do what He has promised. Read the following Scripture. Then respond to the statements that follow.

No temptation has overtaken you but such as is common to man; and God is faithful, who will not allow you to be tempted beyond what you are able, but with the temptation will provide the way of escape also, that you may be able to endure it.
—1 Corinthians 10:13

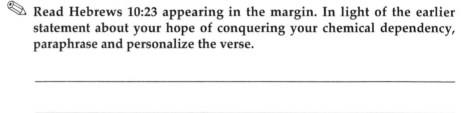 **Mark the following statements as *T* (True) or *F* (False).**

_____ God cannot give me enough strength to endure the difficulty.
_____ I have uncommonly powerful temptations.
_____ Many of my temptations are beyond my ability to resist.
_____ Being tempted is as wrong as sinning.

All but one of the above statements are false. Your temptations may be beyond your ability to resist, but they are not beyond God's power to work in your life. Look for God's faithfulness as you trust Him to help you when you are tempted to drink or to use.

Let us hold fast the confession of our hope without wavering, for He who promised is faithful.
—Hebrews 10:23

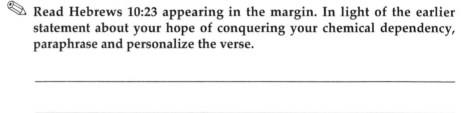 **Read Hebrews 10:23 appearing in the margin. In light of the earlier statement about your hope of conquering your chemical dependency, paraphrase and personalize the verse.**

_____

_____

Steps 1, 2, and 3 serve as preparation for the work you will do in recovery. To move beyond this point will require continued courage.

Following the Path

Step 3 is a decision. Many people make a fatal error at the point of the decision to follow Christ. They think the decision is the destination. They may say, "I'm saved" as though that is the ultimate accomplishment. On the portion of the course map below, note the words on the cross, "Changed Life Ahead."

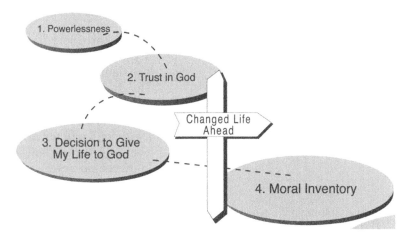

Step 3 brings us to a decision based on the facts that—
- We are powerless—not only over chemicals but over many things including the power of sin (Step 1).
- We are coming to trust the Living God who both loves us and is all power (Step 2).
- Therefore we make the decision—to turn over to God the right to direct our lives.

The journey begins

The decision to follow Christ is not the destination. It is the beginning of the journey.

 Use the course map, the paragraphs above, and all that you have been experiencing in recovery to write your own statement about how you will seek carry out the decision in Step 3. Or, write how you would tell a newcomer how to carry out the Step 3 decision.

_____

_____

_____

In response to the learning activity, one person wrote,"Now I know how to follow Christ. I need to work the Steps!"

In the Old Testament Joshua was Moses' successor. As he prepared to assume leadership and bring the nation of Israel into the promised land, he undoubtedly felt anxious at the enormous task before him. God promised Joshua, "Just as I have been with Moses, I will be with you; I will not fail you or forsake you" (Joshua 1:5). Jesus made the same promise. He said, "I am with you always, even to end of the age" (Matthew 28:20). Three times God told Joshua, "Be strong and courageous" (Joshua 1:6-7,9). In Step 4 you will learn exactly what courageous means and how to be "strong and courageous." As you prepare to take the Step, you may find helpful the words of an old hymn.

"Fear not, I am with thee; O be not dismayed,
For I am thy God and will still give thee aid;
I'll strengthen thee, help thee, and cause thee to stand,
Upheld by My righteous, omnipotent hand.

"When thro' fiery trials thy pathway shall lie,
My grace, all-sufficient, shall be thy supply;
The flame shall not hurt thee; I only design
Thy dross to consume, and thy gold to refine.

"The soul that on Jesus hath leaned for repose,
I will not, I will not desert to his foes;
That soul, tho' all hell should endeavor to shake,
I'll never, no never, no never forsake."[3]

Key Concept for Lesson 5
A new relationship with God can help me overcome my addiction.

Step Review

Write this Step's memory verse.

____

____

Step 3 says: ***We make a decision to turn our will and our lives over to God through Jesus Christ.*** **In your own words write what Step 3 means.**

____

____

____

Have you made that decision? Describe how you will daily apply Step 3 to your life and recovery.

____

____

____

Notes
[1]Alcoholics Anonymous, 26-27.
[2]Ibid, 569.
[3]John Rippon's *Selection of Hymns*, 1787, "How Firm a Foundation," *The Baptist Hymnal* (Nashville: Convention Press, 1991).

We make a moral inventory.

My Moral Inventory

RUNNING FROM PAIN

Peggy expected surgery on her back to solve her problem. Little did she realize that her problems had only begun.

After the surgery Peggy experienced intense pain. She told her doctor she couldn't stand it another moment. She demanded stronger medication. She found the pills did more than make her pain go away. She liked the way they made her feel. In a few days the pain from her back began to lessen, but she found excuses to continue the pills. She rationalized that her pain was greater than other people experienced.

Finally Peggy's doctor refused to write any more prescriptions for the pain medication, but she found other sources to meet her growing need. She went to as many as four different doctors at the same time. She bought her prescriptions from pharmacies in various parts of the city. By the time she exhausted these methods, Peggy had discovered a pharmacist who was willing to sell narcotics "off the record." He had a supply from a false burglary report. When her pharmacist was arrested, Peggy found a contact from whom she could buy pills. The pain—that was the reason she had to do the things she did. She must do whatever it took to avoid the pain.

When Peggy was arrested, her plea-bargain included inpatient drug treatment. There she learned about the Steps and about a searching moral inventory. Her counselor said Peggy would find the truth only by writing her inventory. (Read more about Peggy on page 74)

Step 4   *We make a searching and fearless moral inventory of ourselves.*

Memory verse   *Let us examine and probe our ways, and let us return to the Lord.*
–Lamentations 3:40

Overview for Step 4   Lesson 1: **Why Take a Moral Inventory?**
      Goal: You will describe what a moral inventory is and what a moral inventory is not.
Lesson 2: **Dishonesty and Resentment**
      Goal: You will write an inventory of dishonesty and resentment.
Lesson 3: **Self-Pity and False Pride**
      Goal: You will write an inventory of self-pity and false pride.
Lesson 4: **Criticism and Destructive Anger**
      Goal: You will write an inventory of criticism and destructive anger.
Lesson 5: **Fear and Impatience**
      Goal: You will write an inventory of fear and impatience.
Lesson 6: **Selfishness and Sex**
      Goal: You will write an inventory of selfishness and sexual behavior.

LESSON 1

Why Take a Moral Inventory?

We make a searching and fearless moral inventory of ourselves.

> *He is on the path of life who heeds instruction, but he who forsakes reproof goes astray.*
>
> –Proverbs 10:17

Key Concept:
A moral inventory is an honest look at the good and the bad in my life.

immoral. –adj. Moral means having to do with both right and wrong. Immoral means only that which is wrong.

We learned in Step 2 that *sanity* can mean exercising sound judgment or making wise, rational decisions. In Step 4, we will see that the best way to determine the course of our future—using sound judgment—is to obtain the facts about our past. Reviewing our past enables us to work today toward a successful tomorrow.

Step 4 refers to taking an inventory. Shopkeepers take inventory of their stores so that they will know what they have in stock. They will know what is damaged, outdated, and needs replacing; what they need to order; and what new items they need. A self-inventory is not a list of wrongs one has committed. An inventory is a thorough individual evaluation. It is a complete assessment of our good and bad traits, strengths and weaknesses, assets and liabilities, and how they work for and against us.

Someone in a group said, "When I first came into program, I thought Step 4 meant I was to take a complete *immoral* inventory of myself." Use the information from the last paragraph to explain what the person meant by an "immoral" inventory.

_____

_____

The person referred to the idea of an inventory as self-condemnation. She thought the idea was to beat herself up by reviewing all the bad things she ever had done. She was surprised to learn that an inventory means an honest look at the good and the bad in her life.

In Step 4 we will examine what we've done well and what we've done poorly. Perhaps we have made improvements in an area of life that always has been difficult for us. We may have taken some action to promote love, kindness, consideration, healing, or health. We also must ask what we've done to harm ourselves or others, to cause pain, bitterness, fear or division. Have we allowed anger and resentment to dominate our relationships? Have we manipulated other people? Have we been selfish, dishonest, or disloyal? How have we dealt with our sexuality? By answering these questions we will gain many benefits.

In the following paragraph circle the benefits that come from taking a searching moral inventory.

Far from being a means of condemning ourselves, or of putting ourselves down, a *searching and fearless moral inventory* is a means to develop healthy self-esteem. It is a plan for growth and maturity. It exposes hazards which may lead to relapse. It highlights individual strengths and gifts we possess in our uniqueness as people God created. All of these strengths and gifts support recovery. A moral inventory also helps us discover our weaknesses. Looking at the negative part of our personalities and behavior is difficult but valuable. A review of our past often helps us understand why we behaved in the ways we have in the past and why we act as we do in the present. By understanding the why's of our behavior, we often gain a new acceptance of ourselves.

You may have circled such benefits as building self-esteem, growing in maturity, warning you of relapse, seeing your strengths, admitting your weaknesses, and understanding your behavior. If you fear self-discovery, remember that God desires your healing. His strong love for you will help you overcome your fears.

There is no fear in love; but perfect love casts out fear.
—1 John 4:18

Before you continue, read the verse appearing in the margin. Stop and pray, thanking God that His love overcomes your fear. Ask Him to give you the power to be honest, open, and willing to work the Step.

Finally, an objective review of the past enables us to confront our age-old enemy—denial. In the past we used denial to escape hurtful remarks, avoid facing a deteriorating self-image, and keep from confronting difficult responsibilities and circumstances. In reality, denial prevented us from progressing in our lives. It takes courage to face the aspects you need to change about your personality and behavior. It may be equally difficult to accept your strengths and virtues. You may reject what is good and see only what you dislike about yourself. This is a destructive form of perfectionism.

He who conceals his transgressions will not prosper, but he who confesses and forsakes them will find compassion.
—Proverbs 28:13

Read the proverb that appears in the margin. Describe how hiding your addiction has given it more power over you.

_____

_____

Trying to hide your flaws—from others and from yourself—seems like a good solution. When you hide something about yourself from others, you usually invest a great amount of energy in maintaining appearances. As time passes, keeping the secret hidden consumes more and more of your attention and resources. Your "investment" in self-protection gives the secret more power over you. Secrecy also prevents you from facing squarely the consequences of your behavior. This leads to an inner sense of despair. Thus the cycle of addictive behavior continues. It goes from irresponsible act to denial to guilt and all over again. It is a vicious cycle leading eventually to self-destruction.

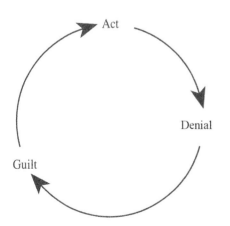

Notice the margin drawing of this vicious cycle. The cycle begins with stress in our lives. When the stress builds to a certain level, we turn to some action that we have found will relieve the stress. We call that behavior our "drug of choice." For some people the drug of choice can be working, gambling, or some other action. For us our drug of choice is a mood-altering chemical. After we have used our drug of choice, we feel guilty. The guilt brings on more stress. We deny the problem. Denial multiplies the stress. Eventually the stress drives us back to the behavior, and the cycle repeats itself.

We can break the cycle of denial-guilt-repeated action, but we only break the cycle by honestly facing the truth. In Step 2, you decided to seek God to restore your sanity through Jesus Christ. To replace denial with courageous honesty may be painful, but we gain control of our lives again because honesty robs our character defects of the power that secrecy gives them. We then can fill with God's truth the emptiness which we tried to fill with a mood-altering substance. This opens the door for freedom. Jesus said, *you shall know the truth, and the truth shall make you free* (John 8:32).

How Will God Respond to Your Honesty?

Because God is steadfast and consistent, you can depend on Him. When you write your inventory and then share it with Him, you will not tell Him anything new or unusual. Nothing about you is strange to Him.

> **Read the two Scriptures at left. According to 1 John 1:8-9, what two things does God do when we confess our sins honestly to Him?**
>
> _____
>
> According to Hebrews 4:15-16, what is Jesus uniquely able to do because He has lived in flesh like our own?
>
> _____

If we claim to be without sin, we deceive ourselves and the truth is not in us. If we confess our sins, he is faithful and just and will forgive us our sins and purify us from all unrighteousness.
–1 John 1:8-9, NIV

For we do not have a high priest who cannot sympathize with our weaknesses, but one who has been tempted in all things as we are, yet without sin. Let us therefore draw near with confidence to the throne of grace, that we may receive mercy and find grace to help in time of need.
–Hebrews 4:15-16

When we confess, God always is faithful not only to accept our confession but also to forgive our sins and cleanse us from all unrighteousness. Because He has shared our experience, He can sympathize with us. He will not reject us. He will give mercy and grace to help us.

As our denial begins to crumble, we will begin to see the truth about our lives. We will see that our addictive behavior caused problems in our relationships, that we had trouble controlling our emotions, that we were desperately unhappy—often filled with fear, a sense of isolation, uselessness, and self-pity. We used alcohol or other drugs to fill our emptiness. They took away the pain for a while, but they increased our emptiness in the process. We worked hard to control circumstances and loved ones to get our needs met. Increasingly unable to tolerate ourselves, we projected onto others our self-hatred. We may have been physically or verbally abusive. Or, we may have repressed our painful emotions and nursed our grudges and resentments. We may have believed we had a "right" to such feelings.

More of Peggy's story

Peggy didn't understand. She stopped using her pills. She had been clean since the month in rehabilitation. She thought her family would appreciate her sacrifice. She believed her problems would resolve themselves and her relationships would improve. Now just the opposite was occurring. Her family seemed more difficult than ever to live with. Her anger and frustration were mounting daily. The counselor's statement echoed in Peggy's mind, "You'll never find the truth without writing your moral inventory."

> **In the next paragraph look for a reason that might explain why Peggy's life and relationships seem to be deteriorating rather than improving. In the activity that appears after the passage describe your conclusion.**

We often think that if I only stop drinking/using then my life will get better. We fail to realize that the chemicals have been our defense mechanism to avoid having to deal with our problems. While we may have stopped our use of chemicals, we cannot resolve these problems unaided. We must confess them, draw them out into God's light and love, and release them. Step 4 is the means to accomplish this task.

In the margin describe a possible reason you found in the paragraph that might explain why Peggy's life is going nowhere.

Did you note that Peggy assumed her problems would go away if she just stopped her drug use? She didn't recognize that she would have to deal with more than just quitting. Someone at a meeting put it this way, "If I have been putting garbage in my basement for years and then suddenly stop putting in more trash, the smell does not automatically go away. I still have to clean the garbage out of my basement." Peggy needed to do more than stop using. She needed to face her life honestly by writing her Step 4 inventory.

This Step in *Conquering Chemical Dependency* will help you to write your inventory. Go slowly. Each lesson covers two or more areas to inventory. Take your time. Try to work through a single area per day. Your only goal in this exercise is to think, to reflect, and to examine your life. Ask God to show you what He wants you to see about your past, and then trust Him to reveal to you *what* you need to know *when* you need to know it. Use extra paper as needed.

> ### Key Concept for Lesson 1
> A moral inventory is an honest look at the good and the bad in my life.

Pray and ask God how this concept can apply in your life. Now please review this lesson. What has God shown you that can help you?

_____

_____

Memorize Lamentations 3:40, this Step's memory verse.

Why Peggy's problems aren't going away—
_____
_____
_____
_____
_____

LESSON 2

Key Concept:
Honesty and forgiveness are essential to my recovery.

Dishonesty and Resentment

We make a searching and fearless moral inventory of ourselves.

> *If, however, you are fulfilling the royal law, according to the Scripture, "YOU SHALL LOVE YOUR NEIGHBOR AS YOURSELF," you are doing well.*
> –James 2:8

Sarah had been anxious about problems within her family when she visited her physician for a routine exam. He prescribed tranquilizers to help her sleep. He intended that she take one each night at bedtime. Sarah followed his instructions for about six months, but her anxiety persisted. Having

Sarah's story

discovered that a tranquilizer soothed her every time she became irritable, she began to increase her dosage. Later, she discovered that the drug's tranquil effect was even more pronounced when she took it with a glass of wine. Within the course of 10 years, Sarah developed a serious addiction to alcohol and prescription drugs.

In an effort to feed her addiction, Sarah conned her parents into "loaning" her money, which she never returned. She took money from her husband's wallet. When he asked her about it, she blamed the children. When her family finally made an attempt at **intervention**, Sarah employed guilt to convince them that they were the source of her troubles, and that they—not she—needed help. She continued to use, and she began hiding her prescription bottles. It wasn't until she was arrested for forging her physician's name at a pharmacy that Sarah realized the truth of her addiction and her dishonesty.

intervention–n. the term for an organized effort by the family and friends of an addict to make him or her see the truth and get help

Answer the following questions to see if you are being honest with yourself and others.

Alibis

We attempt to hide our behavior by making up excuses which only are partially true or which are purely fiction. When have you been dishonest by using alibis?

_____

_____

_____

Denial

Denial appears in an outright lie or a refusal to believe the truth. The classic example occurs when we are addicted to one or more chemicals but are unwilling to admit our condition to ourselves or others. What insights have you experienced about how denial has affected your life?

_____

_____

_____

Displaced blame

Do you sometimes seek to excuse yourself by blaming others rather than facing up to a mistake, error, or sin you have committed? What others have you blamed? How does this affect you and your relationships?

_____

_____

_____

_____

Exaggeration

Describe an incident in which you've stretched the truth to make things seem better or worse than they really were.

_____

_____

_____

Minimizing

In an attempt to make an offense seem smaller than it really is, we understate the truth. A person who has completely dented another person's car door in an accident may attempt to minimize the situation by saying, "The damage was only a scratch." Describe a time when you use minimizing.

_____

_____

_____

Stealing

Stealing occurs in many forms: taking work supplies home; borrowing money we never repay; using the company's photocopy machine for personal copies; stealing time at work by conducting personal business during office hours.

How and from whom have you stolen?

_____

_____

_____

Falsifying the truth would seem obvious, but it often isn't. Many of us flatter people and pretend to care about them when we really want something from them. Or, instead of telling others what we want, we condemn them and make them feel guilty so that we can control and manipulate them. Other forms of pretense include saying "We'll see," when we mean no or, "I'd love to have you come," when we'd rather you didn't. We say we _must_ do something when the truth is that we _want_ to do something. The list is endless. The bottom line is that dishonesty has no place in sobriety.

Lying

Describe how you have been guilty of lying.

_____

_____

_____

All forms of dishonesty have one thing in common. We feel ashamed of something, and we do not want to be found out.

> O LORD, you have searched me and you know me. You know when I sit and when I rise; you perceive my thoughts from afar. You discern my going out and my lying down; you are familiar with all my ways. Before a word is on my tongue you know it completely, O LORD.
> —Psalm 139: 1-4, NIV

Read Psalm 139:1-4. Does realizing that the Lord already knows everything about you—both good and bad—help you to be more honest? Why or why not?

_____

_____

In recovery being honest becomes easier because we have less to hide. One way of stating the purpose of the Steps has to do with honesty. When we work the Steps we eventually desire to reach the life situation that we are "false proof." We won't have to fear that anyone will discover the truth about us—that we are false. We will look in the mirror in the morning and see someone whom we like. More importantly, we'll see someone we respect.

Self-check on Resentment

Resentment is a refusal to let go of anger about some past harm or perceived injury. It is a highly destructive form of self-defense. It often is expressed as a desire to punish the person who offended you.

Brad tells how resentment once governed his life. "I had a video camera and a video screen in my head," Brad said. "I got up in the morning and started my playback. I'd replay every bad thing anyone ever did to me. By the time I was halfway through my resentments, I was ready to get stoned. I deserved to get high. Just look at how everyone was treating me."

How have your thoughts, feelings, and actions been like like Brad's?

_____

_____

_____

Do you sometimes use any of the following expressions of resentment? Check all that you have used.

selective forgetfulness to punish   self-righteous indignation
chronic lateness   blame
gossip, slander, defamation   plotting or seeking revenge
long-term nursing of anger   sarcasm
"justifiable" grudge-bearing   unforgiveness
avoidance/silent treatment   other _____

Holding grudges

Do you tend to hold grudges? Can you think of anyone you aren't willing to forgive? When will you? What will it take?

_____

_____

_____

Sarcasm

Describe recent situations in which you used sarcasm to hide your anger toward others.

_____

_____

_____

Gossip, slander, defamation

Describe a situation when you gossiped or talked about the wrongs or misfortunes of others because you wanted to punish them.

_____

_____

_____

Revenge

What ways—hidden or obvious—do you use to get even with those who hurt you?

_____

_____

_____

Avoidance/silent treatment

Explain any incident in which you've given the "silent treatment" to someone with whom you've been angry. This may have involved punishing that person by refusing to talk with him or her.

_____

_____

_____

Describe any other ways in which you've expressed resentment toward another person.

_____

_____

_____

Mark any of the following authority figures toward whom you feel (or have felt) contempt.

Parent(s)   Spouse
Boss/Supervisor   Church leader
Government official   School official
Other _____

Forgiveness: Reclaiming Damaged Relationships

Forgiveness is mercy triumphing over punishment. When you forgive, you give up your "right" to punish the one who offended you.

Carefully read the following paragraph. From the list of statements that appear after the passage, check all the statements that are true according to the paragraph.

I am responsible

True forgiveness is an informed decision to bear the pain of another's offense without demanding that he or she be punished for it. This does not mean you overlook or accept unacceptable behavior. The process of forgiving may include talking with the person who has hurt you about his or her behavior and/or allowing that person to experience any negative consequences the behavior produces. This enables the offender to understand at least some of the effects of the wrongdoing. However, pointing out another's faults or your willingness to forgive the person may not cause the offender to change his or her behavior or cause your relationship to change. Regardless of another person's response, you are responsible for forgiving anyone who offends you.

Check each statement that is true according to the paragraph you just read.

1. Forgiveness is a feeling.
2. Forgiveness is a decision not to demand repayment of a debt.
3. Forgiveness means I must overlook others' wrong behavior.
4. Forgiveness means the other person does not have to face the consequences of his or her actions.
5. Forgiveness means the other person will change his or her behavior.
6. Forgiveness is my responsibility and does not depend on the other person's response.
7. Forgiveness is my choice to stop torturing myself.

Did you note that most of the answers to the questions were false? Only 2, 6, and 7 are true. The other answers are commonly accepted false beliefs about forgiveness. Number 7 is true even though the paragraph didn't contain the statement. The wisest choice a person can make is to forgive, because resentment is self-destructive.

Three good reasons to forgive are:

- God commands you to forgive others through Jesus Christ. "And whenever you stand praying, forgive, if you have anything against anyone" (Mark 11:25).

- God through Jesus Christ has forgiven you. "And be kind to one another, tender-hearted, forgiving each other, just as God in Christ also has forgiven you" (Ephesians 4:32).

- An unforgiving spirit is self-destructive. Not forgiving often leads to suppressed hurt and anger. Repressing these powerful negative emotions affects every relationship you have and leads to bitterness, depression, and separation from others. This deadly combination can lead to relapse.

forgiveness–n. the act of giving up resentment of or claim to requital for an insult; to grant relief from payment of a debt; to pardon (Webster's)

When Wanda was a child, a relative sexually abused her. Wanda vowed that she never would forgive her abuser. When a counselor confronted Wanda about her need to forgive, she said, "I'm never going to let him off that easy." The problem is "he" was not the one who was suffering; Wanda was. Refusing to forgive injures the one who carries resentment.

What people have offended you or harmed you? What did they do to you?

Person	Offense
_____	_____
_____	_____
_____	_____
_____	_____
_____	_____
_____	_____

resentment equals self-punishment

What would it mean for you to release each person from the penalty he or she owes you?

Person   If I forgive . . .

_____   _____

_____   _____

_____   _____

_____   _____

Key Concept for Lesson 2
Honesty and forgiveness are essential to my recovery.

Write three times in the margin this Step's memory verse.

Pray and ask God how this concept can apply in your life. Now please review this lesson. What has God shown you that can help you?

_____

_____

_____

LESSON 3

Key Concept:
I continue to hurt myself with self-pity, false pride, and false humility.

Self-pity and False Pride

We make a searching and fearless moral inventory of ourselves.

A man's pride will bring him low, but a humble spirit will obtain honor.
—Proverbs 29:23

In this lesson you will study self-pity and false pride/false humility—two more methods we use to defend ourselves. Either method results in self-deception. In certain circumstances, we may attempt to fool ourselves and others into thinking we are better than they are or worse than they are.

Often we play these games for so long that we become completely deceived into believing that we are helpless, worthless, and pitiful. If others don't provide sufficient sympathy, we may wallow in paralyzing self-pity until they either finally feel sorry for us or totally reject us out of frustration and disgust. God wants us to replace these games with gratitude and genuine humility.

Self-pity: How to Be a Life-long Victim

One of the most common causes of self-pity is a sense of being victimized by others. Without attention and care, the wounds continue to ache. Nothing is wrong with acknowledging the fact that you have been hurt. To allow yourself to experience the pain associated with the hurt is essential to healing, but when you let the experience drag out too long in your mind, you run the risk of falling into a "pity trap."

In a pity trap you see yourself as an innocent victim to the extent that you deny to others and to yourself your capacity for doing wrong. In extreme cases you may become emotionally paralyzed. You may blame others for your problems and for your depression. Blaming others gives them control over you. Self-pity may prompt you to control and manipulate others in an attempt to have them do for you what you need to do for yourself.

Blaming others gives them control over you.

Take time to read carefully this list of common characteristics associated with self-pity. Check those you have thought, felt, or said.

Projection: "I feel bad . . . it's your/his/her fault."
Denial: "I never did anything wrong."
Avoiding responsibility by reciting a long list of past hurts.
Avoiding responsibility by pleading physical illness or distress.
Reading the "whine list": "I can't." "I tried once before." "I never get anything right."
Controlling others by making them feel important. "You're the only friend I have." "You're the only one who understands me."

At one time or another all of us have employed some or most of the techniques in the list. Answer the following questions as honestly as you can to explore the hold self-pity has on your life. Remember that freedom comes through rigorous honesty.

Self-check on Self-pity

Denial

Are you afraid to admit when you have done something wrong? If so, why?

_____

_____

"Whine List"

What do you hope to accomplish by seeking others' pity?

_____

_____

Excuses: Physical

Have you relied on physical complaints or illnesses to escape responsibility? If so, explain.

_____

_____

Excuses: Emotional

In what ways do you avoid taking responsibility for yourself because of past abuse or because of some other misfortune you've suffered? How has this increased the burden you've carried?

_____

_____

Manipulation

Have you loaded praise or thankfulness on another person—emphasizing how important he or she is to you—in order to get that person to take care of you or protect you? If so, explain.

_____

_____

Gratitude: Cure for the "Pity Party Blues"

As you work the Steps, you will experience many changes. You will become more thankful. You will realize that the changes you and other people are beginning to see in you result from God's intervention and from your courage.

Gratitude motivates you to share this news with other people. Also, as you start to feel better about yourself and become less preoccupied with your own problems, you begin wanting to exercise responsibility and to share your resources with other people: your time, energies, talents, and sometimes even your finances. You may be surprised to discover that giving yourself to others brings great satisfaction. "Freely you received, freely give" (Matthew 10:8).

List the people, situations, and things for which you are thankful.

_____

_____

Give an example of how gratitude helped you overcome a period of self-pity.

_____

False Pride/False Humility: Two Sides of a Counterfeit Coin

Among the many ailments springing from addiction, false pride and false humility are among the most destructive. These are extreme perspectives in which you swing from feeling like the "general manager of the universe" to being "poor me." As one recovering person said: "Sometimes I think I am God, and the rest of the time I think I'm pond scum."

"Sometimes I think I'm God. Sometimes I think I'm pond scum."

False pride keeps recovery from happening because it is based on the notion that you don't need help from God or other people. You are self-sufficient. This emotional game usually includes an unwillingness to seek help; an unwillingness to be wrong and apologize; and an unwillingness to admit powerlessness over any habit, including drinking or using.

devaluation–n. a lessening of value, status, or stature (Webster's)

False humility is self-**devaluation**. It is putting one's self down because of negative conclusions from past hurts. False humility is marked by self-condemnation, passive behavior, fear, and a sense of hopelessness and defeat.

In recovery, we replace our false pride and false humility with an accurate appraisal of our worth based on our value in God's eyes. The apostle Peter wrote, "You were not redeemed with perishable things like silver or gold . . . but with the precious blood, as of a lamb unblemished and spotless, the blood of Christ" (1 Peter 1:18-19).

Self-check on False Pride/False Humility

Superiority

What situations prompt you to think or act as if you were "the general manager of the universe"?

_____

_____

Why do you think you've sometimes felt this way about yourself?

1. I am better, smarter, and wiser than other people.
2. I criticize anything less than perfect that I or others do.
3. I secretly feel worth less than others, and I cover my feelings up by attempting to prove my worth.
4. I become angry with others when they fail to measure up.
5. I become angry with myself when others fail to measure up.
6. Other _____

Hopelessness

Give examples of situations in which you have you experienced fear, a sense of hopelessness, or defeat.

_____

_____

In what kinds of situations do you tend to act passively? Why do you think you become passive in those situations?

_____

_____

How have these feelings and actions affected you and your relationships?

_____

_____

Humility: Having the Mind of Christ

Humility is the opposite of pride and arrogance. People must be comfortable with themselves in order to practice humility. In the passage that appears in

When someone invites you to a wedding feast, do not take the place of honor, for a person more distinguished than you may have been invited. If so, the host who invited both of you will come and say to you, "Give this man your seat." Then, humiliated, you will have to take the least important place. But when you are invited, take the lowest place, so that when your host comes, he will say to you, "Friend, move up to a better place." Then you will be honored in the presence of all your fellow guests. For everyone who exalts himself will be humbled and he who humbles himself will be exalted.

–Luke 14:8-11, NIV

the margin Jesus told the story of the chief seats at the feast. In Jesus' day how people were seated at a banquet demonstrated their social importance.

Read the story that appears in the margin. Then check each of the following statements which is true of you.

Taking the lowest seat is easy because I feel good about myself.
Taking the lowest seat would be very difficult for me.
I always take the lowest seat. I feel that I don't deserve better.
I would take the lowest seat but I would resent it.
Other _____

Humility begins with acknowledging that you are powerless over alcohol and other drugs. It continues as you submit yourself to God daily. By working the Steps you are moving toward the time when the first response above will describe your feelings. With time, work, and support, you will reach the place that you feel comfortable with who you are. You will look in the mirror and see someone you respect and value.

Imagine for a moment that the first response to the exercise describes how you feel. Imagine that you sit very comfortably in a place out of the limelight—not because you feel unworthy, but because you feel good about yourself. Describe how your life will be different when you feel good about yourself.

_____

_____

As you continue to practice humility and to grow spiritually and emotionally, you may realize you need support from other people. When you feel out of sorts or are tempted to indulge in "stinking thinking" or to use, call on others or attend a support-group meeting. The fellowship you find there will help to meet the needs you once tried to fill with chemicals. By listening to other people who share your predicament, you realize that everyone—including you—has strengths and weaknesses. You realize that it's OK to be human and to be genuine with other people and with God.

Some have experienced abuse or neglect to the point that they fear loss of control. For them the idea of humility may sound like more of the old abuse.

Does the idea of being humble frighten or disgust you? If so, how and why?

_____

_____

Humble yourselves, therefore, under God's mighty hand, that he may lift you up in due time.
–1 Peter 5:6 NIV

Humility does not mean returning to an abusive situation. We are to humble ourselves "under God's mighty hand." Then we appropriately humble ourselves before other people as an expression of that love and trust in God. If the prospect of humility frightens you, remember the work you did in Step 2 on your concept of God. Little by little you can learn to trust your Heavenly Father to protect and care for you.

Describe how humility can be a sign of strength.

_____

_____

Describe how practicing humility can affect or now affects . . .

your life _____

_____

your relationship with God _____

_____

your relationships with other people _____

_____

> ## Key Concept for Lesson 3
> I continue to hurt myself with self-pity, false pride, and false humility.

Pray and ask God how this concept can apply in your life. Now please review this lesson. What has God shown you that can help you?

_____

_____

Take five minutes to continue to memorize this Step's memory verse:
Let us examine and probe our ways, and let us return to the Lord.
–Lamentations 3:40

LESSON 4

Criticism and Destructive Anger

We make a searching and fearless moral inventory of ourselves.

Do not associate with a man given to anger; or go with a hot-tempered man, lest you learn his ways and find a snare for yourself.
–Proverbs 22:24-25

Key Concept:
I replace criticism and destructive anger with love, forgiveness, and honesty.

Fear sometimes drives us to do destructive things, especially when that fear is based on the false belief that we are unworthy of love and deserve to be punished. The resulting fear that others will punish or criticize us causes us to lash out at others in an effort to attack them before they attack us. Whether or not they really plan to attack us isn't the point: fear of punishment drives us to punish them first. We deflect the pain from ourselves and project it onto them.

With enough practice at this game, we eventually can delude ourselves into believing we always are right and others, who may question or criticize us, always are wrong. In essence, we play God. In time, we even may begin to enjoy picking at others, finding and exposing their faults, and punishing their wrongs—real or imagined. We may have left behind a number of victims of our sometimes cruel, vindictive anger.

Two emotional games

In this lesson, you will confront two particularly damaging emotional games you may have played: criticism and destructive anger. It may be a time of painful reflection, but the growth will be worth the pain.

> **Before you continue, stop and ask God to help you see the truth about this part of yourself. Pray for wisdom to know what to do about the truth you see and for a sense of His healing and forgiveness for all past failures.**

Criticism: Verbal Dissection

The criticism described here is not the constructive advice we offer to a friend. It is the negative judgment of others—and ourselves—that is rooted in pride and in our need to be perfect or to be perceived as perfect. Usually this criticism takes the form of verbal abuse, but sometimes it can be more subtle. Sarcasm or silence can mask it.

We use criticism for many different reasons. One is that we see others as a reflection of ourselves. Criticizing them is a form of control to motivate them to conform to our standards.

We may put other people down to elevate ourselves. This usually results from a low sense of self-worth and from the belief that if we criticize others, we can make ourselves look better. Still another reason to criticize others is that it feels right; after all, those who fail *deserve* to be condemned and punished.[1]

At other times we may be critical because we truly believe others need our guidance. We perceive that our correction will benefit them. Later, we are surprised to realize that these people avoid us because our habit of "correcting" has been more *de*structive than *con*structive to them.

Therefore, encourage one another, and build up one another.
                    –1 Thessalonians 5:11

The Scriptures emphasize loving others and building them up rather than tearing them down. In the verses appearing in the margin read how Paul and John described the attitude that ideally supports our interaction with others.

Beloved, let us love one another, for love is from God; and everyone who loves is born of God and knows God. Beloved, if God so loved us, we also ought to love one another.
                    –1 John 4:7,11

Self-check on Criticism

> **Why do you criticize other people? What is your main motivation? What results do you expect? Check all the responses that apply.**

I feel better when someone else is the focus of blame.
I feel threatened when people don't do things well.

I fear criticism, so I criticize others before they can criticize me.
I am critical because others don't do their jobs well.
I'm only trying to help.
Other _____

In what ways do you communicate criticism?

Sarcasm
Pointing out mistakes
Silence, with a raised eyebrow
"Helpful" suggestions
Snide remarks to others (gossip)
Other _____

Communicating criticism

How does a critical attitude affect your relationships, including your relationship with God?

_____

_____

How do you feel about yourself when you criticize others?

_____

_____

Love: the Healing Touch

When you think about love, you may think of the warm feelings, a funny sensation in the pit of your stomach, restlessness, and sense of anticipation you felt toward another person when "falling in love." Fortunately, love is more than emotional feelings experienced at the beginning of attraction. Feelings like these emotional ones tend to come and go.

Genuine love is a matter of choice and of action. John 3:16 says, "God so loved the world that He gave His only Son." Jesus said in John 15:13, "Greater love has no one than this, that one lay down his life for his friends." Titus 3:4-5 says: "But when the kindness of God our Savior and His love for mankind appeared, He saved us, not on the basis of deeds which we have done in righteousness, but according to His mercy, by the washing of regeneration and renewing by the Holy Spirit."

God's love for us is not based on His emotions but is demonstrated by His actions. As we grow in understanding His love and mercy, we increasingly will desire to demonstrate our love for Him and for others by obeying His commands actively.

You shall love the Lord your God with all your heart, and with all your soul, and with all your mind. This is the great and foremost commandment. The second is like it, You shall love your neighbor as yourself. On these two commandments depend the whole Law and the Prophets.
–Matthew 22:37-40

Read the Scripture that appears in the margin. Check the statement below which best describes Jesus' attitude toward love.

Love is a matter of feelings.
Love includes both actions and emotions.
Behavior is what really counts.

Jesus' words demonstrate that genuine love includes actions as well as feelings. The words of the apostle Paul appearing in the margin describe love in terms of actions.

Love is patient, love is kind, and is not jealous; love does not brag and is not arrogant, [love] does not act unbecomingly; it does not seek its own, is not provoked, does not take into account a wrong suffered, does not rejoice in unrighteousness, but rejoices with the truth; [love] bears all things, believes all things, hopes all things, endures all things. Love never fails.
–1 Corinthians 13:4-8

Place an X on the following scale to indicate where your own expression of love falls. Then place an O where you would like it to be.

All feeling/ No action	Balanced feeling and action	All action/ No feeling

Right now, ask God to help you achieve His ideal for your life in expressing love in both attitude and action. As a specific action, you may wish to include replacing criticism with love for others.

Destructive Anger: Human Cannonballs on the Loose

Anger is a God-given emotional response that everyone experiences. Anger can be a response to unmet expectations, irritation, or frustration when things don't go our way. We may show hostility when someone has a different opinion. Anger also can be a defensive response to a hurtful attack or to a real or perceived threat to our self-esteem or our well-being.

Be angry, and yet do not sin; do not let the sun go down on your anger, and do not give the devil an opportunity.
–Ephesians 4:26-27

As with all other emotions, feeling angry is OK. What we do with the feeling of anger is another matter. Too often we use anger destructively rather than constructively. The apostle Paul indicated that we should express anger appropriately. Read his thoughts that appear at left. Appropriate expression of anger is limited in time and effect and is used to help rather than hurt people.

We can express destructive anger outwardly or inwardly. It can result in depression, suspicion, and a low sense of self-worth. Examples of destructive anger are verbal abuse—screaming, criticism, fault-finding—physical abuse, teasing, sarcasm, and in extreme cases, murder. Silence, neglect, and withdrawal also can be destructive expressions of anger.

Destructive anger can have catastrophic effects on your recovery. Expressed outwardly, it can alienate you from others and drive a wedge between you and God. Without relationships with God and others, you likely will return to your addiction to fill the void of emptiness in your life.

Anger turned inward also is very dangerous. As people with an addiction, we already have a low tolerance for the burden of repressed anger. If we do not deal constructively with anger, we may return to chemicals for relief from painful emotions.

How would you describe yourself in the way you express anger? (Place an X in the appropriate spot on the scale below.)

Slow simmer (Silent treatment)	Fireworks (Lots of heat; little damage)	Atomic bomb (Explosive; damaging)

Self-check on Destructive Anger

What specific things do you frequently do when you express anger? Why?

_____

_____

Do particular people or situations seem to trigger your anger? If so, describe those people or situations.

_____

_____

In the box in the margin write one example of how destructive anger has affected you and your relationships.

In recovery you will begin to discover ways in which you can channel anger into positive action. Because you are releasing your grip on denial, you more often can admit feelings of anger. You first can admit them to yourself and then to God.

King David is a good illustration of how to deal in a positive manner with emotions like anger. David's half-crazed father-in-law, Saul, who then ruled Israel, continually attacked David before David began his reign as king. Saul wanted to kill David. Under constant attack, David had every reason to be defensive and angry. Yet David both honored Saul and gained victory over his potentially destructive emotions because he learned to express those emotions to God. You may wish to read more about this in 1 Samuel 26:1-25 and Psalms 42 and 58.

David used his anger constructively; it drove him to his knees. Once you can admit that you are angry, you can ask God for His direction in your response. You can call your sponsor or a friend who can look with a non-biased point of view at your situation. Then, if necessary, you can confront the offender with wisdom and strength.

> ### Key Concept for Lesson 4
> I replace criticism and destructive anger with love, forgiveness, and honesty.

Pray and ask God how this concept can apply in your life. Now please review this lesson. What has God shown you that can help you?

_____

_____

Say this Step's memory verse aloud five times.

A time when my destructive anger affected me was—

_____

_____

_____

_____

_____

He learned to express his emotions to God.

Fear and Impatience

We make a searching and fearless moral inventory of ourselves.

> *Do not be afraid, little flock, for your Father has chosen gladly to give you the kingdom.*
>
> –Luke 12:32

Satan tries to get people to accept another false belief—that they simply are products of their past and unable to change: *I am what I am. I am hopeless.*[2] Fear is one result of this false belief. The combination of impatience and impulsiveness is a second common result.

Fear: God's Warning System

Fear is a God-given emotional response to the awareness of danger. In proper perspective and in certain situations, fear is valuable. Fear prompts you to make decisions necessary for survival. You exercise fear wisely when you warn children to avoid playing with matches, to stay away from strangers, and to look both ways before crossing a street.

When we practice compulsive behavior, however, fear usually controls our lives. Our response to it often is destructive. Fear blocks our ability to love, limits our social involvement, motivates us to avoid the risk of failure or rejection, and exposes our need to be in control. We schedule our lives around our drug use. Sometimes we hide our bottles and our behavior. Sometimes we lie about them. We do all of this in an attempt to gain control and security.

Even when we are in recovery, we still may be consumed by fear. We may be unable to sleep at night for fear we will fail in our work or school performance. Afraid of failing, we may avoid anything that involves risk. The fear of rejection may cause us to avoid meeting people and to avoid attending support-group meetings.

> casting all your anxiety upon Him, because He cares for you.
> –1 Peter 5:7

Feeling afraid is OK, but you do not have to allow this fear to consume you. Recovery gives you an opportunity to learn how to examine fear objectively and to use it constructively. Talk with a trusted friend about your fears to see if they're reasonable. Take your fears to God. He doesn't want you to be imprisoned by fear. In the margin notice the final four words in 1 Peter 5:7. The verse says, "because He cares for you." We can replace fear with confidence in God and in His gracious provision for our lives. We can focus on God's power, strength, and love.

Self-check on Fear

Which of these seems to have the greatest impact on you?

_____ Fear of failure	_____ Fear of being known
_____ Fear of rejection	_____ Fear of trying new things
_____ Fear of punishment	_____ Fear of being creative
_____ Shame: the fear of not being valued	_____ Fear of betraying the family secrets

How does fear control each of the following areas of your life? What are the results? (For example, fear of discovering cancer may cause you to put off going to a doctor. This could allow the disease to become more deadly.)

	How fear controls you	What are the results?
Your attitudes		
Your actions		
Your relationships		
Your sense of freedom		

Trust: the Greatest Medicine of All

As we are released from the tyranny of our addiction, we develop the courage to acknowledge our fears and to move forward with our lives in spite of them. As we do, we exercise trust and discover truth.

Many of our fears are rooted in lies.

Many of our fears are rooted in lies. For example, you may have been convinced that you could not survive without your drug of choice. Now you are learning that while recovery isn't easy, its benefits far outweigh the short-term gratification chemicals once gave you. While that's the truth, you had to exercise some faith to find the truth.

You also needed faith when you placed your trust in Jesus Christ. Now you are discovering that He can do a better job of directing your life than you ever could have done alone. By developing trust in Him, you will begin to learn that you can afford to take the risks of getting to know some people and trying some new things. Fellowship helps your recovery. Remember this also: if a person rejects you, God still accepts you; if you fail, He still loves you.

Learn to trust God

You learn that because no human is consistent enough to merit your complete trust, you can learn to trust God completely and to trust people appropriately.

Go back to the last question you answered in the previous section about fear. Describe how trusting God can help you deal with fear in each of these areas.

In your attitudes _____

_____

In your actions _____

_____

In your relationships _____

_____

In your sense of freedom _____

_____

Impatience: I Want What I Want—Now!

Impatience is a characteristic all addictions share. We have difficulty delaying gratification. We feel anxious as we wait impatiently for the end of the day so we can use. We stop to buy liquor and become angry while the sales person slowly counts our change.

Impatience carries over into our relationships.

Impatience carries over into our relationships. We bark orders. By our actions and attitudes we demand that others "shape up" and "get in line" NOW! We are impatient at work. We hurry to meet deadlines. We hope to prove ourselves and hope to move to the top. Impatience leads to more anxiety and gives the addiction more power. Impatience carries over into other aspects of our lives. We spend money we don't have, make promises we can't keep, and lie to those we love—all because we have little patience.

Self-check on Impatience

In what ways are you impatient or impulsive?

_____

_____

What people and circumstances tend to bring out your impatience?

People   Circumstances

_____   _____

_____   _____

_____   _____

_____   _____

_____   _____

Describe the consequences of impatience in . . .

your schoolwork/vocation: _____

_____

your relationships: _____

_____

your use of chemicals: _____

_____

Slow and Steady Wins the Race

One Christian who was in recovery said, "Jesus does for me in a healthy way what alcohol did for me in a destructive way. Drinking calmed my fears, stabilized my feelings, and gave me the ability to cope. It did those things instantly but at a terrible price. Jesus is meeting those same needs, but He works more slowly. The difference is that with Christ I am learning to cope and to be proud of what He is accomplishing in my life. With my addiction I felt progressively more ashamed and guilty. I am learning that the positive benefits of recovery are worth the wait."

The positive benefits of recovery are worth the wait.

Recovery provides an opportunity to learn patience. Gone is the need for an immediate escape and gratification the chemicals once provided. Gone is the false sense of security when others act as rescuers and caretakers. The result is that we gradually recognize limitations and begin to slow down a little. We learn patience.

In recovery, you demonstrate patience each time you outlast an urge to drink, smoke, pop a pill, or shoot up. You exercise patience when you begin to control your spending and other habits. You develop patience as you look for God's will and wait for His direction. Patience allows you to receive more enjoyment from others and to give more enjoyment to them.

┌───┐
│ **Key Concept for Lesson 5**   │
│ I replace fear and impulsiveness with trust and patience. │
└───┘

Pray and ask God how this concept can apply in your life. Now please review this lesson. What has God shown you that can help you?

_____

_____

_____

Memorize this Step's memory verse.

<table>
<tr><td>

LESSON
6

Key Concept:
I can honestly face my selfishness and sexual misconduct.

Developing patience

And He told them a parable, saying, "The land of a certain rich man was very productive. And he began reasoning to himself, saying, 'What shall I do, since I have no place to store my crops?' And he said, 'This is what I will do: I will tear down my barns and build larger ones, and there I will store all my grain and my goods. And I will say to my soul, "Soul, you have many goods laid up for many years to come; take your ease, eat, drink, and be merry."' But God said to him, 'you fool! This very night your soul is required of you; and now who will own what you have prepared?' So is the man who lays up treasure for himself, and is not rich toward God."
—Luke 12:16-21

</td><td>

Selfishness and Sex

And He said to them, "Beware, and be on your guard against every form of greed; for not even when one has an abundance does his life consist of his possessions."

–Luke 12:15

Give extra attention to these final two areas of your inventory. All mood-altering chemicals share one thing in common—they make us turn inward. We become preoccupied with *our* needs and *our* desires. Remember that addictions are relationships. We turn from healthy, Christ-honoring, life-enhancing relationships with God and other people, to sick, self-centered relationships with a chemical.

Selfishness

As our addictions progress, the desire to get high drives us. We need immediate gratification. The fear that we will not have enough supply on hand makes us increasingly preoccupied with ourselves. This selfishness carries over to all areas of our lives. Selfishness propels our greed, jealousy, denial, manipulation, and anger. We become selfish about sex, possessions, money, and our social and professional status.

Reread on page 71 the Scripture for this lesson. Below describe what you think Jesus meant when He said life is not made up of possessions.

_____

_____

By telling a parable—a story used to teach a spiritual lesson, Jesus went on to explain what He meant. You may have said life is not made up of possessions because other things are more important. Things like character and relationships with God and other people last when things are gone and are unimportant.

Read the parable printed in the margin. Why did God describe the rich man as a fool?

_____

_____

_____

The man was a fool because he made an extremely unwise choice. He chose to serve himself only. Selfishness is self-defeating and destructive. When we put our desires ahead of all else, we destroy our own chance at meaning and purpose in life. Note that taking care of ourselves is not the same as selfishness. Some of us feel selfish when we act appropriately. Learning the difference between selfishness and self-care is an important recovery skill.

</td></tr>
</table>

Describe how you have acted selfishly with money and possessions.

_____

_____

_____

How have you treated others in your pursuit of money or possessions?

_____

_____

_____

How has this affected your relationships?

_____

_____

_____

How has this affected your self-esteem?

_____

_____

_____

How have you been selfish in your pursuit of prestige?

_____

_____

_____

How has this affected your relationships?

_____

_____

_____

How has this affected your self-esteem?

_____

_____

_____

How have you been selfish in your pursuit of attention?

_____

_____

_____

How have you treated others in the process?

_____

_____

How has this affected your relationships?

_____

_____

_____

What have you learned by writing this inventory on selfishness?

_____

_____

_____

Sexual Behavior

Thy hands made me and fashioned me; Give me understanding, that I may learn Thy commandments.
—Psalm 119:73

God, our Creator, made every part of our bodies, including our nerve impulses and sexual responses. Sexuality is God's gift to us. He gave it to us for reproduction and for pleasure. Famous Christian author C.S. Lewis once observed that pleasure is God's invention, not Satan's.[3]

God intended that we enjoy sexual pleasure within marriage. For at least three important reasons, we should confine sexual activity to marriage.

Let us rejoice and be glad and give the glory to Him, for the marriage of the Lamb has come and His bride has made herself ready.
—Revelation 19:7

- The pleasure of sexual union serves as a reminder of the joy we will experience when we, as believers, will be joined together with Christ (see Matthew 9:14-15; 25:1-3; John 3:28-29; Revelation 19:7). God created the marital union itself as a symbol of our relationship with Him.
- Because God made us, He knows under what conditions we will be our best. He created sexual expression for the safe, trusting confines of marriage, not for promiscuity. When we pervert this plan, we bring upon ourselves devastating consequence: a negative self-image; the pain of a broken relationship and sometimes a broken home; marital distrust; shattered lives, distorted perceptions about sex and about members of the opposite sex; and in some cases disease and death.
- Sex is for marriage for the sake of the children. If adult lives are shattered by sexual misconduct, what about its impact on children? Some children

who are victims of rape, incest, or simply a broken parental relationship carry emotional scars into adulthood that haunt them all their lives. Often these scars contribute to compulsions like eating disorders, sexual addiction, or chemical dependency. (Some also suffer from a loss of sexual function or desire, and some develop a same-sex sexual orientation as a result of these traumas.)

The scope of this book is not such that we can address these issues in detail. Nor do we wish to burden our readers with added guilt and shame. The point is this: we may have been involved in one or more sexual sins before our addiction, but chemicals may have added to the problem. Chemical substances work on the central nervous system. They relax our inhibitions which often results in our violating our own values. Then we feel guilty for violating our value system. The guilt drives us back for more chemical relief. We need to bring our sexual misconduct—sometimes we feel guilty for things that are not even misconduct—out into the light of God's forgiveness and love. We will then lessen the hold on our lives of secret shame.

If you have misused your sexuality, below describe how this has harmed others. Be specific. Because of the sensitive nature of the information that comes to mind, you may desire to use a separate sheet of paper for this exercise.

Person (first name or initial only)   Result

_____   _____

_____   _____

_____   _____

_____   _____

_____   _____

How has your sexual misbehavior harmed you? Consider your self-esteem, marriage, parenting, job, physical health.

_____

_____

_____

_____

Flee immorality. Every other sin that a man commits is outside the body, but the immoral man sins against his own body. Or do you not know that your body is a temple of the Holy Spirit who is in you, whom you have from God, and that you are not your own? For you have been bought with a price: therefore glorify God in your body.
　　　　—1 Corinthians 6:18-20

Read the 1 Corinthians 6:18-20 passage that appears in the margin. What does God desire for this area of your life?

_____

_____

_____

What practical actions are you making to achieve God's goal for this area of your life—sexual purity and freedom from sexual slavery?

_____

_____

_____

What do you need to enable you to surrender your sexuality to God?

_____

_____

_____

Key Concept for Lesson 6
I can honestly face my selfishness and sexual misconduct.

Step Review

Step 4 says: *We make a searching and fearless moral inventory of ourselves.* **Write in your own words what Step 4 means to you.**

_____

_____

_____

_____

Describe how you plan to apply Step 4 daily to your life and recovery.

_____

_____

_____

_____

_____

Notes

[1]Robert S. McGee, *Search for Significance* LIFE Support Edition (Houston: Rapha Publishing, 1992), 11.
[2]White, John, *Eros Defined: The Christian and Sexual Sin* (Downers Grove, Il: Intervarsity Press, 1977), 10.

STEP 5

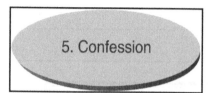

5. Confession

We confess our sins to Him and to another person.

Freedom Through Confession

HOUNDED BY HIS SECRETS

Jim knew he must face it, and he was terrified. Working the program, along with the support he got from the people in his group, had helped him to stay clean and sober for three months now. He even had worked Step 4. Jim spent several weeks writing a searching and fearless moral inventory of himself.

The trouble was Step 5. Everybody kept talking about taking the fifth Step. They talked about how important it was, and they talked about how taking the Step helped them feel better about themselves. What they didn't talk about was what bothered Jim. They didn't talk about the specific things Jim had written in his fourth Step inventory.

Then one Sunday night a deacon spoke at the church service. That deacon said he had learned a new definition for shame. He said shame was the "feeling that something was uniquely wrong about yourself." He went on to explain that shame made him feel that he was wrong or sinful in a way that others were not. He said that taking his fifth Step in a recovery group had enabled him to deal with shame, and he shared several things he had confessed—things that were on Jim's Step 4 inventory.

After the service Jim approached the deacon. "My name in Jim; I'm an alcoholic, and I need someone to hear my fifth Step," Jim blurted out. "Hi Jim, my name is Ron. I'm a recovering addict, and I'd be happy to hear your fifth Step." (Read more about Jim on page 101).

Step 5 *We admit to God, to ourselves, and to another person the exact nature of our wrongs.*

Memory verse *Therefore, confess your sins to one another, and pray for one another, so that you may be healed.*

–James 5:16

Overview for Step 5 **Lesson 1: Why Take the Fifth Step?**
　　　　　Goal: You will define confession, and you will describe four benefits that come from confession.
　　Lesson 2: Taking the Step, Part 1
　　　　　Goal: You will describe a key biblical teaching about confession.
　　Lesson 3: Taking the Step, Part 2
　　　　　Goal: You will make final preparation to share Step 5 with another person.

Why Take the Fifth Step?

We admit to God, to ourselves, and to another person the exact nature of our wrongs.

> *But if we judged ourselves rightly, we should not be judged.*
> –1 Corinthians 11:31

Key Concept:
Taking Step 5 requires courage, but it pays great dividends.

You met Jim and Ron in the story that introduced this Step. Jim's fear mingled with hope as he drove to his appointment with Ron. He saw the need to break the silence surrounding his secret shame. Ron had shown great courage in sharing his story with the whole church. That example gave Jim the strength to keep his appointment.

People working the 12 Steps almost always find two things to be true about Step 5. Of all the Steps, Step 5 is the most terrifying *before*—and the most freeing *after*—they take the Step. Many wonder later, *Why did it take me so long? If only I had known, I would have done this long ago.* The fear of blackmail is a powerful force. Most of us try to keep our "secret sins" hidden for fear that someone will expose us or someone will exploit the information about us. We may be unaware that our addiction has used the fear of exposure to maintain its control in our lives. Satan uses blackmail to rob us of the serenity God wants us to have and to keep us in slavery.

Our addiction has used the fear of exposure to maintain its control in our lives.

If you are like most people, you felt a sudden urge to protect your workbook and keep it confidential after you completed the exercises in Step 4. For the same reason, you may find it particularly difficult to admit your wrongs to God, to yourself, and to another person. Exposure can be threatening. We reason, "Isn't it enough that I tell God?" No, it isn't. Something about our human nature keeps us from change until we have confessed our struggles to another person.

If we reveal ourselves to another human being, we may feel like we have everything to lose and nothing to gain. What will we lose?

- **We will lose our sense of isolation.** Because Step 5 is intended to be a dialogue, not a monologue, we will discover that we are not alone in our sinful deeds and desires. Our sense of aloneness then will begin to vanish.

- **We will lose our unwillingness to forgive.** When people accept and forgive us, we realize that we can forgive others.

- **We will lose our inflated pride.** As we see and accept who we are, we begin to gain humility. Humility involves seeing ourselves as we really are and seeing who God really is.

- **We will lose our pattern of denial.** Honesty with another person tears away denial. We will begin to feel clean and honest.

Circle any of the following that you want to keep in your life:

isolation　　　unwillingness to forgive　　　inflated pride　　　denial

Few of us deliberately would choose to keep any of those traits in our lives, but when we allow fear to keep us from completing Step 5, we choose to stay stuck in our isolation, bitterness, ego, and denial.

Confession

If we confess our sins, He is faithful and righteous to forgive us our sins and to cleanse us from all unrighteousness.

–1 John 1:9

Some people misunderstand 1 John 1:9. They think that confessing purchases forgiveness. The point of the passage is that God is faithful and just. Because our forgiveness already has been paid for at the cross, confession enables us to experience what God already has granted. Confession is a means by which we can experience our forgiveness, not obtain it.

> **Explain in your own words the last sentence of the paragraph you just read.**

> _____

> _____

> _____

The fact that God has forgiven you does not mean that you automatically experience that forgiveness. You still may be in slavery to feelings of guilt and shame. Many of us desperately need to experience forgiveness because deep-seated feelings of shame fuel our addictions. When we bring our hidden guilt and shame into the open with someone who has shown that he or she can be trusted, we somehow find it easier to receive forgiveness and experience freedom from the burden of our sins.

Extending Forgiveness to Others

The more you experience forgiveness, the more you will be able to forgive those who have hurt you. If you are honest with yourself, you may see that failing to forgive results from believing that you are morally superior—that as a victim, you have the right to go on accusing, despising, and denouncing those you refuse to forgive.

> **Imagine that you are your addiction—as if it were a living thing, perhaps a parasite. You must fight to stay alive and in control. Below describe how you would use resentment and lack of forgiveness to maintain control.**

> _____

> _____

> _____

You may have noted that resentment stirs up many unpleasant emotions and memories. If you were the addiction, you could use that pain to drive your host to numb pain by returning to you—the addiction. The more you could isolate your victim, the greater control you could have in his or her life.

Restoring Our Relationships

Isolation is both a cause and a result of compulsive behavior. Addiction thrives on secrecy and aloneness. We avoid getting involved with others because we feel inferior to them or because we fear they will hurt us. To make up for these painful feelings, we turn for comfort to our drug of choice. Our obsessive behavior causes us to fear that others will discover us. Fear then drives us further into the addiction. As a result, we feel the intense pain that accompanies loneliness and isolation. We have the powerful and unshakable feeling that we not only are alone in our struggle but that we also are odd, different, and unique in every bad way.

Something surprising happens when we disclose our harmful behavior to another human being. We learn that unacceptable patterns of behavior do not make us unacceptable people. We also learn that we are not so odd or different or unique after all! This is especially true if we summon the courage to share parts of our moral inventory with a support group. Surprisingly, the thing we feared so much—disclosing what we considered to be our sheer awfulness—becomes the vehicle we need to end our desperate, aching loneliness and isolation. When we disclose ourselves to others and allow them to do the same with us, we obey the apostle Paul's words appearing in the margin.

> Brothers, if someone is caught in a sin, you who are spiritual should restore him gently. But watch yourself, or you also may be tempted. Carry each other's burdens, and in this way you will fulfill the law of Christ.
> –Galatians 6:1-2, NIV

Taking Step 5 opens a door for change and healing because it frees us from our old patterns of secret shame, compulsion, and isolation. In restoring damaged relationships, we not only open ourselves up again to receive help from others, we put ourselves in a position to experience the joy of giving help to those who need it.

Key Concept for Lesson 1
Taking Step 5 requires courage, but it pays great dividends.

Memorize this Step's memory verse, James 5:16.

<table>
<tr><td>

LESSON
2

</td><td>

Taking the Step, Part 1

</td></tr>
</table>

We admit to God, to ourselves, and to another person the exact nature of our wrongs.

> *My enemies speak evil against me, "When will he die, and his name perish?"*
> –Psalm 41:5

Key Concept:
Understanding the biblical teaching about confession makes me willing to take Step 5.

Before going further in Step 5, understand that your confession does not make you forgiven. You are forgiven because Christ died to pay for your sins. Confession is a means for you to experience your forgiveness, not a way to obtain it. As an example look at what happened to King David, one of God's mightiest leaders, when he turned to God under the weight of unconfessed sin.

> Many of us immediately feel shame when we hear the word *sin*. Please understand that when the Bible talks of sin, it refers to the spiritual condition which afflicts every human being. God hates sin because sin harms the people He loves. Admitting to our sin is not shameful. Confessing our sin is honest and courageous. Pretending we have no sin is shameful.
>
> This material is intended to help you overcome shame. It is not intended to make you feel shame.

David: a Man After God's Heart

God called David, the shepherd, psalmist, and king of Israel, a man after His own heart (1 Samuel 13:14). But like all humans, David sinned. He committed what people would consider gross sins. He committed adultery. Then, to cover that sin, he arranged to have Bathsheba's husband killed (See 2 Samuel 11.)

Complete the following checklist to compare your sin with that of King David. Check each sin of which you are guilty.

adultery   betrayal of a loyal friend
lying   premeditated murder

These were only four of the sins of King David, yet God called him "a man after My own heart." You probably did not check all four of the acts in the above list. Even if you checked all four, God is just as loving and willing to forgive you as He was David.

Often we feel that we are different from others—that what we have done is unforgivable. We desperately need to bring some objectivity to our offenses. Yes, all sin is bad. It injures us and others. It grieves God. Unfortunately the most damaging thing may be the way Satan uses what we have done to tell us that we are unforgivable.

God not only forgave King David, He greatly loved him in spite of his sin. Is it reasonable to assume God will forgive you and that He loves you in spite of things you have done?   Yes   No

David's attitude made him a man after God's heart. He not only was sorry for his sin, but he confessed it, and then he repented (turned from it). Look at Psalm 32 to see the process of David's reconciliation to God.

Read Psalm 32:1-2 in the margin at left. What word does David use to describe the one whose transgression is forgiven?

_____

_____

Blessed is he whose transgressions are forgiven, whose sins are covered. Blessed is the man whose sin the LORD does not count against him and in whose spirit is no deceit.
–Psalm 32:1-2, NIV

David describes as blessed the person who is forgiven. Blessed means happy, joyful—as when a person gets something wonderful and undeserved.

Describe what you think it would be like to FEEL forgiven and accepted. What would it feel like to respect yourself?

_____

_____

_____

> When I kept silent, my bones wasted away through my groaning all day long. For day and night your hand was heavy upon me; my strength was sapped as in the heat of summer.
>
> –Psalm 32:3-4, NIV

Read Psalm 32:3-4. What happened to David's body when he kept silent about his sin?

_____

_____

What happens to your body when you keep silent about the things for which you feel guilty? Be specific.

_____

_____

You may have noted some of the following results. Secrecy makes us feel isolated and alone. We become more depressed. The pain becomes greater. Confession is difficult and painful, but it brings blessing in the long run.

Can you pray and thank God for giving you the courage to look honestly at how sin and secrecy have affected your life? In the margin write a prayer expressing your thoughts and feelings.

Read Psalm 32:5. What did David do about his sin?

_____

> Then I acknowledged my sin to you and did not cover up my iniquity. I said, "I will my transgressions to the Lord"— and you forgave the guilt of my sin.
>
> –Psalm 32:5, NIV

What was God's response? _____

_____

David confessed his sin openly to God; that is, he agreed with what God already knew about him. And God forgave him.

Accepting Forgiveness: Part of Confession

All too often, Christians play a game of penance which they believe they must put themselves through before they can feel forgiven. Once convicted of a sin, they might plead with God for forgiveness and then feel depressed for a couple of days just to show that they really are sorry and deserve to be forgiven. They are attempting to _pay for their own sins_ by feeling bad.

You cannot earn forgiveness by punishing yourself. Confession simply involves applying the forgiveness you already have in Christ. Accepting your forgiveness allows you to move on with the Lord and serve Him joyfully.

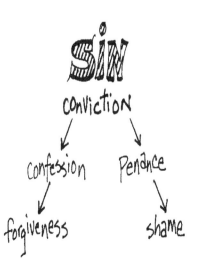

You may be preparing to confess your sins to God for the first time. If you need some help, you might use the prayer below as a guide.

> Dear Father,
> The Holy Spirit has shown me that I sinned when I (*as specifically as possible name your sins of thought and action*). Thank You that I am completely forgiven. I realize that You have declared me to be deeply loved, completely forgiven, fully pleasing, totally accepted, and a new creature—complete in Christ. Amen.

Stop and pray. Ask God to help you develop the habit of immediately confessing your sins to Him as soon as you commit them or recognize them. Thus you will minimize the amount of lost time in your fellowship with God and will maximize His work of healing in and through you.

Key Concept for Lesson 2
Understanding the biblical teaching about confession makes me willing to take Step 5.

Pray and ask God how this concept can apply in your life. Now please review this lesson. What has God shown you that can help you?

_____

_____

In the margin write from memory James 5:16. If necessary see page 100 to check the verse.

LESSON 3

Taking the Step, Part 2

We admit to God, to ourselves, and to another person the exact nature of our wrongs.

> *He who conceals his transgressions will not prosper, but he who confesses and forsakes them will find compassion.*
>
> –Proverbs 28:13

Key Concept:
Keeping secrets results in slavery, while confession brings relief and joy.

Choosing a Good Listener

With a better understanding of what it means to confess your wrongs to God, you are ready to analyze the best way to complete Step 5 successfully. Begin by determining who will be the best person for you to talk with. Choosing a good listener is extremely important. In fact, make this choice only after you consider it prayerfully.

The following may help you in your selection process. With these guidelines in mind, pray for a person to hear you share your fifth Step.

1. Choose someone who has completed several years in recovery, or who at least is familiar with the 12 Steps, especially Step 5 and the issues involved in chemical dependency. This person should see Step 5 as a crucial task. It can mean the difference between recovery and returning to the addiction. A person who is in a 12-Step program, especially for chemical dependency, and who has spent some time in the program, will understand this Step's importance for you and your recovery.

2. Choose someone who can keep a confidence. The information you are preparing to disclose is very personal. Select someone who is completely trustworthy.

3. Choose an objective listener. This is not yet the time (it never may be) to talk openly with those who are emotionally involved with you and who may find that what you have to say is more than they can bear. Be considerate. Sharing is a responsibility.

4. Choose someone who may be willing to share with you personal examples from his or her own life. The person with whom you talk should be a good listener, but often through a two-way exchange you will find the acceptance you especially need right now.

List some people who might be good listeners for you.

_____

_____

Sharing your confession will be a major step in your recovery.

Call the person you have selected and set a time to meet and talk. Your sponsor may be an obvious choice, or you may want to select someone else. Because the sponsor already knows so much of the person's story, some sponsors urge those they sponsor to make their confession to another listener. If you select someone who does not know about the 12-Step process, tell your listener about your involvement in the 12-Step program. Explain that sharing your confession with him or her would be a major step in your recovery.

Give the person the opportunity to bow out graciously if he or she is uncomfortable and chooses not to listen. If that happens, simply select another listener.

Telling Your Story

Once you have found a good listener who has agreed to hear you, prepare your story. The process usually works best when you present it as a story—the story of your life.

Perhaps the best way to prepare is by taking some notes. Start from the very beginning and recall people, circumstances, and events that have affected you most along the way. You can, of course, refer back continually to Step 4 to help you recount all the significant things you have done—positive and negative—over the years.

When you finally sit down with the person you've chosen—your sponsor, pastor, counselor, physician, or trusted friend—you can read from your notes or refer back to them as an outline. This is up to you. The point is to get it ALL out—everything that is significant about your life that you never have told.

> **BOUNDARY ISSUE: Getting it all out does not mean all the ugly details. Notice carefully the wording of the Step. We admit *the exact nature of our wrongs*. The nature of our wrongs refers to their character or qualities, not graphic details and names of people.**

One final word of caution is in order as you write your story. Some people who take Step 5 are disappointed because they experience no immediate feelings of relief afterward. Some people feel guilty because they told the secrets they harbored so closely and so long.

Feelings do not determine the success of the Step.

Feelings do not determine the success of Step 5. The Step is successful when you disclose the significant events in your life which you need to share with another person. Think about this before you complete this Step so that you can be realistic in your expectations.

Finally, remember that this Step is for *you*. Regardless of whom you choose to share yourself with, realize that your purpose in taking this Step is not to please the listener but to gain healing for yourself.

Story Outline

The following outline will help you to write your story. You will need to use additional pages. Use as much paper and as much time as you need to do a thorough job, but do not feel that the Step must be done perfectly. Most people in recovery repeat this Step later when they become more aware of issues and circumstances in their lives.

> **On a separate sheet of paper write out a time line of your life. Include all the significant events—both public and private—that have shaped your life. Include family events, jobs, stages of drug use, emotionally high and low experiences.**

> **What was your life like when you were a child? (Describe your relationships with your parents, brothers, and sisters).**

_____

_____

_____

_____

_____

_____

How has your home life affected you?

_____

_____

_____

_____

_____

When did you first begin to use chemicals?

_____

_____

_____

_____

_____

Go back through the questions in Step 4. Explain in detail how your drug use has affected—

Your self-esteem:

_____

_____

_____

_____

Your relationships with your friends:

_____

_____

_____

Your job or school:

_____

_____

_____

Your health:

_____

_____

_____

Your values:

_____

_____

_____

_____

Your relationship with God:

_____

_____

_____

_____

Congratulations on completing the writing of your story. As you share it, remember the truths of this unit: Keeping secrets brings slavery, while confession brings relief and joy. The Holy Spirit gives us power and encouragement to take Step 5.

Pray about each item you have just written. Surrender to God the memory and impact of each item in the list. Do this whether the memories are good or bad. As you do so, draw a small cross beside each item. The cross indicates that Christ covered the item with His blood at Calvary.

This is where you keep your appointment to tell your story to your chosen listener. Before you begin, pray and ask God to give you a clear mind and a humble spirit. Ask the Holy Spirit to help you speak the truth in love (Ephesians 4:15). Remember, you are *revisiting* your past, not *reliving* it. End by recognizing God's forgiveness and ongoing work in your life.

but speaking the truth in love, we are to grow up in all aspects into Him, who is the head, even Christ.

–Ephesians 4:15

Key Concept for Lesson 3
Keeping secrets results in slavery, while confession brings relief and joy.

Memorize this Step's memory verse, James 5:16.

Step Review

Step 5 says: *We admit to God, to ourselves, and to another person the exact nature of our wrongs.* **Write in your own words what Step 5 means to you.**

_____

_____

_____

_____

_____

_____

Describe how you plan to apply Step 5 daily to your life and recovery.

_____

_____

_____

_____

_____

_____

<table>
<tr><td>

STEP

6

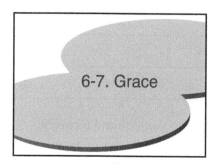

6-7. Grace

We allow Him freedom to change our lives.

</td><td>

Acting in Faith

GIVING UP ON PERFECTION

"I always have been my own worst critic," Karen said as she led the step-study meeting for Step 6. "I almost killed myself because of two of the basic false beliefs that our group studied in Step 2.

"I believed that my worth came from my performance—that *I must meet certain standards to feel good about myself.* Since I based my standards on my own twisted experience and logic, nothing I ever did was good enough. Then I believed that I should blame—beat up on—myself because I wasn't perfect. I believed that *those who fail (including myself) are unworthy of love and deserve to be punished.* I put myself through an endless cycle of demanding perfection, then failing, then blaming and punishing myself.

"When I discovered methamphetamines and cocaine, the drugs fit my pattern three ways. They gave me extra energy to work harder—striving for perfection. Then when I failed to be perfect, as I always did, they helped me forget the pain for a while. Finally—this is the difficult part to admit—as my addiction worsened and as I blamed myself more and more, the drugs were my way to commit suicide. I punished myself by trying to kill myself.

"In Step 6 God showed me the way out of my tangled thinking. I learned that I cannot make myself perfect or good enough for God. God is the only one who can remove the patterns of sin from my life. I realized that I had been trying to do the work of the Holy Spirit for Him. I had been attempting to make myself perfect so that God would accept me and so that I could accept myself. (Read more about Karen on page 116.)

</td></tr>
</table>

Step 6 *We commit ourselves to God and desire that He remove patterns of sin from our lives.*

Memory verse *Humble yourselves in the presence of the Lord, and He will exalt you.*

–James 4:10

Overview for Step 6

Lesson 1: Becoming Willing to Obey
　　　Goal: You will recognize and surrender obstacles to your commitment to Christ.
Lesson 2: Positive Reasons to Obey
　　　Goal: You will evaluate and choose six proper motivations for obedience.
Lesson 3: Harmful Reasons to Obey
　　　Goal: You will evaluate and choose to avoid four improper motivations for obedience.
Lesson 4: Ownership and Conduct
　　　Goal: You freely will choose the role of a servant of the Lord Jesus Christ.

<table>
<tr><td>

LESSON
1

</td><td>

Becoming Willing to Obey

</td></tr>
</table>

We commit ourselves to God and desire that He remove patterns of sin from our lives.

> *Delight yourself in the Lord; And He will give you the desires of your heart.*
>
> *–Psalm 37:4*

Key Concept:
I experience fulfillment when God's desires become my desires.

The verse above from Psalm 37 contains an important principle. The psalmist says, "Delight yourself in the Lord." As a result God will give you the desires of your heart.

If I delight myself in the Lord, which of the following will be desires of my heart?

    1. financial security
    2. the love and acceptance of other people
    3. happiness
    4. fellowship with God
    5. self-respect
    6. becoming what God wants me to be

Whoever wishes to save his life shall lose it; but whoever loses his life for My sake shall find it.
    –Matthew 16:25

The principle the psalm contains is the paradox Jesus stated in the verse appearing in the margin. When we seek financial security, acceptance by others, happiness, or even our own self-respect, we find frustration. But if our goal is to be what God wants us to be—if we delight in Him—He will give us the desires of our hearts. The catch is that he changes the desires of our hearts. We no longer exclusively desire items 1, 2, 3, or 5. The desires of our heart primarily will be for the items listed in answers 4 and 6.

Jesus used many ways to teach the principle behind Step 6. He taught and demonstrated that the key to life was to have the Father's will as our will. He knew the tragic results of being self-centered. When God's will is first in our lives, however, the results ultimately are positive.

When you can grasp this principle, you will begin to understand the power of Step 6. *We cannot overcome our addictions by our own will.* We cannot make ourselves do the things that are best for us. Step 6 is not a decision to accomplish something as much as it is a willingness to have God's priorities as our priorities. When our goal is to be happy, we are certain to fail in the end. When our goal is to love God and to have a relationship with Him, He eventually gives happiness as a by-product.

Seek first His kingdom and his righteousness; and all these things shall be added to you.
    –Matthew 6:33

Read Matthew 6:33 that appears in the margin. This is another way Jesus taught the same principle.

Most of us began treatment or recovery for one of two reasons. Either someone confronted us with our behavior and we couldn't escape the truth, or we wanted relief from the physical and emotional pain our behavior brought in our lives. We wanted relief. What we *really* wanted was to be rid of the negative side effects of our addiction. We wanted the people around us to change. We wanted to feel better physically. We wanted relief from our anxiety. We thought *these* problems were the source of our troubles. When someone said that we were the problem—that our behavior must change—we were less than enchanted.

As we work Step 6 we make a fundamental change in our lives. We seek to become persons who desire God's will. We work the Step knowing that we will experience victory to the degree that we can say with Jesus, "My food is to do the will of him who sent me" (John 4:34). We change our desires to match His desires by honestly facing reality and by overcoming false beliefs about God.

Those of us who are chemically dependent usually share at least one common experience. Our friends and family members don't understand why we can't stop the harmful things we do to our bodies. "Look, I don't understand," they may have said. "Why don't you just stop? It can't be *that* difficult."

Indeed, when you tried to stop your actions in the past, you may have asked yourself the same question. *Why can't I just make up my mind and knock it off?*

Changing our motivations

Then we discovered in Step 1 that we were powerless over our drug of choice. We need spiritual help to overcome our addictions. We examined our lives and confessed our sins. Now we recognize that we need God to change more than just our substance use. Our very motivations need to be changed. We have grown accustomed to a way of thinking which stresses relief from pain over genuine change. We came to recovery to stop the pain rather than to make great changes in our values or ways of relating to others.

If we are honest with ourselves, we will recognize that we have long-established patterns of sinful behavior in our lives. We hang on to these patterns because they *seem* to meet important needs in our lives. They *seem* to help us avoid pain.

> **The following two paragraphs describe some of these patterns of behavior. Underline the two key forms of behavior the paragraphs describe. Think about your life. Circle any phrase that describes an action you have done or are doing.**

> People-pleasing means we need not risk confronting others with the truth. We go to the extremes either by retreating from problems or hiding behind anger. Either way we avoid the risk of honesty and vulnerability. We tell people what we think they want to hear instead of telling them the truth.

These patterns are impossible to conquer by willpower alone.

> Perfectionism leads us to judge others and ourselves without mercy. We try to do everything *just right*. As a result, however, we may blame others for past hurts and thereby feel superior to them. We may learn to lie and steal and shield ourselves in secrecy to maintain our sense of control, and now the truth often is difficult to tell—even about things that have nothing to do with our drug use. It may be easier to lie than to tell the truth; to shoplift instead of pay, even when we have the money; to withdraw and hide from others instead of talking to them. These patterns of sin and others now are as impossible to conquer by willpower alone as is our addiction to a chemical.

The two types of behavior were people-pleasing and perfectionism. Did you identify with such actions as avoiding confrontation, feeling superior, or learning to lie, steal, and keep secrets?

What need in your life is people-pleasing and/or perfectionism an attempt to meet? Write your answer in the margin box on the left.

Avoid falling into the trap of believing, *I am what I am. I cannot change. I am hopeless.*[1] God not only has promised us freedom, healing, and eternal life, but He has promised a changed life. This is the purpose of Step 6. As we place our lives in His hands and willingly agree that His ways are right, we allow Him to remove our self-destructive behavior patterns and to reform our will to match His will.

This is not a one-time event. Our compulsive nature wants the "big fix" and wants it NOW! God is interested in our journey—in how we run the race. Even more important to Him is the runner, not the race. As we run, we grow and mature. And as we run, God perfects us in Himself. But the course of the race itself is a lifetime journey. Step 6, then, is not just a step along the way, but it is a commitment to a new way of life and a continued obedience to the Lord of life.

Fears About God

We may experience difficulty trusting God because we fear Him. Many of us have one or more of the seven attitudes about God that we read about on the next few pages.[2] These faulty views often create powerful obstacles to commitment to God.

1. God is mean. Many people do not believe God has their best interests at heart. They think He chooses us only to use us in a harmful way. Out of fear that God will punish them if they don't please Him, they serve Him through an increasing number of activities.

What about you? Do you ever have this fear? If so, who or what convinced you that God wants to use and abuse you?

_____

_____

2. God demands too much. Some people fear they'll never measure up to the extremely high expectations of the Christian life. A double-edged sword motivates them. They fear failure to meet every Christian standard, and they feel guilt for having failed. They may give lip service to grace and forgiveness, but they experience demands and expectations.

What about you? Do you ever have this fear? If so, who or what convinced you that God demands too much?

_____

_____

_____

These behaviors are my attempt to—

_____

_____

_____

_____

_____

_____

_____

We think God chooses us only to use us in a harmful way.

3. I'm already trying as diligently as I can; what more can I do? When we feel guilt for inadequately meeting the demands of our harsh, strict concept of God, we soon find ourselves also feeling anger. Unfortunately, we often turn this anger against ourselves, a friend, a family member, or the church. Why? Because we believe that *no one* can express anger toward God or can admit feeling anger toward God.

> **What about you? Do you ever have this fear? If so, who or what convinced you that God cannot tolerate your anger?**

_____

_____

_____

_____

More of Karen's story

Karen had been a perfectionist for as long as she could remember. She thought God was the ultimate perfectionist. She believed that He would not accept anything less than absolute perfection, and she believed He certainly would not tolerate anger. Karen was in a terrible double bind. She was angry about many things in her life, but she could not express anger because she feared that God would reject her.

One day Karen's sponsor gave her a most unusual assignment. She said, "I want you to read Jeremiah 20:7-18, and I want you to do what Jeremiah did."

> **Read Jeremiah's words that appear in the margin. What was Jeremiah feeling? What did he do with his feelings?**

_____

_____

O Lord, you deceived me, and I was deceived; you overpowered me and prevailed. I am ridiculed all day long; everyone mocks me. Cursed be the day I was born! May the day my mother bore me not be blessed! Cursed be the man who brought my father the news, who made him very glad, saying, "A child is born to you— a son!" May that man be like the towns the Lord overthrew without pity. May he hear wailing in the morning, a battle cry at noon. For he did not kill me in the womb, with my mother as my grave, her womb enlarged forever. Why did I ever come out of the womb to see trouble and sorrow and to end my days in shame?
–Jeremiah 20:7,14-18, NIV

Karen read the passage and discovered that Jeremiah was feeling depressed and angry. She was amazed to find that he expressed his anger not only to God but at God. Karen began to understand her sponsor's point. If God is able to take Jeremiah's anger—and still love him, then just maybe God could take Karen's anger as well.

4. I don't want to lose control of my life. We live our lives attempting to control every detail, activity, and emotion. We encounter great internal difficulty when we try to turn control of our lives over to another person— even to the Lord.

> **What about you? Do you ever have this fear? If so, who or what convinced you that you never must "lose control" of your life?**

_____

_____

5. God will make me into something "weird." We already are lonely people. We feel distant and alienated from others who are supposed to be close family or friends. When we hear stories of those who stand for Christ and who suffer ridicule or rejection, we are not drawn to the Christian life. We feel neither safety nor assurance in such a choice. We fear that if we really become committed to God, He will send us as a missionary to some far-off place or will make us do all the things we hate.

What about you? Do you ever have this fear? If so, who or what convinced you that God will make you into something weird?

_____

_____

Some Christians see serving God as a means of earning security.

6. I only earn worth by serving God. You've been reading about the fears that push us away from God and from the Christian life. This is the other side of that coin. Some Christians see serving God as a means of earning security and worth. Rather than backing away from extreme kinds of commitment, they plunge headfirst into Christian activities. They hope God and others will recognize their value and worth as persons. They feel the same fears as those listed above, but their thirst for approval drives them to take risks others won't take. They do this to become acceptable to others and to God.

What about you? Do you ever have this fear? If so, who or what convinced you that you only earn worth by serving God?

_____

_____

A larger perspective

7. If God loves me, He won't ask me to do anything difficult. We sometimes read the Scriptures selectively. We pick out passages that soothe, and we overlook passages that prompt us to do what God wants. We may focus entirely on one aspect of God's character such as His love and never hear the balance or see the larger perspective of biblical teachings.

What about you? Do you ever have this fear? If so, who or what convinced you that God won't ask you to do anything difficult because He loves you?

_____

_____

Reread your responses to the seven fears you've studied in this lesson. Use those thoughts to write a prayer to God about how you feel and what you need to share with God about your fears.

_____

_____

_____

> ## Key Concept for Lesson 1
> I experience fulfillment when God's desires become my desires.

Pray and ask God how this concept can apply in your life. Now please review this lesson. What has God shown you that can help you?

_____

_____

Copy the words of James 4:10 three times to help you memorize this Step's memory verse.

_____

_____

_____

_____

Humble yourselves in the presence of the Lord, and He will exalt you.

–James 4:10

LESSON
2

Positive Reasons to Obey

We commit ourselves to God and desire that He remove patterns of sin from our lives.

> _Do not let sin reign in your mortal body that you should obey its lusts._
> –Romans 6:12

Key Concept:
Appropriate motivations lead me to faithful and loving service.

If you love Me, you will keep My commandments. . . . He who has My commandments and keeps them, he it is who loves Me; and he who loves Me shall be loved by My Father, and I will love him, and will disclose Myself to him.

–John 14:15,21

For the love of Christ controls us, having concluded this, that one died for all, therefore all died; and He died for all, that they who live should no longer live for themselves, but for Him who died and rose again on their behalf.

–2 Corinthians 5:14-15

God bases His love and acceptance on His grace—His unmerited favor—not on our ability to impress Him through our good deeds. If He accepts us on the basis of His grace and not our deeds, why should we obey God? According to scriptural principles, at least six proper motivations for obedience exist. In this lesson, you will examine these six motivations.

1. Christ's love motivates us. Our obedience to God expresses our love for Him. We love because He first loved us and at the cross clearly demonstrated His love for us. (See the verses at left.) This great motivation is missing in many of our lives because we really don't believe that God loves us unconditionally. We expect His love to be based on our ability to earn it.

Our perceptions are the basis for how we experience God's love. If we believe that He is demanding or distant, we will not experience His love and tenderness. We either will be afraid of Him or angry with Him. Our concept of God is the basis for all our motivations. As we grow in understanding His unconditional love and acceptance, we increasingly will want our lives to bring honor to the One who loves us so much.

Does the love of Christ motivate you to obey Him? Why or why not?

_____

_____

_____

2. Sin is destructive. God's plans for my life always are for my good. Disobeying God always causes pain and hurt, although the pain may be delayed or disguised. Satan has blinded us to the painful, damaging consequences of sin. Sooner or later sin always will result in some form of destruction. *The wages of sin is death* (Romans 6:23).

Sin is destructive in many ways. Emotionally, it brings guilt, shame, and fear of failure or punishment. Mentally, we spend our time and energy thinking about our sins and rationalizing our guilt. Physically, it contributes to many illnesses. Relationally, it separates us from others. Spiritually, we grieve the Holy Spirit, lose our testimony, and break our fellowship with God.

> **Think of a time you have disobeyed God and experienced painful consequences. In the margin box write a summary of that experience. In your summary include what you can learn from the experience.**

Satan is the master deceiver. He whispers promising suggestions to us. When these thoughts first enter the mind, they speak only about pleasure and never about sin's devastating consequences. When he tempts you, would it help to remember the example you wrote in the margin?   Yes   No

If so, why? _____

_____

3. The Father's discipline trains us. If sin is so destructive, why doesn't God do something about it? The answer is, He does. He lovingly but firmly disciplines His children. See what the verse at left says about disobeying God. Discipline is not punishment. Punishment is venting one's anger about an offense. Discipline is training. God is training us to live effectively and to obey Him for His glory and our good. That God disciplines us is a proof that we belong to Him. The following chart shows the profound difference between discipline and punishment:

A time when I disobeyed—

_____

_____

_____

_____

_____

_____

_____

_____

_____

My son, do not regard lightly the discipline of the Lord, nor faint when you are reproved by Him; for those whom the Lord loves He disciplines.

—Hebrews 12:5-6

God corrects us in love so that we may follow Christ.

Punishment vs. Discipline		
	Punishment	**Discipline**
Source:	God's wrath	God's love
Purpose:	To avenge a wrong	To correct a wrong
Relational result:	Alienation	Reconciliation
Personal result:	Guilt	A righteous lifestyle
Directed toward:	Nonbelievers	His children

Jesus took all our punishment on the cross; we no longer have to fear punishment from God for our sins. We seek to obey out of love and wisdom. When we sin and are disciplined, we can remember that God corrects us in love so that we may follow Christ.

4. God's commands for us are good. God gives commands to protect us from the harm of sin and to lead us to a life of effective service and victory. Many people view God's commands only as restrictions on their lives. We can see these commands as guidelines which God gives us that we may live life to the fullest. God's commands are holy, right, and good. They have value in themselves. To choose to obey God and follow His commands always is best.

Check all the reasons why God's commands for you are good.

1. He knows the complete results of an action.
2. He loves me and has my best interest at heart.
3. He doesn't want me to have any fun.
4. He wants to protect me from harm.
5. Only He knows what joys await my faithfulness.
6. His purpose is to develop my character.

Avoid trying to use legalism and your own efforts to keep God's commands. That leads to bitterness, condemnation, and rigidity. The Holy Spirit will give you power, joy, and creativity as you trust Him to fulfill the commands of God's Word through you. All the answers were correct—except answer 3.

5. God will reward our obedience. Our self-worth is not based on our performance and obedience, but our actions make a huge difference in the quality of our lives and in our impact on others. Disobedience results in spiritual poverty; it short-circuits intimate fellowship with God, causes confusion and guilt, and robs us of spiritual power and the desire to see people won to Christ. Obedience enables us to experience His love, joy, and strength. It also enables us to minister to others, to endure difficulties, and to live for Him. We are completely loved, forgiven, and accepted apart from our performance, but how we live is very important!

How we live is very important!

Which of the results of disobedience the paragraph above mentions have you experienced in your life?

_____

Which were most painful? _____

_____

Which of the benefits of obedience are you enjoying? _____

_____

6. Christ is worthy. Our most noble reason for serving Christ simply is that He is worthy of our love and obedience. Each time we choose to obey, we express the righteousness of Christ. Our performance, then, reflects who we are in Him. We draw on His power and wisdom so that we can honor Him.

Write in the margin the six reasons you have just read for being willing to have Christ as Lord of your life. If necessary review the chapter.

Now go back and rank your list from the most important to the least important. Be prepared to share with your group or sponsor your results.

Six reasons to obey

1. _____

_____

2. _____

_____

3. _____

_____

4. _____

_____

5. _____

_____

6. _____

_____

Pray and ask God how this concept can apply in your life. Now please review this lesson. What has God shown you that can help you?

_____

_____

Memorize this Step's memory verse:
Humble yourselves in the presence of the Lord, and He will exalt you.

–James 4:10

LESSON 3

Key Concept:
My wrong motives lead to false obedience, bitterness, and resentment.

Harmful Reasons to Obey

We commit ourselves to God and desire that He remove patterns of sin from our lives.

> *But the goal of our instruction is love from a pure heart and a good conscience and a sincere faith.*
>
> –1 Timothy 1:5

Unfortunately higher, purer motives alone do not always motivate us. Sometimes lower motivations like fear or greed drive us. We begin to obey to feel accepted or to earn self-worth. We attempt to maintain an image of performance in front of God and people. Jesus repeatedly emphasized that He not only is concerned about *what* we do but also about *why* we do it. The Pharisees obeyed many rules, but their hearts were far from God. Motives are important! The following are poor motives for obeying God and the possible results of those poor motives:

1. Someone may find out. We may obey God because we fear what others will think of us if we don't. Allen visited prospects for his church because he feared what his Sunday School class would think if he didn't. Susan contributed to the employee benevolence fund at her office. She feared what her friend, the fund-drive chairperson, would think if she didn't.

Basing our behavior on others' opinions is not wise. Times will occur when no one is watching. Our desire to disobey eventually may exceed the peer pressure to obey. Once someone finds out we've sinned, we no longer may have a reason to obey. The biggest problem with this type of obedience is that it isn't obedience at all. It is purely self-interest.

Is the fear of someone's finding out a motivation for you to obey God? If it is, identify the specific sin you are trying to avoid; then go back to the last lesson and review the six reasons to obey Him. Which of these

proper motives seems to encourage you most in regard to your specific temptation? Why?

_____

_____

2. God will be angry with me. We sometimes obey God because we think He will get angry with us if we don't. We have discussed the difference between God's discipline and punishment, but we will state this again: God disciplines us in love, not anger. His response to our sin is grief, not condemnation.

Hank was afraid that God would "zap" him if he did anything wrong, so he performed for God. He lived each day fearing God's anger. As you might expect, Hank's relationship with the Lord was cold and mechanical. God doesn't want us to live in fear of His anger but in response to His love. Living in response to His love produces joyful obedience instead of fear.

God doesn't want us to live in fear of His anger but in response to His love.

Pray and ask God to show you ways you can change this feeling of unhealthy fear. Take time to recall what you have been learning in recovery.

Now write as many ways as possible that you can change your attitude toward God from an unhealthy fear to a healthy love and respect.

_____

_____

_____

You may have written such answers as: *I can be honest and voice my feelings and complaints to God; I can meditate on Scripture and on Jesus' love and sacrifice for me; I can write about my feelings; I can share feelings honestly with another person.*

3. I couldn't approve of myself if I didn't obey. Some people obey rules in an attempt to live up to standards they've set for themselves. In doing this they are not yielding their lives to a loving Lord. They are trying to avoid the feeling of shame that occurs when they don't meet their own standards. These people primarily are concerned with do's and don'ts. Instead of seeing the Christian life as an intimate relationship with God, they see it as a ritual—as a life emphasizing rules. If they succeed in keeping the rules, they become prideful. They compare themselves with others. They hope others will accept them because they are a little bit better than someone else.

Philip grew up in a strict religious family. His family taught him that cursing is a terrible sin. All of Philip's friends cursed, but he never did. He secretly thought that he was better than his friends. The fact that God wants pure language is not the reason Philip refrained from cursing. He refrained from cursing because he was compelled to live up to his own standards. Philip needed to base his behavior on God and His Word, not on his own standards.

What things are you not doing because you couldn't stand yourself if you did them? In the margin box describe the things you are doing to obey God with the motivation to meet your own standards.

Things I do to meet my own standards—

_____

_____

_____

_____

_____

_____

_____

_____

God gave us His commands because He loves us. As we obey Him, He protects and frees us to enjoy life more fully.

4. I'll obey to be blessed. God doesn't make bargains. While God does reward obedience, we may try to manipulate God. Our underlying assumption is, "I've been good, so bless me." It's true that we will reap what we sow. It's true that obedience keeps us within God's plan for our lives, but our decision to obey never should be based solely on God's rewards.

Brian went to church so that God would bless his business, not because he wanted to worship God. Penny chose not to spread gossip about Diane because she told God that she wouldn't tell anybody about Diane if He got her the promotion she wanted.

Have you ever bargained with God and said, "I'll obey You if You'll 'fix' me?"   Yes   No

We reason that if we are "fixed," we will be able to serve God and be freed from having to deal with a particular problem or temptation. God sometimes has something important to teach us through our weakness. The apostle Paul three times begged the Lord to remove a "thorn," or difficulty, from him. Read in the margin how the Lord responded to him.

Christ has freed us from the bondage of sin so that we can respond to Him in obedience. We have discussed six reasons the Bible tells us to be involved in good works. As a review, fill in the key words from those reasons.

1. Christ's _____ motivates us to obey Him.

2. Sin is _____.

3. The Father's _____ trains us.

4. His commands for us are _____.

5. God will reward our _____.

6. Christ is _____.

You will find the answers on pages 118-120.

The Lord never said everything had to be perfect in our lives for us to follow Him. He said, "If anyone wishes to come after Me, let him deny himself," (In the context of this passage, "denying yourself" means giving up your selfish desires.) "take up His cross daily, and follow Me" (Luke 9:23). This doesn't mean we should stop working to rid ourselves of our difficulties. We can express our feelings about them to the Lord and with others as appropriate. Then we are to act in faith on His Word.

We don't have to deny the difficulties we have in life, but spiritual growth, character development, and Christian service must not be held hostage by them. God has given each of us a will, and we can choose to honor the Lord in spite of our difficulties.

Bargaining with God

And He has said to me, "My grace is sufficient for you, for power is perfected in weakness." Most gladly, therefore, I will rather boast about my weaknesses, that the power of Christ may dwell in me. Therefore I am well content with weaknesses, with insults, with distresses, with persecutions, with difficulties, for Christ's sake, for when I am weak, then I am strong.

–2 Corinthians 12:9-10

We can choose to honor the Lord in spite of our difficulties.

As you become aware of your motives, you may think, "I've never done anything purely for the Lord in my whole life!" You may feel a sense of pain and remorse because you've had inappropriate motives. Try not to shame yourself for your past attitudes—we all have them. Instead, realize that the Lord wants you to make godly choices today so that you can enjoy the benefits of those decisions in the future. Then ask the Holy Spirit to help you develop an intensity about these choices.

Beloved, now we are children of God, and it has not appeared as yet what we shall be. We know that, when He appears, we shall be like Him, because we shall see Him just as He is.

–1 John 3:2

As the verse at left indicates, your motives won't become totally pure until you see the Lord face to face. The more you grow in your understanding and relationship with Him, the more you will desire to honor Him with your love, loyalty, and obedience.

Recognizing the great reasons for obedience, please write your own statement showing that you intend to grow in your willingness to follow Christ. It will provide you with direction and be your own "pledge of allegiance to Jesus."

_____

_____

┌───┐
Key Concept for Lesson 3
My wrong motives lead to false obedience, bitterness, and resentment.
└───┘

Memorize this Step's memory verse:
Humble yourselves in the presence of the Lord, and He will exalt you.

–James 4:10

LESSON 4

Key Concept:
I am a bond-servant. My Master owns me.

Ownership and Conduct

We commit ourselves to God and desire that He remove patterns of sin from our lives.

> _Do you not know that when you present yourselves to someone as slaves for obedience, you are slaves of the one whom you obey, either of sin resulting in death, or of obedience resulting in righteousness_
>
> –Romans 6:16

An Important Principle

You will find your growth, the control of your emotions, your faithful obedience, and your choice of proper motives for obedience much more natural, and even easier, if you can accept one all-important principle. It is the principle of ownership—the issue of who owns you. The constant struggle between sin and righteousness, between victory and defeat, is mainly a battle about who—Christ or you—is master or owner of your life.

Or do you not know that your body is a temple of the Holy Spirit who is in you, whom you have from God, and that you are not your own? For you have been bought with a price: therefore glorify God in your body.

–1 Corinthians 6:19-20

According to the verse in the margin, who bought you? What was the price? Whose were you before that purchase?

_____

_____

Before you became a Christian, you were a slave to sin—sold into slavery to sin, as the apostle Paul puts it (Romans 7:14). God, at great cost, redeemed you, or "bought you back," and set you free. The cost was the sacrifice of His own Son on the cross. He paid the price of any claim sin had on you.

Accepting the fact of Christ's ownership frees you to trust Him with your life and provides courage to act in faith. While he trusted in Christ as Lord, the apostle Peter was able to do the impossible.

Peter answered Him and said, "Lord, if it is You, command me to come to You on the water." And He said, "Come!" And Peter got out of the boat, and walked on the water and came toward Jesus.

–Matthew 14:28-29

Read the Scripture in the margin. Peter asked what seemed to be impossible. What seemingly impossible request would you like to bring to Jesus?

_____

Obedience is faith in action. Trust Him as your Lord to take responsibility for your requests and for your life. Step out in faith.

Under the ownership and lordship of Christ, you are asked to glorify God in your body (1 Corinthians 6:20). List six ways you can do that. Put a star (★) by one you'll start this week.

1. _____   4. _____

2. _____   5. _____

3. _____   6. _____

In the margin list two troublesome areas in your life that still need work. Present them to the Lord so that He might receive glory by helping you. (Do not be discouraged if you attempt to do this more than once. Keep on asking, acting, and trusting God for the outcome.)

You recognize that your compulsion has robbed you of life and has cheated you of the life that should have been yours, but in recovery, you discover the gift of new life.

The comedian Jack Benny performed a routine in which a mugger demanded at gunpoint, "Your money or your life!" Benny, whose comedian character centered around his supposed extreme tightness with money, always got a laugh as he stalled and mulled over this demand and finally answered, "Don't rush me! I'm thinking, I'm thinking!" How well we could identify with this in our compulsions, because we could not bring ourselves to consider what we thought were the horrors of life without alcohol or other drugs. In recovery, we learn that life is worth living, for God has given us infinite worth and meaningful purpose for a full life. In Step 7 we will discover some new means for experiencing the transformation necessary to enjoy that life.

Life with my drug of choice is struggling merely to survive. Life with sobriety is real living.

Key Concept for Lesson 4

I am a bond-servant. My Master owns me.

Pray and ask God how this concept can apply in your life. Now please review this lesson. What has God shown you that you can use?

_____

_____

Memorize this Step's memory verse:

Humble yourselves in the presence of the Lord, and He will exalt you.

–James 4:10

Step Review

Step 6 says *We commit ourselves to God and desire that He remove patterns of sin from our lives.* **Write in your own words what Step 6 means.**

_____

_____

_____

_____

Describe how you daily will apply Step 6 to your life and recovery.

_____

_____

_____

_____

_____

_____

Notes

[1]McGee, Robert S., *Search for Significance* LIFE Support Edition (Houston: Rapha Publishing, 1992), 11.

[2]Pat Springle, *Untangling Relationships: A Christian Perspective on Codependency* (Houston: Rapha Publishing, 1993), 156-157.

STEP

7

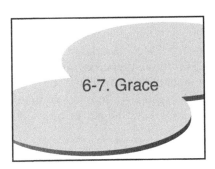

6-7. Grace

We seek Him to renew our minds and transform us.

Ready for Change

APPLYING GRACE

Julie finally "got" Steps 6 and 7. She genuinely applied them to her life and behaviors. In Step 6 she realized that she had been attempting to work to make herself acceptable to God. The Step said that "we commit ourselves to God," but it also said that "we *desire that He* remove the patterns of sin from our lives." She understood that even all her attempts at Christian service still were efforts to make herself good enough. She still was trying to do God's work for Him.

The day Julie finally took Step 7, she wrote in her personal journal, "Step 7 is not just about asking God to help me. It is about grace. Grace is undeserved. I am powerless. I have wanted God to lend me His power so I no longer will be powerless—so I could overcome my compulsions with God's help.

"I have been asking God to help me to be perfect, to overcome my drug habit, and to gain others' approval. I was asking the wrong question and praying the wrong prayer. I now realize that I need God to do the work. I can begin to accept myself. I can 'Let Go and Let God.'" (Read more about Julie on page 128.)

Step 7   *We humbly ask God to renew our minds so that our sinful patterns can be transformed into patterns of righteousness.*

Memory verse   *And do not be conformed to this world, but be transformed by the renewing of your mind, that you may prove what the will of God is, that which is good and acceptable and perfect.*

          –Romans 12:2

Overview for Step 7

Lesson 1: The Grace Step
Goal: You will identify why you need a renewed mind.

Lesson 2: The Performance Trap
Goal: You will determine how trying to gain a sense of worth through your performance affects you negatively, and you will describe the solution.

Lesson 3: The Approval Addict
Goal: You will learn how an addiction to approval affects you negatively, and you will describe the solution.

Lesson 4: The Blame Game
Goal: You will study how habitual blaming affects you negatively, and you will describe the solution.

Lesson 5: Shame
Goal: You will evaluate how low self-esteem affects you negatively, and you will describe the solution.

Lesson 6: Taking the Step
Goal: You will describe three practical actions necessary to work this Step.

The Grace Step

We humbly ask God to renew our minds so that our sinful patterns can be transformed into patterns of righteousness.

> *for it is God who is at work in you, both to will and to work for His good pleasure.*
>
> –Philippians 2:13

Key Concept:
A solid, biblical, belief system is the key to my healthy behavior.

In Step 1 we discovered that we are powerless. In Step 7 we begin to apply God's power to our situation. Philippians 2:13 above describes grace in a distinctive way. God gives us both the desire and the power to do His will. God does not merely overlook our sin. He works in our lives to make genuine change. God's grace creates a renewed mind so we can be rid of our self-destructive patterns of sin.

Read Philippians 2:13 again. Why is it important that God give us the will (desire) as well as the work (ability) to follow Him?

_____

_____

We often define grace as God's unmerited favor. Grace is His free, undeserved gift of loving and accepting us. God's gift includes the desire and the power to follow Him. We do not naturally desire what is best. We do not, on our own, have the ability to do God's will.

Why Do I Need My Mind Renewed?

Julie said, "In the early days of using drugs I was arrogant and proud. I thought I was smarter than anyone else. I was smarter than my parents, smarter than my teachers, smarter than the cops. Later I got smarter than my probation officer. I even thought I was smarter than God. I thought I could do anything and get away with it. When my life began to fall apart, I came to this group. One of the men jokingly referred to his 'keen alcoholic mind.' *That's me,* I thought. *I have a sharper mind than other people.* Only later did I realize that he was making fun of his distorted thinking. When I became more honest, I began to realize how stupid I had been. I allowed myself to believe all that stuff about how smart I was. I learned that I need my mind renewed because I think in a distorted manner. My pastor explained that sin has damaged every one of us—sin caused this distorted thinking. I even learned that a big word exists to describe the damage sin has done to us all. The word is depravity."

> An ox knows its owner, And a donkey its master's manger, But Israel does not know, My people do not understand.
>
> –Isaiah 1:3

> walk no longer just as the Gentiles also walk, in the futility of their mind, being darkened in their understanding, excluded from the life of God, because of the ignorance that is in them, because of the hardness of their heart; and they, having become callous, have given themselves over to sensuality, for the practice of every kind of impurity with greediness.
>
> –Ephesians 4:17-19

The Scriptures in the margin speak about our depravity. From Julie's story and the Scriptures, describe how sin has affected our thinking.

_____

_____

And do not be conformed to this world, but be transformed by the renewing of your mind, that you may prove what the will of God is, that which is good and acceptable and perfect.

–Romans 12:2

You are of your father the devil, and you want to do the desires of your father. He was a murderer from the beginning, and does not stand in the truth, because there is no truth in him. Whenever he speaks a lie, he speaks from his own nature; for he is a liar, and the father of lies.

–John 8:44

Julie went on to say, "I thought that drugs were my habit and my problem. I have discovered that a deeper problem exists. My distorted thinking is my real habit. In Step 7, I am asking God to renew my mind and change my distorted thinking."

God wants to renew our minds and transform our lives, as our memory passage at left indicates. Satan desires to keep us in darkness with our minds unrenewed so that our lives won't be transformed. The ugly truth is that we are depraved. John 8:44 says Satan is the source of our behavior, and we naturally are like him. Sin shapes our thoughts, our actions, and our feelings.

Sin in our lives occurs largely because of our distorted belief system. The following diagram shows this process:

Most of the time we act because of habit rather than because of clear choices. Our thoughts, feelings, and actions mostly are habit. They result from learned behavior. We all must deal with a variety of situations in life. Between the situation and our thoughts, emotions, and actions is a filtering system—our beliefs.

Julie, in the story above, discovered that her thought patterns were the deeper habit that supported her drug addiction. She began to identify and cooperate with God to change those habitual thought patterns. Here is another example of learned and practiced thought patterns:

> My boss doesn't seem to like the job I do. I believe that my worth comes from doing a good job and being approved by others. I begin to think depressing thoughts about myself. This causes me to feel bad about myself. I then drink or use to soothe my frayed emotions.

As long as I believe my worth comes from my performance and from others' approval, I always will be stuck. Habit is almost impossible to change without confronting and changing the underlying belief system.

Our beliefs represent our deepest, most basic thoughts. They affect the way we feel, the way we perceive others and ourselves, and ultimately, the way we act. They determine whether we will live according to God's functional truth or the world's dysfunctional value system. Read the verse appearing at left.

As (a man) thinks within himself, so he is.

–Proverbs 23:7

Below check the response which shows the root from which our habits originate.

     1. our thoughts
     2. our actions
     3. our beliefs
     4. our emotions

Our beliefs (number 3) are the roots from which our habits of thinking, feeling, and acting grow.

Check all of the following that are false basic beliefs:

1. I must gain the approval of others to feel good about myself.
2. I cannot change, I am hopeless.
3. I am feeling depressed because I failed to meet expectations.
4. I must meet certain standards to feel good about myself.
5. Those who fail are unworthy of love and deserve to be punished.

If you checked numbers 1, 2, 4, and 5, you were correct. Answer 3 is a feeling that grows out of the false belief that my worth is determined by my performance. In our opinion, people usually concentrate on habitual thoughts, feelings, and actions. They seldom deal with the genuine problem—a false belief system.

How our filters work

Our beliefs represent the filters through which we interpret the situations we encounter. Some of these interpretations are conscious reflections; however, most are based on unconscious assumptions—habits. These beliefs trigger thoughts, which in turn lead to emotions, which drive actions.

False Beliefs

If we use the truth of God's Word as the basis for what we believe about ourselves, we likely will have a positive sense of self-esteem. However, as we mentioned in Step 2, Satan has deceived most of us by convincing us that:

Our Self-Worth = Performance + Others' Opinions

The four false beliefs serve as a summary of the many lies Satan tells us. Below we again list these beliefs for you. To what extent do they affect you? Estimate the percentage, from zero to 100 percent, which you think indicates how much you live by each belief.

_____% *I must meet certain standards in order to feel good about myself.*

_____% *I must have the approval of certain others* (boss, friends, parents) *to feel good about myself. If I don't have their approval, I can't feel good about myself.*

_____% *Those who fail are unworthy of love and deserve to be punished.*

_____% *I am what I am. I cannot change. I am hopeless.* In other words, I am the sum total of all my past successes and failures, and I'll never be significantly different.

In your work on this Step you will examine how each of those false belief systems operates in your life. Remember from Step 2 that for each of the false beliefs God has a life-changing truth.

Read the following two lists. The first list contains the four basic false beliefs. The second list contains four of God's truths. At the left of each false belief write the letter of the corresponding truth.

_____ 1. *I must meet certain standards to feel good about myself:* results in fear of failure; perfectionism; being driven to succeed; manipulating others to succeed; withdrawing from healthy risks for fear of failing.

Beliefs, consequences

_____ 2. *I must have the approval of certain others to feel good about myself*: results in fear of rejection; becoming a people-pleaser; being overly sensitive to criticism; withdrawing from others to avoid disapproval.

_____ 3. *Those who fail, including me, are unworthy of love and deserve to be punished*: results in fear of punishment; a tendency to punish others; blaming self and others for personal failure; withdrawing from God and fellow believers; being driven to avoid punishment.

_____ 4. *I am what I am. I cannot change. I am hopeless*: results in feelings of shame, hopelessness, inferiority, inactivity; lack of interest; loss of creativity; isolation, withdrawing from others.

A. *Propitiation*, which means we have the capacity to experience God's love deeply because we no longer will fear punishment or punish others. Results include: increasing freedom from the fear of punishment; patience and kindness toward others; being quick to forgive; deep love for Christ (1 John 2:2).

B. *Justification*, which means we are completely forgiven and fully pleasing to God. Results include: increasing freedom from the fear of failure; desire to pursue the right things: Christ and His kingdom; love for Christ (Romans 5:1).

C. *Regeneration*, which means we have been made brand new, complete in Christ. Results include: no longer experiencing the pain of shame; Christ-centered self-confidence; joy, courage, peace; desire to know Christ (Colossians 1:21).

D. *Reconciliation*, which means we are totally accepted by God. Results include: increasing freedom from the fear of rejection; willingness to be open and vulnerable; ability to relax around others; willingness to take criticism; a desire to please God no matter what others think (2 Corinthians 5:18).

These four basic truths are the foundation on which we can build an effective, Christ-honoring life. The responses are 1. B, 2. D, 3. A, 4. C.

> ## Key Concept for Lesson 1
> A solid, biblical, belief system is the key to healthy behavior.

Please pray and ask God how this concept can apply in your life. Now please review this lesson. Below write what God has shown you that can help you.

_____

_____

_____

_____

Begin memorizing this Step's memory verse, Romans 12:2.

Key Concept:
I am completely forgiven by God and am fully pleasing to Him.

The Performance Trap

We humbly ask God to renew our minds so that our sinful patterns can be transformed into patterns of righteousness.

> *knowing that a man is not justified by the works of the Law but through faith in Christ Jesus, even we have believed in Christ Jesus, that we may be justified by faith in Christ, and not by the works of the Law; since by the works of the Law shall no flesh be justified.*
>
> –Galatians 2:16

The false belief that I must meet certain standards in order to feel good about myself results in a fear of failure. Take the following test to determine how strongly this belief affects you.

Fear of Failure Test

Read the statements below. Then, from the top of the test, choose the term which best describes your response. Put in the blank beside each statement the number above the term you chose.

1	2	3	4
Always	Sometimes	Seldom	Never

_____ 1. I avoid participating in some activities because I am afraid I will not be good enough.

_____ 2. I become anxious when I sense I may fail.

_____ 3. I worry.

_____ 4. I have unexplained anxiety.

_____ 5. I am a perfectionist.

_____ 6. I feel I must justify my mistakes.

_____ 7. I feel I must succeed in some areas.

_____ 8. I become depressed when I fail.

_____ 9. I become angry with people who interfere with my success and who make me appear incompetent.

_____ 10. I am self-critical.

_____ Total (Add up the numbers you placed in the blanks.)

My score means—

Interpreting Your Score
If your score is . . .

34-40
God apparently has given you a very strong appreciation for His love and unconditional acceptance. You seem to be free of the fear of failure that plagues most people. (Some exceptions exist: Some people who score this high either are greatly deceived or have turned off their emotions as a way to suppress pain. Examine your heart and talk to your group members to see if these exceptions apply to you.)

28-33
The fear of failure rarely controls your responses or does so only in certain

situations. Again, people who are not honest with themselves represent the major exceptions to this statement.

Fear of failure

22-27
A sense of failure and fear of criticism is a cause of pain in your life. As you reflect on many of your previous decisions, you probably will find that you can relate many of them to this fear. The fear of failure also will affect many of your future decisions unless you act directly to overcome this fear.

16-21
The fear of failure forms a general backdrop to your life. Probably, few days exist in which this fear does not affect you in some way. Unfortunately, this fear robs you of the joy and peace your salvation is meant to bring.

10-15
Experiences of failure dominate your memory. They probably have caused you to experience a great deal of depression. These problems will remain until you take action. In other words, this condition will not simply disappear. You need to experience deep healing in your self-concept, in your relationship with God, and in your relationships with others.

Effects of the Fear of Failure

Remember from the last lesson the following diagram:

We interpret situations through our belief system. This results in a cycle of thoughts, feelings, and actions. The key beliefs behind the fear of failure are our self-imposed standards. Fear of failure stems from the false belief, *I must meet certain standards in order to feel good about myself.*

In *The Search for Significance* author Robert S. McGee tells the story about how he experienced the fear of failure during his teenage years. During those years he practiced basketball a lot and became a good player. In the process he learned that he could attempt many maneuvers when he practiced on the court or when he played basketball with friends.

But during a game when he felt intense pressure, he was afraid to do those same maneuvers. "I now realize that same fear has prevented me from attempting things in several other areas of my life," he wrote. "Although God has enabled me on many occasions to conquer this fear, I still struggle with the risk of failing. This story may surprise some people who know me and who think of me as a successful person." Success does not reduce the amount of fear of failure we experience in our lives.[1]

> **Do you see any of the following patterns at work in your emotions and actions? Check all that apply:**
>
> avoiding failure at all costs by attempting only things in which I feel offer limited risk of failure.

spending time around those who are not a threat to me.

avoiding people who by their greater success make me feel like a failure.

feeling angry at those who stand in the way of me meeting my standards and goals.

blaming myself or others for my inability to meet my standards.

other_____

Think of a situation in which your performance did not measure up to the standard you had set for yourself. Try to remember what thoughts and emotions arose because of that situation. What action did you take in response to those emotions? Read the example below, then write your thoughts.

Situation: I failed to make a sale.
Standard: I must meet my quota to feel good about myself.
Thoughts: I'm a failure. I'll never make my quota. I'll never
            get promoted. I'll probably be fired any day now.
Emotions: Fear, anger, depression.
Actions: I avoided my boss for three days. I yelled at my
            wife and kids. I took out my anger on them.

Situation: _____

Standard: _____

Thoughts: _____

Emotions: _____

Actions: _____

_____

Most of us have become experts at avoiding failure.

If we believe that our self-worth is based on our success, we will try at all costs to avoid failure. Most of us have become experts at avoiding failure. We attempt only those things in which we are confident of success. We avoid activities in which the risk of failure is too great. We spend time around people who are not a threat to us. We avoid people who, either by their greater success or by their disapproval, make us feel like failures. We have trained ourselves very well!

Do you have to be successful in order to feel good about yourself?
Yes   No

What would you have to be or do to feel like you are a success?

_____

When we evaluate ourselves by our performance, we ultimately lose no matter how successful we are. As we answer the previous question, many of us discover that even reaching our goals would not make us feel successful.

In the following paragraph underline two additional dangers of living by the lie of performance-based self-worth.

Meeting certain standards in order to feel good about ourselves also causes us to live a rules-dominated life. We know people who have a set of rules for everything and who always place their attention on their performance. They miss the joy of walking with God. The gospel is about relationships, not regulations. The opposite danger is feeling good about ourselves because we are winning the performance game. We can't afford to mistake this pride for positive self-worth. God can bring about circumstances to stop us from trusting in ourselves. God intends to bring us to Himself through prayer and through studying His Word so that we can know, love, and serve Him. Sometimes He will allow us to fail so that we will look to Him instead of to ourselves for our security and significance. Before becoming upset that God would allow you to experience failure, remember that any life less than God intended is a second-class existence. He loves you too much to let you continue to obtain your self-esteem from the empty promise of success.

The gospel is about relationships, not regulations.

What do you think the writer meant when he wrote the verse appearing in the margin? Write your own version of the verse.

It is good for me that I was afflicted, That I may learn Thy statutes.

    –Psalm 119:71

_____

_____

The two dangers that appear in the paragraphs above are: a rules-dominated life and pride in our seeming success. My own version of the psalm read: "God loves me so much that He is willing to allow me to learn from experiencing my failure and inadequacy. Failure can lead me to the joy of a love and trust relationship with Him."

God's Answer: Justification

Impute means to credit something to one's account. My sins were imputed to Jesus, and His righteousness was imputed to me. God loves us and has provided a solution to the nightmare of the performance trap. That solution is called *justification*. Someone explained the meaning of *justified* very simply. God makes me "JUST as IF I'D" never sinned. As a result of Christ's death on the cross, our sins are forgiven and God has imputed Christ's righteousness to believers. Christ has justified us. Therefore, we are fully pleasing to God.

The solution

Some people have trouble thinking of themselves as being pleasing to God because they link pleasing so strongly with performance. They tend to be displeased with anything short of perfection in themselves, and they suspect that God has the same standard. The point of justification is that we never can achieve perfection on this earth, yet God loves us so much that He appointed His Son to pay for our sins. God credited to us Christ's own righteousness, His perfect status before God.

What does it mean to be justified? _____

_____

He made Him who knew no sin to be sin on our behalf, that we might become the righteousness of God in Him.

–2 Corinthians 5:21

Justification is one of the central messages of Scripture. 2 Corinthians 5:21 at left is an example. We have not pulled out a couple of isolated passages to prove a point. Literally hundreds of passages all through the Bible teach this liberating truth. If you have accepted Christ, God considers you just as holy and righteous as the Lord Jesus Himself because He has taken your sins and placed His righteousness in its place.

Read this statement: *I am completely forgiven by God and am fully pleasing to Him.* **How does being justified and having Christ's righteousness lead you to the conclusion reached in that statement?**

_____

_____

This doesn't mean that our actions don't matter and that we can sin all we want. Our sinful actions, words, and attitudes make the Lord sad, but our status as beloved children remains intact.

Taking sin seriously

Some people may read these statements and become uneasy. They may believe that we are not taking sin seriously. As you will see, we are not minimizing the destructive nature of sin. We are trying to make sure we see Christ's payment on the cross as very, very important.

Visualize two ledgers like the ones appearing below. On one is a list of all your sins; on the other, a list of the righteousness of Christ. In the left column write your name and list some of your sins.

All _____ 's (your name) Sins	All Christ's Righteousness

Now in the right column list some of Christ's wonderful characteristics, such as His love, faithfulness, holiness, and kindness.

God transferred our sin to Christ and His righteousness to us.

Now exchange names on the ledgers. Mark out the name of Christ and write your name in place of Christ's. Mark out your name and write His name in place of yours. This represents an example of justification: transferring our sin to Christ and His righteousness to us. In 1 Corinthians 5:21 Paul wrote "He (God) made Him (Jesus) who knew no sin to be sin on our behalf, that we might become the righteousness of God in Him."

Key Concept for Lesson 2
I am completely forgiven by God and am fully pleasing to Him.

Please pray and ask God how the concept you just read can apply in your life. Now please review this lesson. What has God shown you that can help you?

_____

_____

<table>
<tr><td>

LESSON

3

</td></tr>
</table>

Key Concept:
I am totally accepted by God.

The Approval Addict

We humbly ask God to renew our minds so that our sinful patterns can be transformed into patterns of righteousness.

> _For am I now seeking the favor of men, or of God? Or am I striving to please men? If I were still trying to please men, I would not be a bond-servant of Christ._
>
> —Galatians 1:10

Living by the false belief that I must be approved by others to feel good about myself causes fear of rejection. We cannot be free to serve Christ as long as this fear makes us conform our attitudes and actions to others' expectations. Take the following test to determine how strongly you fear rejection.

Fear of Rejection Test

Read each of the statements below. Then, from the top of the test, choose the term that best describes your response. Put in the blank beside each statement the number above the term you chose.

1	2	3	4
Always	Sometimes	Seldom	Never

_____ 1. When I sense that someone might reject me, I become anxious.
_____ 2. I spend lots of time analyzing why someone was critical or sarcastic to me or ignored me.
_____ 3. I am uncomfortable around those who are different from me.
_____ 4. It bothers me when someone is unfriendly to me.
_____ 5. I am basically shy and unsocial.
_____ 6. I am critical of others.
_____ 7. I find myself trying to impress others.
_____ 8. I become depressed when someone criticizes me.
_____ 9. I try to determine what people think of me.
_____ 10. I don't understand people and what motivates them.

_____ Total (Add up the numbers you have placed in the blanks.)

My score means—

Interpreting Your Score
If your score is . . .

34-40
God apparently has given you a very strong appreciation for His love and unconditional acceptance. You seem to be free of the fear of rejection that

plagues most people. (Some exceptions exist: Some people who score this high either are greatly deceived or have turned off their emotions as a way to suppress pain. Examine your heart and talk to your group members to see if these exceptions apply to you.)

28-33

The fear of rejection controls your responses rarely or only in certain situations. Again, the only major exceptions are those who are not honest with themselves.

22-27

Emotional problems you experience may relate to a sense of rejection. Upon reflection you probably will relate many of your previous decisions to this fear. The fear of rejection also will affect many of your future decisions unless you take direct action to overcome that fear.

Take direct action

16-21

The fear of rejection forms a general backdrop to your life. Probably few days go by in which this fear does not affect you in some way. Unfortunately, this robs you of the joy and peace your salvation is meant to bring.

10-15

Experiences of rejection dominate your memory and probably cause you to experience a great deal of depression. These problems will persist until you take definitive action. In other words, this condition will not simply disappear; time alone cannot heal your pain. You need to experience deep healing in your self-concept, in your relationship with God, and in your relationships with others.

Effects of the Fear of Rejection

By working the following exercises you will understand more clearly the fear of rejection, and you will clarify the impact of the fear in your life.

Does anyone's disrespect or disapproval have negative effects on you? If so, below list those individuals.

_____   _____

_____   _____

_____   _____

To see how others affect you, select one of the people from your first group of responses. Then answer the questions that appear below. For example you might write, "My father would be more pleased with me if I had excelled in sports," or "My husband is proud of me when I wear the clothes that he likes."

1. _____ would be more pleased with me if I would _____

_____

_____

2. _____ is proud of me when I _____

_____

_____

3. How does _____ attempt to get me to change by what he or she says or does?

_____

_____

4. Things I do or say to get _____ to approve of me include:

_____

_____

Use as many extra sheets of paper as you need and repeat the exercise with each of the individuals or groups you listed on page 138.

We think that when our performance is unacceptable, we are unacceptable.

Evaluating our self-worth by what we and others think about our performance leads us to believe that any time our performance is unacceptable, we are unacceptable as well.

Do you identify in your life any of the following results of fear of rejection? Check all that apply:

being easily manipulated
being hypersensitive to criticism
defensiveness
hostility toward others who disagree with me
superficial relationships
exaggerating or minimizing the truth to impress people
shyness
passivity
other _____

Virtually all of us have internalized the following sentence into our belief system. We hold to it with amazing strength:

I must have the acceptance, respect, and approval of others in order to have self-worth.

This is the basic false belief behind all peer pressure. We seek acceptance and respect from people who don't have what we need and wouldn't give it to us if they did. Then when the pain of rejection—or the fear of potential rejection—becomes too great, we seek a form of chemical relief from the pain.

God's Answer: Reconciliation

reconcile-v. to restore to friendship or harmony; to settle or resolve differences (Webster's)

God's answer to the pain of rejection is **reconciliation**. Christ died for our sins and restored us to a proper relationship with God. We are both acceptable to namely, that God was in Christ reconciling the world to Himself, not counting their trespasses against them, and He has committed to us the word of reconciliation.

–2 Corinthians 5:19

And although you were formerly alienated and hostile in mind, engaged in evil deeds, yet He has now reconciled you in His fleshly body through death, in order to present you before Him holy and blameless and beyond reproach.

–Colossians 1:21-22

He saved us, not on the basis of deeds which we have done in righteousness, but according to His mercy.

–Titus 3:5

Him and accepted by Him. We are not rejected! We are His. The verse at left from 2 Corinthians explains how God reconciled us to Himself. He chose to bear the penalty for our sin and not count the sins against us.

When God chose to redeem us, He did not go part way. He did not make us partially righteous because of our poor performance. The blood of Christ is sufficient to pay for all sin. His blood makes us holy and righteous before God, even in the midst of sin. This does not minimize the destructiveness of sin. It glorifies the sacrifice of Christ. We are restored to a complete and pure love relationship with God.

We may neglect this teaching more than we may neglect any other in Scripture. The passage from Colossians at left says it plainly. Enjoy those last words. God sees us as holy and blameless and beyond reproach at this very moment. This is not merely a reference to our future standing; it describes our present status as well. We are totally accepted by God. God received us into a loving, intimate, personal relationship the moment we placed our faith in Christ. We are united with God in an eternal and unbreakable bond (Romans 8:38-39). Knowing that no sin can make a Christian unacceptable to God is faith in a pledge sealed with the Holy Spirit (Ephesians 1:14).

Since our relationship with God was bought entirely by the blood of Christ, no amount of good works can make us more acceptable to Him. Read Titus 3:5, which appears in the margin. Because Christ has reconciled us to God, we can experience the incredible truth that we are totally accepted by and acceptable to God.

Review the last two paragraphs and look for reasons to thank God for reconciling you to Himself. Write a prayer thanking Him for totally accepting you.

_____

_____

_____

As in the last lesson, this truth is a central theme of Scripture.

What can we do when we have failed or when someone disapproves of us? We can learn to use the truth in this lesson and say:

> "It would be nice if _____ (my boss liked me, I could fix the refrigerator, my complexion were clear, James had picked me up on time, or _____), but I'm still deeply loved, completely forgiven, fully pleasing, totally accepted and complete in Christ."

This statement doesn't mean that we won't feel pain or anger. We can be honest about our feelings. The statement simply is a quick way to gain God's perspective on what we experience. It is not magic, but it enables us to reflect on the truth. We can apply this truth in every difficult situation, whether it involves someone's disapproval, our own failure to accomplish something, or another person's failure.

On the lines below, write the following statement: I am deeply loved, completely forgiven, fully pleasing, totally accepted, and complete in Christ.

_____

_____

_____

Now go back and read the statement three times. Cathy's sponsor assigned her to look in the mirror and read that truth to herself each day for a month. Cathy said it was the most difficult thing she ever did. Today Cathy gratefully acknowledges that this statement was a key to changing her life.

Memorize the truth in the above statement and begin to apply it in your situations and relationships. Also continue to work on this Step's memory verse.

> ### Key Concept for Lesson 3
> I am totally accepted by God.

Please pray and ask God how this concept can apply in your life. Now please review this lesson. What has God shown you that can help you?

_____

_____

LESSON 4

Key Concept:
I am deeply loved by God.

The Blame Game

We humbly ask God to renew our minds so that our sinful patterns can be transformed into patterns of righteousness.

> *He has not dealt with us according to our sins, Nor rewarded us according to our iniquities.*
>
> –Psalm 103:10

The false belief that *those who fail, including me, are unworthy of love and deserve to be punished,* is at the root of our fear of punishment and our tendency to punish others. Take the following test to determine how much this lie influences you.

Fear of Punishment/Punishing Others Test

Read each of the statements that appear in the exercise on the next page. Then, from the top of the test, choose the term that best describes your response. Put in the blank beside each statement the number above the term you chose.

	1	2	3	4
	Always	**Sometimes**	**Seldom**	**Never**

_____ 1. I fear what God might do to me.

_____ 2. After I fail, I worry about God's response.

_____ 3. When I see someone in a difficult situation, I wonder what he or she did to deserve that situation.

_____ 4. When something goes wrong, I tend to think that God must be punishing me.

_____ 5. I am very hard on myself when I fail.

_____ 6. I find myself wanting to blame others when they fail.

_____ 7. I get angry with God when someone who is immoral or dishonest prospers.

_____ 8. I am determined to make sure others know about it when I see them doing wrong.

_____ 9. I tend to focus on the faults and failures of others.

_____ 10. God seems harsh to me.

_____ Total (Add the numbers you have placed in the blanks.)

My score means—

Interpreting Your Score

If your score is. . .

34-40

God apparently has given you a very strong appreciation for His unconditional love and acceptance. You seem to be freed from the fear of punishment that plagues most people. (Some exceptions exist: Some people who score this high either are greatly deceived or have turned off their emotions as a way to suppress pain. Examine your heart and talk to your group members to see if these exceptions apply to you.)

28-33

The fear of punishment and the compulsion to punish others control your responses rarely or only in certain situations. Again, the only exceptions are those who are not honest about how strongly these matters affect them.

22-27

When you experience emotional problems, they may have to do with a fear of punishment or with an inner urge to punish others. Upon reflection you probably can relate many of your previous responses to this fear. The fear of punishment and/or the determination to punish others also will affect many of your

Take direct action

future responses unless you take direct action to overcome these tendencies.

16-21

The fear of punishment forms a general backdrop to your life. Probably few days go by that the fear of punishment and the tendency to blame others do not affect you. Unfortunately, this robs you of the joy and peace your salvation is meant to bring.

10-15

Experiences of punishment dominate your memory. You probably have suffered a great deal of depression as a result. This condition will not simply disappear; time alone cannot heal your pain. You need to experience deep healing in your self-concept, in your relationship with God, and in your relationships with others.

The Fear of Punishment and Tendency to Punish Others

A wife spent her hour in the counselor's office attempting to show that a marital problem was all her husband's fault. When it was time for her husband's appointment, he tried to prove that she was to blame. People often are more interested in avoiding blame and pinning it on someone else than they are in solving problems.

Using the example of the couple above, explain the meaning of the slogan appearing in the margin.

_____

_____

An addict is someone who would rather be in control than be happy.

We seem to believe that we deserve blame for our shortcomings and that others deserve the same. You may have written that we would rather be in control by proving something isn't our fault than by solving the problems and remove the pain. This exercise will help you understand the fear of punishment and the false belief, *Those who fail are unworthy of love and deserve to be punished.*

Do you believe that you really deserve to feel good about yourself? Below explain why, or why not.

_____

_____

Describe three recent incidents in your life in which you feared being blamed or punished. What prompted this fear?

1. _____

_____

2. _____

_____

3. _____

_____

What are the three most negative terms you use to describe yourself? What names do you call yourself?

_____

After sinning, do you ever believe you have to feel badly about yourself before you can feel good about yourself?   Yes   No

Most of the reasons we spend time condemning ourselves stem from the false belief that *when we fail we deserve to be blamed and punished*. We have been conditioned either to accept personal blame or to blame somebody else when our performance is unsatisfactory. You may think that this false belief does not affect you at all—but it probably does. Do you generally have an urge to find out who is at fault when something fails?

Rather than evaluating our problems objectively, we tend to defend ourselves. We sometimes do this by attacking others. The more we criticize other people, the more defensive they become, and the less likely they are to admit their errors, especially to us. Criticism can lead to a counterattack from both sides, and pretty soon it's like a volleyball game, with each person intensifying the pace while returning blame to the other person's side.

Some of us have learned to accept blame without defending ourselves. Under his wife's constant condemnation Tom was becoming an emotional zombie. Instead of fighting back he kept thinking, "Yes, Suzanne's right. I am an incompetent fool." He was like a worn-out punching bag. Both self-inflicted punishment and the compulsion to punish others result from the false belief: *Those who fail are unworthy of love and deserve to be punished.*

God's Answer: Propitiation

God's plan for us is centered in the cross. At the cross, God poured out His wrath against sin. To understand His plan we can look at what **propitiation** means. Propitiation is difficult to define because it brings together the following four concepts:
1. God is holy.
2. His holiness leads to the necessity of justice—His actions must be expressions of justice. He must punish sin.
3. God lovingly chose to provide a substitute—His beloved Son took the punishment our sins deserved.
4. As a result, God's justice is satisfied—no more punishment is required.

Write the number of the appropriate part of propitiation in the blanks following the parts of the following paragraphs. I have done the first one for you.
   a. # __1__ The problem with our sinfulness is that God is absolutely holy, pure, and perfect. Absolutely nothing is unholy in Him.
   b. #_____ Therefore, since God is holy, He can't overlook or compromise with sin.
   c. #_____ It took one sin to separate Adam from God. For God to condone even "one" sin would instantly defile His holiness.
   d. #_____ The Father did not escape witnessing His Son's mistreatment: the mocking, the scourging, and the cross. He could have spoken and ended the whole ordeal, yet He kept silent.
   e. #_____ Confronted with the suffering of His Son, God chose to let it continue so that we could be saved. What an expression of love!
   f. #_____ God loves you, and He enjoys revealing His love to you. He enjoys being loved by you, but He knows you can love Him only if you are experiencing His love for you.
   g. #_____ Propitiation means that His wrath has been removed and that you are deeply loved!
   h. #_____ God is holy, and therefore He must punish sin. But He loves us and therefore provided a substitute to take the punishment we deserve.

propitiation–n. describes what happened when Christ, through His death, became the means by which God's wrath was satisfied and God's mercy was granted to the sinner who believes on Christ

Welcome to:
The Blaming Game

Jesus has satisfied completely the righteousness of God so God's only response to us is in love. One possible set of answers to the learning activity are: a. 1, b. 1, c. 2, d. 2, e. 3, f. 3, g. 3, h. 4.

By this the love of God was manifested in us, that God has sent His only begotten Son into the world so that we might live through Him. In this is love, not that we loved God, but that He loved us and sent His Son to be the propitiation for our sins.
—1 John 4:9-10

Read the verse at left. Does the Father love you? Yes   No
How do you know He loves you?

_____

Do you feel loved?   Yes   No

Explain _____

Try to recall an experience in which you felt someone loved you. That person cared about you and wanted to be with you. You didn't have to perform; just being you was enough. The thought of that person selecting you to love was intoxicating. He or she loved you, and that love was soothing to you and satisfied many of your inner longings. If a person's love can make us feel this way, consider how much greater fulfillment the Heavenly Father's love can bring. We can't truly appreciate the Father's love unless we realize that it goes beyond any experience of being loved by another human being. If you've never felt that kind of love from a person, God wants you to feel it from Him.

Many of us have a distorted concept of the Heavenly Father. We believe that God is thrilled when we accept Christ and are born into His family. But many of us also believe that He is proud of us for only as long as we perform well, and that the better we perform, the happier He is with us.

Many, O LORD my God, are the wonders which Thou hast done, And Thy thoughts toward us.
—Psalm 40:5

In reality, as the Scripture at left indicates, not a moment goes by that God isn't thinking loving thoughts about us. We are His children, and we are special to Him because of Christ! Propitiation means Jesus Christ by His death satisfied the Father's righteous condemnation of sin. God loves you!

Applying the Principle to Others

The more we understand God's love and forgiveness, the more we will be willing and able to forgive others. If we think about it, the things that others do to us all are trivial compared to our sin of rebellion against God that He graciously has forgiven. This is why Paul encouraged the Ephesian Christians to forgive each other just as God in Christ also has forgiven you—completely and willingly (Ephesians 4:32).

And be kind to one another, tender-hearted, forgiving each other, just as God in Christ also has forgiven you.
—Ephesians 4:32

Do you have trouble forgiving some sins, or even personality differences, in others? If so, list them and confess to God your lack of forgiveness.

_____

_____

How do these compare to your sins that deserved God's wrath but that received the payment of Christ's substitutionary death?

_____

Stop and pray. Ask God how this concept can apply in your life. Now please review this lesson. What has God shown you that can help you?

_____

_____

LESSON 5

Key Concept:
I am complete in Christ.

Shame

We humbly ask God to renew our minds so that our sinful patterns can be transformed into patterns of righteousness.

> *And now, little children, abide in Him, so that when He appears, we may have confidence and not shrink away from Him in shame at His coming.*
> —1 John 2:28

The fourth false belief binds people to the hopeless pessimism of poor self-esteem. Take the following test to establish how strongly you experience shame.

Shame Test

Read each of the following statements. Then, from the top of the test, choose the term that best describes your response. Put in the blank beside each statement the number above the term you chose.

1	2	3	4
Always	Sometimes	Seldom	Never

_____ 1. I often think about past failures or experiences of rejection that have occurred in my life.

_____ 2. I cannot recall certain things about my past without experiencing strong, painful emotions (such as guilt, shame, or anger.)

_____ 3. I seem to make the same mistakes over and over again.

_____ 4. I want to change certain aspects of my character, but I don't believe I ever can do so successfully.

_____ 5. I feel inferior.

_____ 6. I cannot accept certain aspects of my appearance.

_____ 7. I am generally disgusted with myself.

_____ 8. I feel that certain experiences basically have ruined my life.

_____ 9. I perceive of myself as an immoral person.

_____ 10. I feel I have lost the opportunity to experience a complete and wonderful life.

_____ Total (Add the numbers you have placed in the blanks.)

My score means—

If your score is. . .

34-40
God apparently has given you a very strong appreciation for His love and unconditional acceptance. You seem to be free of the shame that plagues most people. (Some exceptions exist: Some people who score this high either are greatly deceived or have turned off their emotions as a way to suppress pain. Examine your heart and talk to your group members to see if these exceptions apply to you.)

28-33
Shame controls your responses rarely or only in certain situations. Again, the only major exceptions are those who are not honest with themselves.

22-27
Emotional problems you experience may relate to a sense of shame. When you think about some of your previous decisions, you may relate many of them to your feelings of worthlessness. Feelings of low self-esteem may affect many of your future decisions unless you take direct action to change those feelings.

16-21
Shame forms a generally negative backdrop to your life. Probably, few days go by when shame does not affect you in some way. Unfortunately, this robs you of the joy and peace your salvation was meant to bring.

10-15
Experiences of shame dominate your memory and probably have caused you to experience a great deal of depression. These problems will remain unless you take definite action. In other words, this condition will not simply disappear one day; time alone cannot heal your pain. You need to experience deep healing in your self-concept, in your relationship with God, and in your relationships with others.

Effects of Shame

Shame comes from our own negative estimate of 1) our past performance; and/or 2) our physical appearance. Shame leads to the false belief: *I am what I am. I cannot change. I am hopeless.*

Even when others don't know of our failure, we assume their opinion of us is poor.

Shame often results from instances of neglect or abuse; then failures in our performance or "flaws" in our appearance reinforce it. Even when others don't know about our failure, we assume their opinion of us is poor, and we adopt what we think their opinion might be.

Study the paragraph above and check all of the following statements that are part of the paragraph:

1. My perception that I am physically imperfect adds to my sense of shame.
2. Feeling shamed becomes a habit so that I feel others disapprove of me even when they really approve.
3. My shame will decrease if I can improve my performance enough.
4. Shame may begin when I am ignored or mistreated.

5. Christians are wrong to feel shame.
6. The feeling that I have failed feeds my sense of shame.
7. The only way to be rid of shame is to experience love and acceptance.

The paragraph describes four critical issues concerning shame. Shame originates from not being loved and accepted—usually very early in life. The feeling that our performance and appearance is flawed feeds our sense of shame. Once shame has become our habit, we shame ourselves. Answers 3, 5, and 7 were not in the paragraph. Answer 3 is a lie because working harder will not remove my feeling of shame. Answer 5 is a more damaging lie; we cannot get rid of our shame by dumping more shame on ourselves. Answer 7 is true. The only way to change the habit of shaming myself is to replace it with love and acceptance. I can get that love and acceptance from the Lord and from healthy believers. Answer 7 simply wasn't in the paragraph.

Describe an incident in your life for which you felt shame for your addictive behavior.

_____

_____

Did the shame cause you to improve? Or, did the shame drive you into depression and more drinking, using, or other behavior?

_____

Shame fuels our compulsions and assures our failures.

We so easily fall for the performance lie, "If only I could make myself feel ashamed enough, I would be motivated to succeed." The truth is that the shame fuels our compulsions and assures our failures.

Stop to pray. Ask God to remind you each time that you try to shame yourself into better behavior. Ask Him to replace your shame with the awareness that you are loved, accepted, and absolutely perfect in His eyes.

Shame and Performance

If we base our self-worth on our performance long enough, our past behavior eventually becomes the sole basis of our worth. We see ourselves with certain character qualities and flaws because that's the way we have always been. We then include Satan's lie, "I always must be what I have been and live with whatever self-worth I have, because that's just me," in our belief system.

We then risk going to one of two extremes. Some of us act out our low self-worth through false humility, and we become self-abusers. Others go to the opposite extreme and become arrogant.

Describe a time when you have gone to one of the two extremes of acting out low self-worth by abusing yourself or others.

_____

_____

We may think that humility is belittling ourselves, but true humility is an accurate appraisal of our worth in Christ. Because of our sin we deserved God's righteous condemnation, yet we receive His unconditional love, grace, and righteousness through Christ. We are deeply loved, completely forgiven, fully pleasing, totally accepted, and complete in Him. Thankfulness, generosity, kindness, and self-confidence constitute true humility! Arrogant persons strive to fill the hole in their souls by appearing strong and independent. They only make matters worse by driving people away.

True humility is an accurate appraisal of our worth in Christ.

Shame and Appearance

Another aspect of poor self-concept relates to personal appearance. Most of us have some aspect of our appearance that we wish we could change but can't. Are you angry with God for the way He made you? Can you ever be satisfied with your appearance? Do you compare your appearance to that of others? If you do, at some point in your life you will suffer because someone prettier, thinner, stronger, or more handsome always will be around. Even if you are beautiful or handsome, you still will suffer because you will fear losing your good looks—the basis of your self-worth.

Are you angry with God for the way He made you?

Check all of the following you feel when you consider your physical appearance.

I hate the way I look.
I am grateful that God made me like He did.
I am more beautiful / handsome than others.
I am unhappy with _____ about my appearance.
My appearance makes me feel that I am worth more / less than others.

If we insist on valuing our worth by our appearance and performance, sooner or later God graciously will allow us to see how futile that struggle is. God created our need for a sense of significance. However, He knows we never will come to Him until we find the importance of people's opinions to be empty and hopeless. At that point we can turn to Him and find comfort and encouragement in the truths of His Word.

God's Answer: Regeneration

God created an answer to shame. His answer is unique and powerful. He makes you a new you. He makes me a new me. Imagine that you are guilty of all manner of crimes. The police come to your home to arrest you, but just before they break down the door, God works a miracle. He turns you into . . . SOMEBODY ELSE! That is the miracle of regeneration. God recreates us. He changes our identity.

The miracle described above is real. Through your relationship with Jesus Christ, you are a new person. Think of a time in your life when someone shamed, ridiculed, or ignored you. With the awareness that you are a new person, write below what you would say to your accuser.

_____

_____

Jesus answered and said to him, "Truly, truly I say to you, unless one is born again, he cannot see the kingdom of God."
–John 3:3

Therefore, if any man is in Christ, he is a new creature; the old things passed away; behold, new things have come.
–2 Corinthians 5:17

Read the two Scriptures appearing in the margin. Write below the key words the passages use to describe regeneration.

_____

Did you note the words _born again_ and _new creature_? To the person who shamed you wouldn't it be fun to say, "I'm terribly sorry, but you must be talking about somebody else. That person doesn't live here anymore"?

The problem is that many of us rationalize away the practical power of regeneration by thoughts like this, _Well, yes, God did make me brand new in the past, but I've sinned since then. I'm not brand new any more._

put on the new self, which in the likeness of God has been created in righteousness and holiness of the truth.
–Ephesians 4:24

Read the words of the apostle Paul to the Ephesians—remember, these were Christians to whom he was writing. The words appear in the margin. Write below what you think Paul meant by the command, "put on the new self."

_____

_____

_____

If you looked in the Bible, you found that Ephesians 4:23, the verse before Ephesians 4:24, tells us to _be made new in the attitude of our minds._ "Putting on the new self" means to make choices to act in ways that are consistent with our new identity in Christ. We are to train our minds to reflect the fact that we are new creatures.

The LORD's lovingkindness indeed never cease, for His compassions never fail. They are new every morning.
–Lamentations 3:22-23

Read Lamentations 3:22-23 appearing in the margin. How do you feel about the promise that God's mercies are _new every morning_?

hopeful   doubtful
afraid   relieved
joyful   other _____

Jeremiah recognized that only God's continuing mercy keeps God from punishing us for our sin. His mercy is certainly as great toward His children as it is toward lost persons. God expresses His mercy through regeneration. Moment by moment He continues to make us new.

┌───┐
│   │
│   **Key Concept for Lesson 5**   │
│   I am complete in Christ.   │
│   │
└───┘

Please pray and ask God how this concept can apply in your life. Now please review this lesson. What has God shown you that can help you?

_____

_____

_____

Write from memory Romans 12:2.

_____

_____

<table>
<tr><td>

LESSON

6

</td><td>

Taking the Step

We humbly ask God to renew our minds so that our sinful patterns can be transformed into patterns of life and health and righteousness.

</td></tr>
</table>

Key Concept:
I can cooperate with God as He renews my mind.

Finally, brethren, whatever is true, whatever is honorable, whatever is right, whatever is pure, whatever is lovely, whatever is of good repute, if there is any excellence and if anything worthy of praise, let your mind dwell on these things.

–Philippians 4:8

In this Step you examined in detail the effects of the key false beliefs. You have considered the truths you need for recovery. Now you can do the work necessary to apply these truths. That work includes: making a Truth Card, exposing ungodly thoughts, and identifying and stopping the bargaining process.

New options for life

Speaker and author Earnie Larsen compared our habits to a ravine washed out by desert rains. For years we have thought, felt, and acted in certain ways. When the rains fall, the water naturally runs in the same channel. The false beliefs are the channels for our guilt, shame, and dysfunctional behaviors. Now we want to change our behavior, thinking, and feeling. When the pressure builds up, we naturally will fall back into the old channels. We can decide what is more healthy behavior and begin to scratch out a new channel. When the rains come, much of the water still will run in the old ditches, but with time and persistence, we will make new paths.[2]

Write your own statement of the message in the story of the ravine and the desert rain.

_____

_____

We begin to scratch out that new channel by repeatedly feeding our mind with the truth. Here is an exercise in how to do just that: make a Truth Card. A simple three-by-five-inch card can be a key factor in helping you base your self-worth on the liberating truths of the Scriptures. To make the Truth Card, use a three-by-five-inch card. On the front, write the following truths and their corresponding verses from Scripture.

- I am deeply loved by God (1 John 4:9-10).
- I am completely forgiven and fully pleasing to God (Romans 5:1).
- I am totally accepted by God (Colossians 1:21-22).
- I am a new creation, absolutely complete in Christ (2 Corinthians 5:17).

On the back of the card, write out the four false beliefs. Carry this card with you at all times. For one month, each time you do a routine activity, like drinking your morning cup of coffee or tea, look at the front side and slowly meditate on each phrase. The Scripture at left tells us how we are to meditate on God's Word. Thank the Lord for making you into a person with these qualities. By doing this exercise for the next month, you can develop a habit of remembering that you are deeply loved, completely forgiven, fully pleasing, totally accepted, and complete in Christ.

If you have not already done so, memorize the supporting verses the card lists. Look in your Bible for other verses that support these truths. Memorize them. Doing this will establish God's Word as the basis for these truths. Also memorize the false beliefs. The more familiar you are with these lies, the more you can recognize them in your thoughts. Then, as you recognize them, you more readily can replace them with the truths of God's Word.

> Let the word of Christ richly dwell within you, with all wisdom teaching and admonishing one another with psalms and hymns and spiritual songs, singing with thankfulness in your hearts to God.
> —Colossians 3:16

Exposing Ungodly Thoughts

Habitual lies

One reason the lies we believe are so destructive is because they are habitual rather than conscious. We have a running conversation with ourselves, often without even realizing it. When we make a mistake, we begin to call ourselves names. Our thoughts reveal what we really believe, yet most of us have difficulty being objective in our thinking simply because we haven't trained ourselves to be. We usually let any and every thought run its course in our minds without analyzing its worth.

We need to develop the skill of identifying thoughts that reflect Satan's deceptions. Then we can reject those lies and replace them with scriptural truth.

As a first step in developing this skill, write down your thoughts in response to the four truths we've examined. For example, you might respond to the truth that you are fully pleasing to God by thinking, "No, I'm not! I mess up all the time, and to be fully pleasing, I'd have to be perfect!" When we see it written out, we more easily recognize that response as a lie. Write your own personal response, not necessarily what you may believe is the "correct" response.

I am deeply loved by God: _____

_____

_____

_____

I am completely forgiven and fully pleasing to God: _____

_____

_____

_____

I am totally accepted by God: _____

_____

_____

_____

_____

I am complete in Christ: _____

_____

_____

_____

_____

_____

Thoughts that contradict these truths are lies. Reject them and replace them with passages of Scripture to reinforce the truth in your mind. We have listed some passages on which to reflect.

Growing in Him

> **Propitiation:** Matthew 18:21-35; Luke 7:36-50; Romans 3:25; 8:1-8; Colossians 3:12-14; Hebrews 2:17
>
> **Justification:** Romans 3:19-24; 4:4-5; 5:1-11; Titus 2:11-14; 3:4-7
>
> **Reconciliation:** John 15:14-16; Romans 5:8-10; Ephesians 2:11-18
>
> **Regeneration:** 2 Corinthians 5:17; Galatians 5:16-24; Ephesians 2:4-5; 4:22-24; Colossians 3:5-17

As we become increasingly aware of the battle within us between the Spirit and the flesh and as we identify false beliefs that prompt sinful behavior and renew our minds with the truth of God's Word, we confidently can ask God to remove our sinful patterns of behavior. We can begin to live in His resurrection power. We never will be sinless until we reign with Him in His kingdom, but as we grow in Him, we will sin less.

Identifying and Changing Bargaining Behavior

When we see how our lives are damaged, we often respond by trying to bargain with ourselves, with our families, and with God. After learning about dysfunctional families, Christy quickly saw those painful effects in her own life. She asked a friend, "How can I get my father to love me?"

Pretend that you are Christy's friend. How might you respond to her question?

_____

_____

_____

Her friend explained, "Christy, it's not up to you to get your father to love you. It's up to you to be secure in the Lord, whether or not your father ever loves you."

Bargaining takes many shapes and forms, but its goal is to get other people to change by offering some change in ourselves. We'll say, "I'll be a better husband to her," or "I won't nag him any more; then he'll love me the way I want to be loved."

We can come up with all kinds of "deals" to get people to love us, but bargaining still is not totally objective. The responsibility still remains on us alone. Believing the best about others usually is good and right. But sometimes a person, through months and years of irresponsible and manipulative behavior, proves he or she is emotionally unhealthy. Then believing the best about that person is naive and foolish.

Bargaining expresses hope—hope that the other person will change and give us the love and worth that we need. But it is a false hope. Observing objectively leads us to a painful but honest conclusion: We need to give up the vain hope that the other person will change and will give us what we need. Giving up doesn't sound very godly, but it is. Giving up reflects reality. It involves abandoning the idol of pleasing others and having them love and accept us as the way to win self-worth. Actually, it is an act of worship to the Lord. It is loving the other person unconditionally, whether or not the person ever changes.

The Awkwardness of Change

Many of us will experience wide swings in feelings and behavior during these early stages of growth. As we take the cap off our emotions for perhaps the first time, we may feel more hurt, anger, and fear than we ever thought possible. We may become afraid of how intense our emotions are, and we may put the cap back on until we have more courage to experiment again with these feelings. We also may feel more joy and freedom and love than ever before. We may cry for the first time in years. We may feel loved and comforted for the first time ever. We may ask hundreds of questions, or we may become more introspective than we've been before. These wide swings in mood and behavior are understandable. Don't try to clamp them; instead, realize that surges of emotion are perfectly understandable for one who has repressed them for years. Be patient.

Please pray and ask God how this concept can apply in your life. Now please review this lesson. What has God shown you that can help you?

_____

_____

_____

Step Review

Please review this Step. Pray and ask God to identify the Scriptures or principles that are particularly important for your life. Underline them. Then respond to the following:

Restate Step 7 in your own words: _____

_____

_____

_____

What do you have to gain by practicing this Step in your life?

_____

_____

_____

Reword your summary into a prayer of response to God. Thank Him for this Step, and affirm your commitment to Him.

_____

_____

_____

_____

Notes
[1]Robert S. McGee, _Search for Significance_ LIFE Support Edition (Houston: Rapha Publishing, 1992), 48.
[2]Earnie Larsen, _Stage II Recovery_, E. Larsen Enterprises, Inc., 1990.

STEP 8

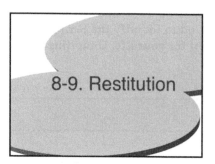

8-9. Restitution

We choose to forgive and become willing to make amends.

Forgiveness and Amends

BABY-STEPPING IT

Phil learned about the program from a relative who was recovering from alcoholism. What he learned proves the old saying, "A little knowledge is a dangerous thing." Phil misunderstood two things about the message of recovery. First, he thought the 12-Step *program* was the answer to his drug addiction. He failed to understand that the program serves as a vehicle for *God* to change our lives. Phil's second problem grew out of that misunderstanding. He looked at all 12 Steps, read as far as Step 9, and concluded that he never could accomplish the amends Step. As a result, he believed he never would be able to stay sober because he couldn't work Step 9. In his twisted, addictive logic, the biblical principle of restitution—intended to set us free from shame and guilt—locked Phil into his addiction.

For many months Phil wrestled with his dilemma. He would attend meetings and stay clean for a while based on the encouragement of the members. Then he would fall back into his world of drugs. He even learned that some of the old-timers have a name for his failed attempts. They call it trying to get clean and sober on the *fellowship* rather than the power of God.

In one of Phil's attempts at sobriety, he asked Richard to be his sponsor. Richard agreed to do so on one condition. He said he would not waste his time on someone who refused to work the Steps. He asked what kept Phil from working the Steps. Phil admitted he feared Step 9.

Richard laughed and hugged Phil. He said, "Son, you're going to have to learn about baby steps. Forget the amends. Don't fight tomorrow's battles today." (Read more about Phil on page 168.)

Step 8   *We make a list of all persons who have hurt us and choose to forgive them. We also make a list of all persons we have harmed, and we become willing to make amends to them all.*

Memory verse   *And just as you want people to treat you, treat them in the same way.*

–Luke 6:31

Overview for Step 8   **Lesson 1: People to Forgive**
        Goal: You will accept responsibility for forgiving others.
     Lesson 2: Forgiving Others
        Goal: You will describe the negative consequences of failing to forgive.
     Lesson 3: Taking the Step, Part 1
        Goal: You will make a list of people to forgive.
     Lesson 4: Taking the Step, Part 2
        Goal: You will make a list of the people you have harmed.

156

<table>
<tr><td>

LESSON

1

Key Concept:
My refusal to forgive is self-destructive.

</td><td>

People to Forgive

We make a list of all persons we have harmed, and we become willing to make amends to them all.

> *The wise woman builds her house, but the foolish tears it down with her own hands.*
> —Proverbs 14:1

If we want to progress further in our journey of recovery, we must prepare to rid ourselves of the burden of guilt, fear, and shame. The guilt, fear, and shame we carry prompts us either to avoid certain people or to feel uncomfortable around them. We never will be free from guilt, fear, and shame on the one hand and from anger and resentment on the other until we do two things. For our own sakes, we must make amends to those we have harmed, and we must forgive those who have harmed us.

For many of us, the fear of making amends and granting forgiveness freezes us into inaction. Instead we remain stuck in our fears and resentment. Step 8 provides an answer. Until we have objectively examined our shame, guilt, and resentments, we are not ready to take further action. So we encourage you to work Step 8. Step 8 calls us to forgive. We will not make amends until Step 9. Step 8 is an exercise in objectivity. By writing this Step you will begin to gain the objectivity to go on. You may find that people exist to whom you feel inappropriate guilt—to whom you owe no amends. You are not yet ready to make your amends—that is Step 9—but as you work Step 8 you may find that what was impossible will become possible. Work the Steps one at a time!

Forgiveness

Proverbs 14:1, quoted above, powerfully applies to the issue of forgiving. When we refuse to forgive, we harm ourselves. We tear down the house in which we must live.

</td></tr>
</table>

Forgiveness means that we choose to give up our self-proclaimed "right" to blame others.

Up to this point we have used chemicals as part of our strategy to repress or deny strong emotions like fear and anger, and to prevent them from causing pain in our lives. Unfortunately, it didn't always work—we still got hurt. We hid our true feelings. For years we nursed grudges, hatred, and jealousy. Bottled-up emotions grew. Those strong emotions supported our addiction. The process of recovery requires that we deal with hidden or denied feelings. Forgiveness means that we choose to give up our self-proclaimed "right" to blame, condemn, find fault, punish, and retaliate against others.

A list of methods we often substitute for forgiveness appears below. Check each method which you have used or currently are using.

1. Forgetting an offense or pretending it never happened;
2. Trying to bury the pain or avoid the issues by drinking or drugging the rage away;
3. Punishing your offender by passive-aggressive forms of revenge, like procrastination, the "silent treatment," or getting drunk;
4. Assuming responsibility for others' offenses—being a blame sponge;
5. Taking revenge.

Rather than pretending the offense never happened or burying the pain by practicing our addiction, we learn in recovery to deal with the offense as it is—raw, ugly, and painful. Instead of secretly punishing the offender, we learn to put aside our pride and deal in humility with the offender. We gain freedom from the burden of remembering the offense. We allow everyone involved to settle the issue and get on with their lives. Rather than accepting the blame for others' actions, we develop healthy boundaries. Rather than taking revenge, we forgive.

As long as we hold a grudge against another person for his or her offense—no matter how long ago it happened—*we* carry the full impact of the offense. Many hurting people go to their graves needlessly bound by the chains of past injuries because they failed to forgive! If any of this strikes a painful nerve within you, pay close attention to the exercises in this Step. Along with the inner working of the Holy Spirit, the exercises will help you experience freedom from the tyranny of a bitter, unforgiving spirit.

Our unwillingness to forgive others also blocks our ability to experience God's forgiveness. This compounds the deep feelings of shame and self-hatred and strengthens the old cycles of performance, perfectionism, and hopelessness. Step 8 helps us to seek liberation from this slavery!

We often want to avoid the responsibility to forgive. We rationalize that the way we responded to someone else was exactly what he or she deserved. Read the words appearing in the margin from the apostle Paul to the Roman Christians.

Never pay back evil for evil to anyone. Respect what is right in the sight of all men. If possible, so far as it depends on you, be at peace with all men. Never take your own revenge, beloved, but leave room for the wrath of God, for it is written, "Vengeance is Mine, I will repay," says the Lord.

–Romans 12:17-19

Which of the following statements do you think most accurately describes what Paul meant by *be at peace with all men***?**

1. Never argue with anyone.
2. Let others always have their way.
3. Settle disagreements as quickly as possible.
4. Don't let anyone walk over you.

Arguments and disagreements with others are normal and may be justified or even necessary. But as quickly as possible, we should repair the broken peace the arguments cause among people. Although we may not resolve all issues and disagreements, forgiveness and restoration of fellowship are better than bitterness and hatred. The physical, emotional, and spiritual toll of unforgiveness is just not worth it. The answer in the exercise is number 3. Sometimes we also need to apply number 4.

How would your life be different if you allowed God to take care of your grievances, rather than if you yourself tried to take revenge on someone else?

_____

_____

The one who is forgiven much, loves much.

One of the benefits we experience from Step 5 is acceptance. Once we have experienced acceptance from another person, we more easily can accept and forgive other people. In fact, our ability to love and forgive is related directly to how much we have experienced love and forgiveness. As Christ said, "He who is forgiven little, loves little" (Luke 7:47). The reverse also is true.

In the past we found it easier to block out or temporarily repress feelings of resentment against others. We waited for the right moment to get revenge. We buried the painful emotions so deeply that we no longer recognized them as resentments.

Do you simply not like to be around some people? Do you have a difficult time looking some people in the eye? Do you get angry when you even think about certain people? The following exercise is designed to help you see the need to forgive others and accept the responsibility to do so when necessary.

Why make a list?

In Matthew 18:21-35 Jesus told the story of the unmerciful servant. He said a king called in a servant who owed him 10,000 talents. The talents were measures of money. Depending on whether the talents were of silver or gold, the value of the debt was between $20 million and $300 million (Unger's Bible Dictionary). The servant was unable to pay, so the king forgave him the debt. Then the servant found one of his fellow servants who owed him a very small amount of money. The servant who had just been forgiven the huge debt grabbed his fellow servant and began to choke him. "Pay back what you owe me!" he demanded. Read the rest of the parable which appears in the margin.

His fellow servant fell to his knees and begged him, "Be patient with me, and I will pay you back." But he refused. Instead, he went off and had the man thrown into prison until he could pay the debt. When the other servants saw what had happened, they were greatly distressed and went and told their master everything that had happened. Then the master called the servant in. "You wicked servant," he said, "I canceled all that debt of yours because you begged me to. Shouldn't you have had mercy on your fellow servant just as I had on you?" In anger his master turned him over to the jailers to be tortured, until he should pay back all he owed. This is how my heavenly Father will treat each of you unless you forgive your brother from your heart.
–Matthew 18:29-35, NIV

Was it possible for the first servant to pay back the $20 to $300 million that he owed?   Yes   No

Likewise, before you trusted Christ, how great was your debt to God for your sin? Was it possible for you ever to repay it?

_____

The debt of the first servant—like our debt of sin—was beyond any hope of payment. Yet the man who the king graciously forgave so much refused to forgive even a small debt.

Write your own statement of the meaning of the parable.

_____

_____

You could have stated the meaning of the parable in one of many ways. You may have written that since God forgave you of so much, you are responsible to forgive others.

God wants you to forgive others to the same degree He forgave you. Circle all the terms below that describe how God has forgiven you.

1. fully and completely
2. after much begging
3. at personal cost to Him
4. after I become sinless
5. without earning it
6. without my deserving it
7. until I sin again
8. without reservation
9. with little concern
10. in spite of my sin
11. after earning it
12. after deserving it

People will offend you in this life. You may go through periods when it seems that almost everybody is letting you down. Both your experience of the offense and your reliving it over and over in your mind hurt you. However,

Deal with offenses

the first pain of the wrong usually amounts only to a small fraction of the total hurt. You cannot avoid being offended, but you can avoid most of the pain if you will learn to deal quickly and completely with offenses rather than mentally reliving them countless times. Failing to forgive cuts the flow of God's power in your life. Unforgiveness brings about many negative consequences which you will examine later in this Step. Answer numbers 1, 3, 5, 6, 8, and 10 describe God's way of forgiving.

Key Concept for Lesson 1
My refusal to forgive is self-destructive.

Pray and ask God how this concept can apply in your life. Now please review this lesson. What has God shown you that can help you?

_____

_____

And just as you want people to treat you, treat them in the same way.

–Luke 6:31

The suggested memory verse appears in the margin. Repeat it five times. In the space in the margin attempt to write the verse from memory.

Ask God to help you make this verse a reality in your life in a way that you unmistakeably could point others to Christ. Commit yourself to working through this Step as fully as you can in the power of His Spirit.

LESSON 2

Key Concept:
Failing to forgive others can cause me to injure myself again and again.

Forgiving Others

We make a list of all persons we have harmed, and we become willing to make amends to them all.

> *I am writing to you, little children, because your sins are forgiven you for His name's sake.*
>
> –1 John 2:12

Even though God has forgiven us, we seem to forget about this fact when we decide how we will treat others. We inflict punishment on those around us—and on ourselves—by refusing to forgive them. We add up all the times someone has wronged us and all the things we don't like about the person.

Much of the material in this lesson comes from *Search for Significance* LIFE Support Edition.[1] When you have completed *Conquering Chemical Dependency*, you may wish to participate in a *Search for Significance* group to develop a more Christ-centered sense of self-worth.

Reasons We Don't Forgive

We often fail to forgive others (and ourselves) because we don't think it's possible to forgive. We forget how God through Christ's death graciously has forgiven all of our sins, and we come up with reasons we can't forgive.

The following represent many of the countless excuses we make for our unwillingness to forgive ourselves and others. Write the letter of the matching reason in the left margin beside each of the case studies below.

a. The person never asked for forgiveness.

b. The offense was too great.

c. The person won't accept responsibility.

d. I simply don't like the person.

e. The person did it too many times.

f. The person isn't truly sorry.

_____1. Grant's wife left him for another man, and Grant became bitter toward his wife. Her infidelity was too great a sin for him to forgive.

_____2. Janet's mother emotionally abused Janet as a child. Her mother never has admitted her harsh treatment of Janet. Janet refuses to forgive her mother.

_____3. John pulled a practical joke on you. His prank caused you to be late for class, and your professor refused to accept your paper because you didn't turn it in on time. John doesn't see anything wrong with a little joke. Oh, he made some rather insincere statements about being sorry, but he still thinks the incident was hilarious.

_____4. Darrell knew he made you angry when he deliberately didn't invite you to his Christmas open house. He never asked you for forgiveness. You decide to withhold forgiveness until he requests it.

_____5. Candy's husband stayed out late playing cards every Friday night for three years. Some nights he didn't come home at all. "Forgive that jerk? Look how many times he's wronged me!" Candy exclaimed.

_____6. Cindy just plain didn't like Martha, who constantly tried to make Cindy look bad at work. Every emotion in Cindy called for getting back at her co-worker. She certainly didn't want to forgive her.

Which of the above reasons in the past has kept you from forgiving? Below, describe how that reason interfered with your ability to forgive.

_____

_____

_____

_____

_____

_____

Possible answers include 1. b, 2. c, 3. f, 4. a, 5. e, 6. d.

Here are more of the excuses we make for our unwillingness to forgive ourselves and others. Again, write the letter of the matching reason in the left margin beside each of the case studies.

a. I've found an excuse for the offense.

b. Someone has to punish the person.

c. The person did it deliberately.

d. Something keeps me from forgiving.

e. If I forgive, I'll have to treat the offender well.

f. I'll forgive but I won't ever forget.

_____1. George's best friend, Hal, swindled George out of $10,000. George's mind raced through times he had been generous to Hal. Hal had carefully planned the swindle. George felt he never could forgive the planned betrayal.

_____2. Ben excused himself for slandering Steve by pointing out how Steve had offended him. He felt justified in lying to destroy Steve's reputation. Forgiving him might mean Ben would have to be nice to this scoundrel.

_____3. Shirley had been cold for two weeks to Greg, who had offended her. She would forgive him, all right—as soon as she finished punishing him.

_____4. Steve knew he should forgive Joe, but something kept him from it. He told others that the devil kept him from having a forgiving spirit toward Joe, but Steve showed no signs of trying to resist Satan, either.

_____5. Mary thought she had forgiven her brother for his cruelty to her when they were children, but during arguments between the two, Mary kept bringing up past incidents. When Mary and her brother were together, it seemed that she always was stewing about these past misdeeds.

_____6. Hank behaved irresponsibly. His wife, Sally, attempted to forgive him by placing the blame on his mother, who babied Hank even after he was grown. Sally thought she had forgiven Hank when really she had just excused him.

With which of the above case studies do you most readily identify? Below, describe a situation in which the excuse used in that case study has kept you from forgiving.

_____

_____

_____

_____

_____

Possible answers include 1. c, 2. e, 3. b, 4. d, 5. f, 6. a.

When We Don't Forgive

When we fail to forgive others, our lives and our relationships suffer. Let's take a look at some problems in our lives that stem directly from a lack of forgiveness.

Describe a time in which stress from a past wrong someone has done to you made you physically ill.

_____

_____

_____

_____

• **Stress:** Sarah announced to the group that her husband did not deserve forgiveness. She vowed that she would not forgive him even if it meant her life. It turned out that it did. Sarah died of kidney failure which physicians said was related to the extreme stress under which she lived. She wanted to kill her husband, but in reality, she caused her own death.

Many people experience extreme stress because they hold inside bitterness and anger. Their stress occurs because they have not forgiven. In the margin write about a time when you have experienced physical illness because of the stress of unforgiveness.

• **Self-inflicted Reinjury:** Robert recalled this incident: "As I drove home, I saw flashing through my mind the face of a guy I played basketball with in college. He was a great enemy of mine. He was one of the few people I ever met whom I truly wanted to punch out. I began to remember the unkind things he did to me. Soon anger started creeping up inside of me. I had not thought about this fellow for years, and I'm sure that he doesn't remember me at all. Yet my reliving this event caused me a lot of pain. I had not properly dealt with it in the beginning."

• **No More Love:** "I don't know if I ever can love someone again" is a frequent complaint from those offended by someone about whom they care deeply. Our deepest hurts occur at the hands of those we love. One way we deal with the pain of being offended is simply to withdraw, refusing to love anymore. We often make this unconscious decision when we have not adequately dealt with an offense. We desperately may want to love again but feel that we cannot do it. Refusing to experience love and feeling unable to love devastate us.

Which of these three problems stemming from lack of forgiveness do you most readily spot in your life? Describe it here.

_____

_____

Has failing to forgive put an ugly snarl on your face?

• **Bitterness:** Emotions trace their lines on our faces. We think others don't notice what's going on inside us, but even the casual observer usually can detect our anger. Kristin recalled seeing a neighbor go through difficulties in her marriage. Hatred was so much a part of the neighbor's life that her face became permanently snarled. Kristin described the neighbor as still having that ugly look on her face. Unforgiveness produces ugliness of all sorts.

• **Perpetual Conflict:** A husband and wife, both of whom had been married previously, received counseling several years ago. Having been hurt in their first marriages, each anticipated hurt from the present spouse. At the smallest offense each reacted as if the spouse were about to deliver the final blow. This husband and wife constantly were on the defensive. They protected themselves from the attacks they imagined their mate would deliver. Having been offended in the past, they anticipated more hurt in the present and the future. They reacted in a way that perpetuated the conflict.

• **Walls that Keep Others Out:** Many of us refuse to experience love from those who love us. We often may become anxious and threatened when personal intimacy becomes possible. Jane hoped and prayed that her husband

Frank would come to know the Lord. She thought that if he were a Christian, he would be more loving toward her and toward their children. One day Frank accepted Christ. His life began to change. He paid more attention to Jane and started spending time with her and the children. He became sensitive and loving. Was it a dream come true? Instead of rejoicing, Jane deeply resented Frank for not changing sooner! *If Frank is able to love us like this now, then he's always had the ability,* she thought. She also felt confused and guilty about her anger.

Jane used anger as a defense mechanism to keep distance between Frank and herself. The closer they might get, the more pain she might experience if he reverted to his old ways. She never really had forgiven Frank, so the bricks of unforgiveness formed a wall that kept him from getting too close. Hiding behind a wall of unforgiveness is a lonely experience.

Hiding behind a wall of unforgiveness is a lonely experience.

Do you see any of these results of unforgiveness in your life? Review these last three results of unforgiveness; think about them for a few moments. Describe below a time one of these problems affected you.

_____

_____

_____

We have looked at what happens to us when we don't forgive. God loves us and expects us to care about ourselves because we are His creation. When we abuse our bodies and our emotions by not forgiving, we are not living the way God wants us to live. Not forgiving also hinders our relationships with others—our brothers and sisters in Christ about whom God cares deeply. We can choose to stop acting in a way that harms ourselves and others.

Stop and pray, asking God to help you forgive others and to help you remember that forgiving others is a part of His plan.

Key Concept for Lesson 2
Failing to forgive others can cause me to injure myself again and again.

Pray and ask God how this concept can apply in your life. Now please review this lesson. What has God shown you that can help you?

_____

_____

Below write from memory Luke 6:31. Look on page 156 to check your memory work.

_____

_____

<table>
<tr><td>

Key Concept:
Forgiving means counting the
debt paid in full.

And be kind to one another,
tender-hearted, forgiving each
other, just as God in Christ has
forgiven you.

–Ephesians 4:32

</td><td>

Taking the Step, Part 1

*We make a list of all persons we have harmed, and we become willing to
make amends to them all.*

*Whenever you stand praying, forgive, if you have anything against
anyone; so that your Father also who is in heaven may forgive you your
transgressions.*

–Mark 11:25

Sometimes we think that forgiveness is like a large eraser that wipes our
offenses off the books. God never has forgiven like this. For each offense He
demanded full payment. This is the reason for the cross. Christ paid for our
sins in full.

Christians have a special ability to forgive because they can forgive as God
does. God has forgiven us fully and completely. We, of all people, know the
experience of unconditional forgiveness. As a result, we in turn can forgive
those around us. Think of it this way: I will not have to forgive anyone else for
anything that can compare with what Christ already has forgiven me for
doing.

We can look at others' offenses in a different light when we compare them to
our sin of rebellion that Christ has forgiven completely. Read the verse
appearing in the left margin about this kind of forgiveness.

**List 10 things for which you are glad God in Christ has forgiven you.
This can prompt you to be willing to forgive those who have done
wrong to you.**

1. _____   6. _____

2. _____   7. _____

3. _____   8. _____

4. _____   9. _____

5. _____   10. _____

**Stop and pray, thanking God for forgiving you for the matters you
mentioned above.**

Your Book of Forgiveness

The exercise on the following pages will help you to recognize any lack of
forgiveness in your life and will help you move toward a lifestyle of forgiving
others just as God in Christ has forgiven you. It is not a mechanical formula

</td></tr>
</table>

but a living opportunity to exercise a life-changing power. Forgiving is one of the many awesome responsibilities God has given His children. It is holy work not to be taken lightly.

On a separate sheet of paper write the headings listed on this page. In the appropriate spaces, complete the information requested below. Add to this forgiveness guide when you need to and refer to it frequently. Focus on the forgiveness and not the offenses.

- **Persons to be forgiven:** List everyone who participated in the offense.
- **Offense:** Describe in some detail an event which caused you pain.
- **Date:** When did the offense take place?
- **Reasons for not forgiving:** Review the summary of reasons for not forgiving. Which ones apply?

As an act of your will, and with God's help, choose to forgive. Remember the complete forgiveness you have in Christ.

At the conclusion of the exercise, use the prayer provided at the end of this lesson (or use your own) as an exercise of faith for each offense.

Below is an example of the guide.

> If you forgive the sins of any, their sins have been forgiven them; if you retain the sins of any, they have been retained.
> –John 20:23

People to Be Forgiven	My brothers, Harry and Frank	
Offense	lying to me, blaming me for their mistakes	
Date	1992-now	
Reasons for Not Forgiving	1, 2, 4, 5, 9	

Prayer of Forgiveness

Dear Lord,
I forgive _____ (name) for _____ (offense) on the basis that you have forgiven me freely and have commanded me to forgive others. I have the capacity to do this because Christ has completely forgiven me. I do not excuse this person's offense in any way, nor do I use any excuse for not forgiving. Thank You, Lord Jesus, for helping me to forgive him (her). I also confess that I have sinned by using the following excuses for not forgiving: _____ (name any). Thank You for forgiving me and for helping me to have victory in this important area of my life. Amen.

Review today's lesson. Name at least one thing God wants you to do in response to this study. Ask Him for the grace to help you do it.

_____

_____

LESSON 4

Key Concept:
I begin to make amends by writing a list.

Taking the Step, Part 2

We make a list of all persons we have harmed, and we become willing to make amends to them all.

God has not given us a spirit of fear, but of power and of love and of a sound mind.

–2 Timothy 1:7, NKJV

This lesson is designed to prepare you to ask forgiveness of and to make amends to the people you have offended. The task before you is simply to list their names and the offenses. Don't get ahead of yourself on this Step.

You probably do not know for certain whether or not you need to make amends to certain individuals. Sometimes you may feel you need to make amends when you really don't need to. For now, make your list. You will determine in Step 9 how to deal with each situation. Use additional paper and refer to Step 4 as often as necessary. Use the following guidelines as you write your amends list.

Questions to Ask in Filling Out Your List of Offenses

Whom did I harm?

- From whom did I cheat or steal?
- What promises and/or confidences did I break (sexual infidelity, lying, sharing something someone told me in confidence) and whom did I hurt or betray?
- For whom did I cause pain by missing family obligations (birthdays, anniversaries) or other special days or commitments?
- What social responsibilities (laws, commitments) did I break or avoid? Who did my actions harm?
- What financial obligations did I avoid or wrongly create? Who did my behavior harm?
- What have I done to harm those with whom I have worked?
- What harm has my chemically-dependent behavior caused? Who did I harm?
- To whom have I neglected to show gratitude?
- Who was victimized by my anger, resentment, blame, or fear?

My List of Offenses

People I Have Harmed	How I Harmed Them
_____	_____
_____	_____
_____	_____
_____	_____
_____	_____
_____	_____
_____	_____

Phil's baby steps

Phil began to work the Steps seriously. Every time he got ahead of himself by worrying about a future amend, Richard would say, "Baby steps, son; remember to take baby steps." By the time Phil reached Step 8, the list didn't seem so impossible. One by one he wrote the names of the people he had harmed. His list included people he had hurt because of his drug use, but it also included people he had hurt before he began to use and people he hurt apart from his chemical dependency.

Though Phil still feared the reaction of some people on his list, he also began to feel a sense of freedom and relief. Just having the names of the people written on paper helped clear away the fog of guilt and shame he felt.

Richard shared a favorite Bible verse with Phil. Richard said the verse was a blessing Moses shared with one of his sons, but Richard said the blessing applies for any believer who seeks to obey God. Deuteronomy 33:25 appears in the margin.

Thy shoes shall be iron and brass; and as thy days, so shall thy strength be.
—Deuteronomy 33:25, KJV

> **Describe below what the phrase, "As thy days, so shall thy strength be," means to you.**

_____

_____

Phil began to think, *God is giving me the strength to make my amends list—something I thought I could never do. Maybe God really will give me the strength to make my amends just as the verse says.* You may have written that God gives us the strength to fight our battles, or to make our amends, one day at a time.

I will pray the Father, and he shall give you another Comforter, that he may abide with you forever.
–John 14:16, KJV

In John 14 Jesus called the Holy Spirit the "comforter." The word Jesus used pictures the Holy Spirit "coming alongside" or "getting under the load" with us. The Spirit of God gives us the strength to face our tasks, one baby step at a time. He does not give strength today for tomorrow's tasks.

```
┌─────────────────────────────────────────┐
│            Key Concept for Lesson 4       │
│      I begin to make amends by writing a list. │
└─────────────────────────────────────────┘
```

Key Concept for Lesson 4
I begin to make amends by writing a list.

Review today's lesson. Name at least one thing God wants you to do in response to this study. Ask Him for the grace to help you do it.

_____

Step Review

Please review this Step. Pray and ask God to identify the Scriptures or principles that are particularly important for your life. Underline them. Then respond to the following:

Restate Step 8 in your own words: _____

_____

_____

Reword your summary into a prayer of response to God. Thank Him for this Step, and affirm your commitment to Him.

_____

_____

Memorize this Step's memory verse:
And just as you want people to treat you, treat them the same way.

–Luke 6:31

Notes
[1]McGee, Robert S. *Search for Significance* LIFE Support Edition (Houston: Rapha Publishing, 1992), 129-130.

STEP 9

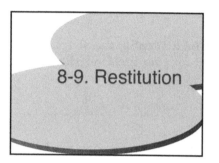

8-9. Restitution

We make amends.

Making Amends

CONFRONTING THE PAST

This was it . . . the big one. Peggy's sponsor instructed her to begin with her smaller amends. She said Peggy would build the strength and faith to make the more difficult amends. Peggy followed that advice. She felt much stronger and better about herself as she thought about the relationships she had mended.

Now Peggy had reached the amend she feared most. During the darkest days of her drug addiction, she regularly had stolen from her former employer. At first she padded her expense account to pay her druggist. Later, when she became hooked on heroin and morphine, she took money from accounts and doctored the books to hide her theft. Eventually her boss fired Peggy because she no longer was able to do her job, but the boss never said anything about the stolen funds.

Since Peggy had been in recovery, her past actions and feelings of guilt followed her like a dark cloud. She knew she never would be free as long as she feared disclosure. After counseling with her sponsor and her pastor, Peggy made up her mind and made her appointment.

Visions of prison bars filled Peggy's head as she walked through the door and into her old business. To the company president she said, "When I worked for the company, I stole cash and embezzled funds. I've come to do whatever is necessary to make up for my actions." (Read more about Peggy on page 174.)

Step 9 *We make direct amends to such people where possible, except when doing so will injure them or others.*

Memory verse *Therefore, however you want people to treat you, so treat them, for this is the Law and the Prophets.*

–Matthew 7:12

Overview for Step 9 **Lesson 1: The Benefits of Amends**
Goal: You will describe some of the benefits that occur when you make amends.

Lesson 2: The Mechanics of Amends
Goal: You will describe the specific actions necessary to make amends.

Lesson 3: Taking the Step
Goal: You will record the results as you make your amends.

<table>
<tr>
<td>

LESSON

1

Key Concept:
Step 9 requires faith and courage, but it pays great dividends.

</td>
<td>

The Benefits of Amends

We make direct amends to such people where possible, except when doing so will injure them or others.

> *See that no one repays another with evil for evil, but always seek after that which is good for one another and for all men.*
>
> –1 Thessalonians 5:15

Step 9 picks up where Step 8 left off—preparing to make amends as appropriate and to restore wounded relationships. In this Step you will design and carry out your amends.

Many benefits await you if you are willing to make amends to those you have hurt and to deal appropriately with those who have hurt you. Making amends will release you from other people's control. Think about people you have been avoiding—those whom you've been dodging, hoping they won't see you, or those you've been excluding altogether from your circle of friends. Have you ever considered that your guilt and fear are controlling you and are keeping you from the life God wants you to have?

</td>
</tr>
</table>

Released from prison

When you make amends, you are released from the emotional prisons of your past. This is true whether or not the other person accepts your amend. This releases you from the fear that someone will discover something about you that you don't want known. As you probably know, this fear could haunt and control you for the rest of your life if you don't confess it.

What do you fear most about making amends?

_____

_____

Do you think this is a realistic fear? Why or why not?

_____

_____

Are you willing to lay aside this fear and make amends even though you may experience pain when you do?   Yes   No

What possible joys might result from making amends? _____

_____

_____

To which of these do you most look forward? Why? _____

_____

_____

Amends: Not Just Apology

Dan said he thought before he entered recovery that Step 9 was the "I'm sorry" Step. He said, "I was like someone with 'I'm sorry' stenciled across my forehead. I was so accustomed to taking the blame that I apologized for anything that I had done—and a lot of things I hadn't done!"

Many people confuse making amends with apologizing. The two concepts are not the same. Read carefully Lamentations 3:40 appearing in the margin. Check which of the following statements most nearly reflects the meaning of the verse:

> Let us examine and probe our ways; And let us return to the Lord.
>
> –Lamentations 3:40

1. We are to examine our behaviors and ask forgiveness.
2. We are to ignore our past actions.
3. We are to examine our behaviors and take corrective action.

> **amend**–v. to make better by some change; improve; to improve one's conduct (Webster's)

As you see from the definition appearing in the margin, **amend** means to change behavior. Asking forgiveness sometimes is the appropriate change, but the change in behavior is the key. The answer is number 3.

We can begin to understand about amends when we think about a debt to be paid. When you owe a debt, to confess and apologize does not solve the problem. The debt needs to be paid.

A friend in Alcoholics Anonymous rejoiced that he had completed the final amend on his list. He had paid off the last of the debts he ran up during his drinking days. When someone asked how long he had been paying on the debt, he replied, "Only 14 years." His story represents genuine amends. He genuinely owed the debt, he accepted full responsibility, and he worked until he could pay off the debt. To the best of his ability he genuinely corrected the offense.

Does the idea of taking a long time to make amends encourage you or discourage you?   It encourages me.   It discourages me.

Below explain why you feel encouraged or discouraged.

_____

_____

Some of us respond that the idea of taking a long time to make amends discourages us. We would prefer to get them over more quickly. Others respond that the prospect encourages them because they realize that making amends is a process.

Making amends is a difficult step—with great rewards. As you prepare to take it, follow these suggestions:
1. Pray for strength and courage as you determine to make your amends.
2. You won't make all your amends at once. You may benefit from making the easiest first.
3. Make your amends one by one as the Lord leads.
4. For strength and motivation, keep in mind two pictures: 1. the relief you may experience when you have made your amends, and 2. how pleased Jesus is as you make the difficult choices to make amends.

Pray and ask God how this concept can apply in your life. Now please review this lesson. What has God shown you that can help you?

_____

_____

In faith, thank God that He will show Himself strong in this area of your life and will help you to correct any long-standing unresolved relationships. Begin praying for the people to whom you will make amends in the last lesson of this Step.

LESSON 2

Key Concept:
Amends are actions.

The Mechanics of Amends

We make direct amends to people where possible, except when doing so will injure them or others.

> _If therefore you are presenting your offering at the altar, and there remember that your brother has something against you, leave your offering there before the altar, and go your way; first be reconciled to your brother, and then come and present your offering._
>
> –Matthew 5:23-24

Direct Amends

In this lesson we'll study reasons to make direct amends to others. Many reasons exist for doing so.

In the paragraph below, circle each reason to make direct amends.

Be direct in making amends. Avoid making anonymous phone calls, letters, or payments to those we wronged. Unless we're extremely far away, we can go in person. Once we have looked someone squarely in the eye to confess our wrongdoing, we always can look that person and others in the eye. Having gained their respect, we will regain our self-respect. If a personal interview is impossible, a phone call is our second choice. One of our objectives is to open a door for dialogue.

You may have circled: _to confess our wrongdoing,_ so we can _look that person and others in the eye,_ to _regain our self-respect,_ and _to open a door for dialogue._

Be direct

Being direct also means assuming complete responsibility for our wrongs. We don't do this by pointing the finger at someone else and saying, "I'm very sorry, but if you hadn't done what you did. . . ." Nor do we want to lessen our responsibility by blaming a third party and saying something like, "Well, I'll admit to using poor judgment, but if Joe hadn't told me. . . ." Your point in making amends is not to admit how someone misled you, though this may have been the case. Your point is to confess that you had a choice in the matter and that you made the wrong one.

restitution–n. the act of restoring to the rightful owner that which was lost or has been taken away (Webster's)

Read the definition at left of restitution. Then below write your own definition.

_____

_____

Making amends is more than just making apologies. Restitution means setting things back in order—righting our wrongs. We demonstrate not only that we know we are wrong but also that we have a change of heart that results in a change of action. When our actions demonstrate a positive change of direction, we have repented.

If a wicked man restores a pledge, pays back what he has taken by robbery, walks by the statutes which ensure life without committing iniquity, he will surely live; he shall not die.
–Ezekiel 33:15

What does the Scripture passage in the margin say to you about making restitution with creditors, the government, local law enforcement agencies, or in instances of theft?

_____

_____

_____

Peggy trembled with fear as she faced her former employer and made her confession. "When I worked for the company, I stole cash and embezzled funds. I've come to do whatever is necessary to make up for my actions," she said. "I would like to have an opportunity to pay back the money I have taken, but you may call the police and prosecute me if you desire." She expected him to reach for the phone and call the police. Instead, a look of amazement appeared on his face. Since he said nothing, Peggy went on to confess her past actions. She explained that she now was in recovery and that she wanted to be honest with both God and others.

More about Peggy

Next, Peggy's former boss said something that amazed her. He said that the company knew about Peggy's thefts. After Peggy was fired, an auditor discovered them. The company executives elected not to prosecute Peggy because she once had been a valued employee and because they knew about her drug problem. He said the company would allow Peggy to repay the money with small payments that she could afford. He thanked Peggy for her honesty. Peggy wept with joy and relief as she walked from the office. She felt that the weight of the world had been lifted from her shoulders.

Indirect Amends

Step 9 states that *we will make direct amends to others where possible.* Again something we cannot change—the past—confronts us. The children we may have wronged now may be grown. We cannot go back and erase the poor example we might have been for them or the abuse we might have given them. Nor can we make restitution with persons who have died or who now have moved to unknown places.

In these instances we can take some positive, constructive steps by way of indirect amends: We can learn from our mistakes and apply that knowledge to present and future situations. If people we wronged have died, we can pay what debts we may owe to one of their survivors or make a charitable donation in their name; we can treat their survivors with a special act of kindness.

Pray for people still living but whom we cannot locate.

We can do for other people's children or parents what we wish we'd done for our own. We can do this not as an act of guilt but as an act of love. We can pray for those whom we know are still living but whom we cannot locate.

Below list any other suggestions you can think of about how to make indirect amends.

_____

_____

_____

Avoiding Injury to Others

Some situations call for making partial restitution. This may mean partially disclosing your wrongdoing. Sexual infidelity may be one situation calling for this kind of action. Telling your spouse about your sexual escapades possibly could cause him or her severe mental and emotional anguish and could damage your marriage beyond repair. In the same way, disclosing the person(s) with whom you committed infidelity possibly could damage them. Causing others such pain is both needless and harmful. Our goal in making amends is not to do further damage to others but to right our wrongs.

Our goal in making amends is not to do further damage but to right our wrongs.

How can we make restitution in such instances? First, we can repent. If we haven't already, we can break off the adulterous relationship(s). We can resolve that with God's help, we will remain faithful to our spouse for the rest of our lives (one day at a time). We also can show renewed interest toward our spouse by giving him or her time and attention.

Some of us are so conscientious that we can't tell when partial restitution is appropriate. Others of us are so irresponsible that we will use any excuse to avoid making amends at all. God knows your situation. Pray about the matter. Consult an objective minister, a Christian counselor, or your sponsor. Find someone with whom you can talk candidly and from whom you can expect a godly response.

Think about the people or circumstances in your life which may call for making partial amends. Because of the sensitive nature of the information that comes to mind, you may desire to use a separate sheet of paper for this exercise. Using the format on the next page, write down each instance. Then by the side of each instance, identify the possible damage that could result from making full disclosure.

Person or Situation:	Damaging Result	Specific Action:
_____	_____	_____

As you reread your list, think about ways you by a change of action can demonstrate partial restitution. Using the format below list those on your separate paper.

Person or Situation:	Damaging Result	Specific Action:
_____	_____	_____

Still other situations may call for delayed restitution. You may have hurt someone so recently that any discussion now might end in a broken relationship. In these cases, you can wait to act. Careful, prayerful consideration, combined with wise counsel and timing, are very important in successfully completing Step 9.

List below the people or circumstances in your life which may call for delayed amends. (These may include situations where you still have not resolved your own negative emotions.) Beside each instance, list the possible harm that you could cause by making amends now. You may desire to use a separate sheet of paper for this excersise, also.

Person or Situation:	Damaging Result	Specific Action:
_____	_____	_____
_____	_____	_____

Below describe some things you can do about these situations while you are waiting for the right time to make amends.

_____

_____

_____

Take all of these issues to your sponsor, pastor, or counselor; ask him or her to pray through each with you, and wait with an open mind for God's direction.

At Peace with All

Making restitution often brings favorable results. Many people are completely disarmed when we are willing to be open and honest and when we admit wrongdoing. These people usually respond with gracious appreciation. But this isn't always the case. Some people will respond in anger, shock, indifference, or disapproval. The fear of such a response should not deter us from completing our errand. We can remember that we cannot control others' responses. Scripture tells us that "their" response is not the issue. Romans 12:18 says, ". . . so far as it depends on you, be at peace with all men."

We cannot control others' responses.

Please pray and ask God how this concept can apply in your life. Now please review this lesson. What has God shown you that can help you?

_____

_____

LESSON 3

Key Concept:
We can record our own progress and growth in discipleship.

Taking the Step

We make direct amends to people where possible, except when doing so will injure them or others.

Let us examine and probe our ways, And let us return to the Lord.
–Lamentations 3:40

Turn back to page 168 in Step 8 where you listed all the people you have harmed. In the spaces below, rewrite those names. Beside each, list the action you plan to take, the date you will complete the action, and the result of your interview with him or her. Use extra pages of paper as necessary for additional names and actions. This exercise may take weeks or even months to complete as you prayerfully determine your best course of action. The point is to have a reminder of both those to whom you need to make amends and of what you are going to do to demonstrate repentance toward them. Success in smaller amends also will encourage you when you need courage to face more difficult amends.

Name: _____

Action Planned: _____

_____

_____

Date Planned: _____   Completed: _____

Name: _____

Action Planned: _____

_____

_____

Date Planned: _____   Completed: _____

Name: _____

Action Planned: _____

_____

_____

Date Planned: _____ Completed: _____

Respecting ourselves

Remember that we make amends so that we can respect ourselves, not so we can obtain any particular response from others. However, we do often see positive results from making amends. As you make amends, note here any resulting changes. Watch for changes in the response of those to whom you make amends, in your relationships with others, in your prayer life, marriage, or any other result. Below write any observed results. Add extra pages if necessary.

_____

_____

_____

_____

Step Review

Please review this Step. Pray and ask God to identify the Scriptures or principles that are particularly important for your life. Underline them. Then respond to the following:

Restate the Step in your own words: _____

_____

_____

What do you have to gain by practicing this Step in your life?

_____

_____

Reword your summary into a prayer of response to God. Thank Him for this Step, and affirm your commitment to Him.

_____

_____

Memorize this Step's memory verse:
Therefore, however you want people to treat you, so treat them, for this is the Law and the Prophets.

–Matthew 7:12

STEP 10

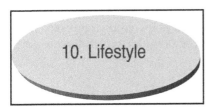
10. Lifestyle

We continue to take inventory.

Recognizing and Responding

> ## BETTER THAN AN AMEND
>
> "I finally did it," Allison proclaimed. The others at the meeting could see from the smile on her face that Allison had accomplished something significant. "As I have worked my Steps, I saw a pattern I have repeated over and over," Allison said. "I offend someone, and I don't recognize until later what I've done. Then I have an amend to make. Other times I fail to stand up for myself. Then I have to go back to the person and say what I wish I had said the first time.
>
> "Since I've been working on Step 10, I realize the importance of the little word 'promptly.' I've been trying to recognize promptly when I am wrong and promptly admit it so I spare myself the worry of having an amend to make. Now here comes the good part. This week I have gotten it right three times! Once with my boss, once with my daughter, and—if you can believe it—this morning with my husband, I have worked Step 10.
>
> "My boss asked me about a project that was due at work. I started to make excuses, but then my recovery kicked in. I simply told her, 'I don't have it ready yet.' All she did was ask if I could have it by the morning. I said, 'I'll have it ready.' That was all there was to it! If I had followed my old pattern, the whole day would have been ruined. I would have been filled with guilt, resentment, and self-pity, and by five o'clock I would have been ready to go get stoned."

Step 10 *We continue to take personal inventory, and when we are wrong, promptly admit it.*

Memory verse *Trust in the LORD with all your heart, And do not lean on your own understanding. In all your ways acknowledge Him, And He will make your paths straight.*
–Proverbs 3:5-6

Overview for Step 10

Lesson 1: Guilt: A Devastating Burden
　　　Goal: You will distinguish between guilt and godly sorrow.
Lesson 2: More About the Process
　　　Goal: You will identify ways that conviction and guilt occur in our lives and how they affect us.
Lesson 3: Identifying False Beliefs
　　　Goal: You will develop the skill of identifying false beliefs.
Lesson 4: Catching the Signals
　　　Goal: You will practice identifying the warning signals of harmful behavior.

Guilt: A Devastating Burden

We continue to take personal inventory, and when we are wrong, promptly admit it.

> *He is on the path of life who heeds instruction, But he who forsakes reproof goes astray.*
>
> –Proverbs 10:17

Key Concept:
Guilt is destructive to believers, but godly sorrow for our sins is important for us to grow.

Read the following review of the Steps, and mark your progress. Circle each Step that you practice with reasonable regularity. Underline each Step with which you are struggling.

In Step 1 we admitted that we had a problem which was controlling our lives and admitted that this problem was making our lives unmanageable. In Step 2 we recognized the existence and power of God—a power greater than, and outside of, ourselves—and acknowledged that He alone could restore us to sanity. In Step 3 we became willing to let Him change us by accepting His lordship. In Step 4 we "cleaned house" and uncovered some of the self-defeating patterns that had governed our lives.

In Step 5 we agreed with God about what we had learned about ourselves in Step 4, and we confessed to another person the things we had kept secret in the past. In Step 6 we submitted our inventory to God and asked Him to remove the patterns of sin from our lives. In Step 7 we asked God to replace our false belief systems—which governed our thought patterns and resulting actions—with the truth of His Word. In Step 8 we listed those to whom we needed to make amends, and in Step 9, we carried that further by not only addressing those whom we had offended but forgiving those who had offended us. In that Step we began to learn to change the way we typically relate to others.

Now in Step 10, as faithful stewards of the lives God has given back to us, we continue to take responsibility for our attitudes and actions. We can be aware that the old patterns of thinking and acting can reappear—and will from time to time.

Beware of the feelings of failure that occur because of Satan's accusations.

Did you underline some Steps because you are still struggling with them? If so, congratulations for your awareness and honesty. Remember the slogan, "We seek progress, not perfection." Beware of the feelings of failure that occur because of Satan's accusations.

Remember that recovery is like swimming upstream. It is difficult work. Old thoughts and feelings do not just go away. We replace them with new, Christ-honoring habits. In the process we must watch for and avoid danger areas. We use our inventories to identify these areas and to bring them to the Lord in confession and repentance as soon as we discover them. We learn to monitor them on a daily basis as a form of maintenance.

The potential for slipping does not have to rob us of the joy we have in our new life. Our old self was nailed to the cross with Christ. We can say victoriously, "I have been crucified with Christ; and it is no longer I who live, but Christ lives in me; and the life which I now live in the flesh I live by faith in the Son of God, who loved me and delivered Himself up for me" (Galatians 2:20).

> **To help you memorize this passage, write Galatians 2:20 in the margin. Think about the passage as you answer the following question.**
>
> What evidence do you have that Christ is living His life in you?

_____

_____

You may not always feel like Christ is living in you. All too frequently you may be reminded of the presence of your old, sinful nature. That nature seems to cover up all evidence that you even are a Christian. But feelings, or lack of them, do not change the fact that you are dead to the old ways and alive to the new in Christ.

Step 10 is a means of daily confirming that your old way of life is dead and of affirming the life which Jesus Christ is living in you. Working Step 10 will help you identify: (1) the destructive patterns of behavior which keep creeping up out of the swamps of the past, and (2) new patterns of behavior which are the emerging evidence of Christ's life in you.

In order to walk by the Spirit in the light of honesty, we take a daily inventory. Before we do this, however, we will examine the effect of guilt on our lives. The following material in lessons 1 and 2 is adapted from *Search for Significance* LIFE Support Edition. We hope you will find it helpful in understanding how you can be free from this always-present burden.

Guilt's Destructiveness

If we say that we have no sin, we are deceiving ourselves, and the truth is not in us. If we confess our sins, He is faithful and righteous to forgive us our sins and to cleanse us from all unrighteousness. If we say that we have not sinned, we make Him a liar, and His word is not in us.
                      –1 John 1:8-10

confess–v. to declare by way of admitting oneself guilty of what one is accused of, the result of inward conviction (Vine's)

conviction–n. the act of convincing a person of error (Webster's)

Even after we've trusted Christ and are freed from eternal condemnation, we still sin. First John 1:8-10 appearing at left tells us about this. We miss the mark; we make mistakes; we turn from God's ways. What happens at that point? Should we then feel guilty about what we've done?

The Bible indicates that God intends for us to feel *something* when we sin, and we don't stop feeling that *something* just because we accept Christ. God doesn't intend that just because we accept Christ, we can go on sinning without our sins ever bothering us.

Here's what happens: When we sin, the Holy Spirit urges us to **confess** those sins. (We also studied the term **confess** in unit 4.) The definition at left says that we confess sin by admitting ourselves guilty of what we are accused. This comes about through **conviction** (see definition at left)—the Holy Spirit works in our lives to get us to agree with God about the wrong we've done. Our sense that something is wrong occurs because the Holy Spirit is **convicting** us of sin.

God wants us to feel a godly sorrow, or grief, for our sins. He does not want us to experience guilt that eats away at us and destroys our self-esteem.

I now rejoice, not that you were made sorrowful, but that you were made sorrowful to the point of repentance; for you were made sorrowful according to the will of God, in order that you might not suffer loss in anything through us. For the sorrow that is according to the will of God produces a repentance without regret, leading to salvation; but the sorrow of the world produces death.

–2 Corinthians 7:9-10

Second Corinthians 7:9-10 at left describes this kind of sorrow. This verse says godly sorrow brings us to the point of repentance.

Once we confess our sin, repent, and accept Christ's forgiveness, we may continue to have regret and remorse, but we can be assured that Christ has forgiven us completely. Forgiveness enables us to overcome the fear of condemnation.

What Guilt Does to Us

When people allow guilt to burden them even after God forgives them, they can find themselves harmed emotionally. This kind of lingering guilt causes a loss of self-respect. It causes the human spirit to wither, and it eats away at our personal significance and self-esteem. It causes us to condemn ourselves.

Guilt plays on our fears of failure and rejection; therefore, it never can ultimately build, encourage, or inspire us in our desire to live for Christ.

Go back to Step 4 and select two incidents from your personal inventory that have caused you to feel guilty. List for each the destructive effect this guilt had on your life.

Incident #1: _____

_____

The destructive effect on my life was: _____

_____

Incident #2: _____

_____

The destructive effect on my life was: _____

_____

Unfortunately, some people tell us that even after God has forgiven us of a particular sin, we still are guilty. And sadly, we hear this statement in churches—places that loudly and clearly should proclaim God's forgiveness. Sometimes people may try to make us feel guilty in order to motivate us to respond in certain ways.

Guilt, however, is not a healthy motivator for us. In the margin box briefly describe a time when you felt that someone tried to make you feel guilty to motivate you to do something.

Perhaps some people think that if they don't use guilt motivation, people won't respond. Because guilt motivation is so deeply ingrained in us, we will require time to develop more healthy motivations. The grace of God, who is in us, produces these motivations. Be patient with yourself as you learn to develop healthy motivations.

Describe a time when someone tried to use guilt to motivate you.

_____

_____

_____

_____

Recognize the Lies

Learn to identify the results of guilt in your thoughts. Then focus instead on the unconditional love and forgiveness of Christ. His love is powerful, and He deserves our intense zeal to obey and honor him.

Christians are subject to grief, or sorrow, over our sins. The Bible often speaks about the Holy Spirit's work to convict believers of sin. He directs and encourages our spiritual progress by revealing our sins in contrast to the holiness and purity of Christ. The purpose of conviction is to lead us back to God's way for our lives. The Holy Spirit does not intend to produce pangs of guilt long after we've been forgiven of our sins. The Holy Spirit convicts us to show the error of our performance in light of God's standard and truth. His motivation is love, correction, and protection. Godly sorrow that comes about through conviction enables us to realize the beauty of God's forgiveness and to experience His love and power. After we repent and God has forgiven us for that sin, no reasons exist from God's perspective for feelings of guilt to be a part of our lives.

In the margin box describe a time when conviction caused you to experience godly sorrow for a sin.

> **A time when I felt godly sorrow for sin:**
>
> _____
>
> _____
>
> _____
>
> _____

> **Key Concept for Lesson 1**
> Guilt is destructive to believers, but godly sorrow for our sins is important for us to grow.

Please pray and ask God how this concept can apply in your life. Now please review this lesson. What has God shown you that can help you?

_____

_____

LESSON 2

Key Concept:
I can understand that I am forgiven, accepted, loved, and totally secure because of Christ.

More About the Process

We continue to take personal inventory, and when we are wrong, promptly admit it.

> *Sanctify them in the truth; Thy word is truth.* –John 17:17

How Guilt Affects Us

Although God does not condemn Christians, we probably won't be free from the destructive power of condemnation until we learn that we no longer have to fear judgment. The Holy Spirit wants us to be convinced that God forgives us, accepts us, loves us, and makes us totally secure because of Christ. The Holy Spirit is the Paraclete, or "one called alongside," to uplift and encourage us. He faithfully makes us aware of any behavior that does not reflect the character of Christ. He helps us understand both our righteousness before God and the failures in our performance.

Knowing this, how can we deal with feelings of guilt? In the following chart, we can study a little more about how guilt affects us.

GUILT

Basic Focus—Guilt focuses on self-condemnation. We believe, "I am unworthy."

Primary Concern—Guilt deals with the sinner's loss of self-esteem and wounded self-pride. We think, "What will others think of me?"

Primary Fear—Guilt produces a fear of punishment. We believe, "Now I'm going to get it!"

Behavioral Results—Guilt leads to depression and more sin. We think, "I am just a low-down, dirty, rotten person." Or, it leads to to rebellion. We believe, "I don't care; I'm going to do whatever I want to do."

Interpersonal Results—The interpersonal result of guilt is alienation, a feeling of shame that drives one away from the person wronged. We think, "I never can face him again."

Personal Results—Guilt ends in depression, bitterness, and self-pity. We think, "I'm just no good."

Remedy—The remedy for guilt is to remember that if you have repented of your sin, Christ has forgiven you and remembers your sin no more.

Look back in the box at the statements about guilt. Check any that you might have experienced in your life.

To deal with feelings of guilt, we first can affirm that Christ has forgiven us. As believers we are not condemned when we sin, but that sin is harmful and dishonors God. We can confess our sin to God, claim the forgiveness we already have in Christ, and then move on in joy and freedom to honor Him. The prayer appearing in the margin expresses this attitude. You may want to pray the words of this prayer of confession or use similar words of your own.

We can affirm our righteousness in Christ as well as confess our sins. God does not need to be reminded of our right standing in Him, but we do. Make this prayer a daily experience and let it fill every corner of your thoughts.

As you yield to the gentle urging of God-given conviction, confess your sins and affirm your true relationship with Him, God gradually will shape and mold you to increasingly "honor Him who died and rose again on (our) behalf" (2 Corinthians 5:15).

Father, I affirm that I am deeply loved by You, fully pleasing to You, and totally accepted in Your sight. You have made me complete and have given me the righteousness of Christ, even though my performance often falls short. Lord, I confess my sins to You. (List them. Be specific.) I agree with You that these are wrong. Thank You for forgiving me for these sins. Do I need to return anything, repay anyone, or apologize to anyone in order to fully make amends? Give me the courage to take these steps. In Jesus' name. Amen.

Please pray and ask God how this concept can apply in your life. Now please review this lesson. What has God shown you that can help you?

_____

_____

_____

Begin memorizing this Step's memory verse, Proverbs 3:5-6

LESSON 3

Key Concept:
Changing my belief system is the key to changing my behavior.

You brood of vipers, how can you, being evil, speak what is good? For the mouth speaks out of that which fills the heart.
—Matthew 12:34

Identifying False Beliefs

We continue to take personal inventory, and when we are wrong, promptly admit it.

For the mouth speaks out of that which fills the heart.   —Matthew 12:34

You earlier identified how our belief system is the key to our behavior. In this lesson you will further develop this process and begin to practice identifying the beliefs that control your life from behind the scenes. By taking a personal inventory we learn to identify the false beliefs that govern our actions, so that we can replace them with the truth of God's Word. We can recognize the source of our emotions and actions. Read Matthew 12:34 appearing in the margin to learn what Jesus said about this. Our communication, which reveals our thoughts, emotions, and the intent of our actions, comes from our heart (or belief system). Our beliefs interpret the events in our lives; therefore, our belief system, not the situation, usually is the key to our response! The following diagram helps us understand our thinking process from situation to action.

Situations ⇨ **Belief System** ⇨ Thoughts ⇨ Emotions ⇨ Actions

Tracing Emotions to Root Beliefs

Let's suppose Bill picked you up late, so you are late to work (or school, church, committee meeting). You respond in anger. You can trace that anger back to its root false belief in order to replace it with corresponding truths from the Scriptures or a characteristic of Christ Step 3 presents.

"Why am I angry?"

How do you determine the false belief responsible for your anger? Ask yourself, "Why am I angry? Am I angry because . . . ."

- ". . . I hate to be late" (your "certain standard,") "and my lateness makes me feel badly about myself?" (*I must meet certain standards. . .*)

- ". . . my boss will be displeased with me because I'm late, and her opinion of me means so much?" (*I must be approved by certain others. . .*)

- ". . . Bill failed by being late to pick me up? It was *his* fault, that creep!" (*Those who fail are unworthy of love and deserve to be punished.*) "No matter what I do, something always goes wrong?" (*I am hopeless. I cannot change.*)

Note that the proper response is not "I'm not angry." You *are* angry. Denial only compounds our problems; it is not a solution. We can be honest with the Lord and with ourselves about our feelings.

If the situation about being picked up late in the previous example had happened to you, what would your emotion(s) likely have been?

_____

_____

To which false belief(s) could you trace it? _____

_____

_____

Learned Habits We Can Overcome

The process described above works in every person's life, but it may be more difficult for those of us who come from hurtful backgrounds. Our emotions also are habits—products of our family backgrounds, our past experiences, relationships, and patterns of responses. They are learned habits we can overcome.

We use many different methods to block pain in our lives, but we can begin reversing this trend by finding someone who will encourage us to be honest about our feelings. We then can use our feelings as a gauge to determine if our response to a situation is based on the truth or a lie.

Feelings are signals which tell us something about our environment.

Only by getting in touch with our feelings will we overcome these self-destructive defense mechanisms. Feelings are neither right nor wrong. They are signals which tell us something about our environment. If we are not aware of those feelings, we miss an entire range of information we need to live life effectively. When we are honest about our emotions, these emotions can tell us what we need to know about our perceptions. When our emotions are painful or distressing, we can ask, "Why am I responding this way? Am I believing a lie? If so, which one?" Learning to take a daily inventory—to take Step 10—is our path to a growing lifestyle of victory and obedience.

Key Concept for Lesson 3
Changing my belief system is the key to changing
my behavior.

Please pray and ask God how this concept can apply in your life. Now please review this lesson. What has God shown you that can help you?

_____

_____

_____

LESSON 4

Key Concept:
In recovery we recognize and deal with the dysfunctional behaviors in our lives.

A wise person can take correction and apply it to his or her life.

Catching the Signals

We continue to take personal inventory, and when we are wrong, promptly admit it.

> *Do not reprove a scoffer, lest he hate you, Reprove a wise man, and he will love you.*
> —Proverbs 9:8

The Book of Proverbs gives a test for a wise person. Proverbs states this test repeatedly. Can you figure it out from reading the passage above?

Look at the verse above. What is the one difference between a wise and a foolish person?

_____

_____

Step 10 is about looking at myself honestly and regularly. A wise person is one who can take correction and apply it in his or her life.

Warning Signs

Throughout these pages, we have looked at many examples of harmful behavior—these represent warning signs for us. As we read them we may identify by saying, "That's me; that's what I do!" or "My wife does that to me!" or "I respond that way to my husband."

We can learn to see the truth about ourselves. Some of us see a few particular events but don't see any deep-rooted patterns in our behavior.

A friend named Ralph told me about his relationship with his condemning, manipulative father. "I've been angry with my father several times, so I guess I'm pretty objective," he surmised. He didn't see the obvious—that his life was filled with insecurity and all sorts of defense mechanisms that he had developed. We need to see both the patterns of our behavior and the specific events that make up those patterns.

We have divided the following chart into the two extremes of thinking. In one extreme we think we are God—absurdly exaggerated thinking. At the other extreme we think we are pond scum. We call these savior and Judas thinking. Sometimes we act as if we are the Savior—faultless and indispensable. Other times we act as if we are a Judas—always at fault. Review these common feelings and behaviors and determine which of these, or variations of these, you can identify in your life. Do you find a pattern?

Circle the feelings you identify in your own life.

Savior	Judas
Feelings: important, superior, certain, euphoric, confident, appreciated, angry, self-righteous, jealous, possessive, easily hurt	**Feelings:** depressed, lonely, angry, helpless, confused, afraid, hurt, inferior, hopeless, guilty, numb, trapped, martyred, persecuted, lethargic, worthless, ashamed, tired
Thoughts and Words: *It's all your fault.* *You made me fail.* *I can help.* *He (she) needs me.* *Why aren't people as perceptive as I am?* *I deserve their respect and love.* *I can make life good.*	**Thoughts and Words:** *It's all my fault.* *I'm a failure.* *I can't do anything right.* *Everything I do is wrong.* *Yes, but I mean no.* *No, but I mean yes.* *I don't deserve their respect and love.* *Life never will be good for me.*
Black-and-White: *People really need me.* *I am indispensable to the kingdom of God.* *People won't be helped and the Great Commission can't be fulfilled without me.*	**Black-and-White:** *People really need me, but I'll only let them down.* *Good Christians wouldn't think or act this way.* *God must be mad at me. He'll punish me.*
Actions: positive exaggeration, self-promotion, overcommitment, workaholism, susceptibility to manipulation, control of others through praise and condemnation, rescue of people without being asked, denial of reality, compulsion to avoid failure, giving, helping, trying to please people, defensiveness, overly responsible, prone to outbursts of anger.	**Actions:** negative exaggeration, self-belittling, withdrawal, avoidance of people and risks, susceptibility to manipulation, control of others through self-pity, denial of reality, passive-aggressive behavior, fear of failure leading to passive behavior, defensive, irresponsible, prone to outbursts of anger, rationalizing.

Sometimes I think I'm God and at other times I think I'm pond scum!

Do we feel people can't do without us? Or do we feel like we're always at fault?

Growing in objectivity

Did you identify with several of the feelings, thoughts, and actions in both columns? Identifying this behavior indicates your growing honesty and objectivity.

> **Pray and ask God to give you insight and objectivity. This exercise is not about putting yourself down but about honestly identifying the patterns in your life. Using the Savior/Judas chart, describe your feelings, thoughts, statements, and actions. Be specific. Use an extra sheet of paper, or write in the margin, if necessary.**

When I feel like a savior, I have these/do these:

Feelings: _____

Thoughts and words: _____

Actions: _____

When I feel like a Judas, I have these/do these:

Feelings: _____

Thoughts and words: _____

Actions: _____

> No temptation has overtaken you but such as is common to man; and God is faithful, who will not allow you to be tempted beyond what you are able, but with the temptation will provide the way of escape also, that you may be able to endure it.
> –1 Corinthians 10:13

Identifying our behaviors usually brings out a flood of emotions as we realize how deeply we have been affected. The Lord can give us wisdom and strength, and a friend can give us the encouragement we need to fight our battles. However, what you see probably is only the first layer. As you deal with these hurts, fears, anger and habits, you will expose yet another layer. The Lord will give you the grace to endure and progress. Be encouraged by what Paul said to the believers in Corinth. Read the verse at left.

The way of escape so that we may endure begins when we *identify* our destructive behavior; *detach* and reflect on reality; and finally, *decide* on the best course of action. For the next 15 days, develop a habit in your scheduled activities which can change your life permanently. Select a specific time and place to complete the daily inventory that follows. Everything else of value in your life—a time to eat your meals, a time to rest, a time to begin the work day—usually happens as a result of scheduling.

Schedule a time to take a daily inventory in which you—

- seek to *identify* situations that bring out a dysfunctional response.

- *detach* to reflect on the situation. Were you acting like a savior or a Judas? What were you thinking? What did you say? How did you feel? Which false belief(s) were you believing? What is God's truth?

- *decide*. For what are you responsible in this situation? What will be your plan of action? How will you implement it? Finally, pray. Thank God for the insights He has given you. Claim the truth of His Word, and ask Him to provide what you need to gain victory over a similar situation in the future.

Use the chart that follows to help you identify, detach, and decide. Use extra paper if you need to. Copy the chart for the remaining 14 days in which you take your daily inventory.

Identify   Situation:_____

_____

Destructive response: _____

_____

_____

Detach   Were you acting like a savior or a Judas? _____

What were your feelings? _____

_____

What thoughts and words did you use? _____

_____

What actions did you take? _____

_____

Which of Satan's lies apply to this situation? How? _____

_____

Which of God's truths apply to this situation? How? _____

_____

_____

Decide   What are you responsible for in this situation? _____

_____

What are you not responsible for? _____

_____

What would have been a healthy response to this situation? _____

_____

What is your plan of action? _____

_____

_____

> ## Key Concept for Lesson 4
> In recovery we recognize and deal with the dysfunctional behaviors in our lives.

Please pray and ask God how this concept can apply in your life. Now please review this lesson. What has God shown you that can help you?

_____

_____

Step Review

Please review this Step. Pray and ask God to identify the Scriptures or principles that are particularly important for your life. Underline them. Then respond to the following:

Restate the Step in your own words.

_____

_____

What do you have to gain by practicing this Step in your life?

_____

_____

Reword your summary into a prayer of response to God. Thank Him for this Step and affirm your commitment to Him.

_____

_____

_____

_____

_____

Memorize this Step's memory verse:
Trust in the LORD with all your heart, And do not lean on your own understanding. In all your ways acknowledge Him, And He will make your paths straight.

–Proverbs 3:5-6

11. Prayer

We grow in relationship with God by prayer, meditation, and Bible study.

A Growing Relationship

WHY THE WAIT?

Bill had been a Christian since he was 10 years old. His drug use began with "bagging." Bill and his friends found that they could get high by spraying paint into a paper bag and breathing the fumes. By the time Bill became a high school student, he was using inhalants, alcohol, and pills regularly.

Even in the depths of his addiction, Bill still believed in God. He sometimes still attended church, and he still prayed. Mostly he prayed that God would give him the power to stay away from drugs, but his prayers seemed to go unanswered.

When Bill first began working the Steps, he said the placement of Step 11 was a mystery. *We've all heard about how important prayer is, so why is it placed so far down the list in the Steps?* he wondered.

Now Bill says God changed his life—including a change in his feelings about and approach to prayer. "Before I began to work the Steps I prayed, but I felt so guilty because I didn't pray as much as I thought I should. I felt too ashamed to talk to God. Then as I worked the first three Steps, I began to pray out of desperation and need. Now in Step 11, I am learning about the character and pattern of prayer."

As you work this Step, you may find the answer to why your prayer life has been such a source of frustration instead of the joyous relationship God has in store for you. (Read more about Bill on page 200.)

Step 11 *We seek to know Christ more intimately through prayer and meditation, praying only for knowledge of His will and the power to carry that out.*

Memory verse *But seek first His kingdom and His righteousness; and all these things shall be added to you.*

–Matthew 6:33

Overview for Step 11

Lesson 1: **What Is Prayer?**
 Goal: You will identify the primary purpose of prayer.
Lesson 2: **Meditation**
 Goal: You will describe Christian meditation.
Lesson 3: **God's Word and Obedience**
 Goal: You will examine some methods to help you work Step 11.

What Is Prayer?

We seek to know Christ more intimately through prayer and meditation, praying only for knowledge of His will and the power to carry that out.

> *But if any of you lacks wisdom, let him ask of God, who gives to all men generously and without reproach, and it will be given to him. But let him ask in faith without any doubting, for the one who doubts is like the surf of the sea driven and tossed by the wind.*
>
> –James 1:5-6

Key Concept:
The essence of prayer is a loving relationship with God.

Jesus Christ's primary purpose in becoming human and being crucified on our behalf was to reconcile us to God. He desires to have a relationship with us. He wants us to know Him intimately.

Think about a time when you desired to have a relationship with someone—possibly a person you admired or a person you wanted to date. What did it feel like to desire that relationship? Did you feel—

shy and afraid to speak?
fearful of rejection?
hopeful that you would be accepted?
excited?
happy?
other? _____

Can you carry that feeling over to your relationship to God? He desires to have an intimate love relationship with you. He cares for you so deeply that He was willing to give His Son to die in your place. In the above exercise one thing you probably did not write was that you felt critical of the person you love. In the margin box write why many of us so quickly assume God desires to reject us.

We assume God desires to reject us because—

_____

_____

_____

_____

_____

In the John 10 passage at left, Jesus described himself as the shepherd who cares for the sheep. Why do the the sheep that the verses at left mention follow the shepherd?

because they fear the shepherd
because they love and trust the shepherd

Mark prayed regularly each night before he went to bed. One night after he stayed up late reading, Mark fell asleep without having his prayer time. The next morning when he realized what he had done, Mark was terrified. He was afraid something horrible would happen to him because he slept through his prayer time the previous evening. He felt that God never would forgive him for getting off his schedule. Many of us try to build a prayer life out of fear. We think God will be disappointed in us or punish us if we don't pray. We can learn from the sheep to follow and pray because we love our Shepherd and respond to His love. See what the bottom verse at left says about this.

> To him the doorkeeper opens, and the sheep hear his voice, and he calls his own sheep by name, and leads them out . . . he goes before them, and the sheep follow him because they know his voice. I am the good shepherd; and I know My own, and My own know Me.
>
> –John 10:3-4,14

Scripture describes Jesus as the Good Shepherd who is faithful to lead and to provide for His sheep. Just as sheep know the shepherd's voice, we can know Jesus' voice. We can't distinguish His voice from any other voice unless we

> We love, because He first loved us.
>
> –1 John 4:19

develop an intimate relationship with Him. Such a relationship takes time, but God clearly wants this relationship. He took the initiative to have a relationship with us.

Elements of Effective Prayer

Have you wondered, "So how do I pray?" Here is a simple summary of the elements in an effective prayer life. If you practice these kinds of prayer on a regular basis, you will be working Step 11.

Praise

The 12 Steps are a program of humility. A warped sense of self-importance and shame accompanies our addictions. When we are prideful, we act as if we are God. When we are down, we believe we are pond scum. Either way the addiction wins. It remains in control. Humility involves recognizing that we are people of infinite worth because God loves us, but we are not God. Growing in humility includes recognizing the greatness of God. We praise God in prayer, not because He needs our praise (see Psalm 50:7-15), but because we need the humility which accompanies acknowledging God as God. In praise we direct thoughts and words of worship to God for who He is: His character, His lovingkindness, His power, His handiwork.

Write a prayer of praise to God. Express to Him your love and adoration for who He is. You may want to use additional paper.

_____

_____

_____

_____

_____

Petition

You present your petitions, or requests, to Him in prayer as well. He wants your concerns and the burdens of your heart. In fact, He asks that we hand these things over to Him (see 1 Peter 5:7 at left). Philippians 4:6 expresses the attitude of trust you can have. You can trust Him to do what is best for you and for those for whom you pray.

> casting all your anxiety upon Him, because He cares for you.
> —1 Peter 5:7

> Be anxious for nothing, but in everything by prayer and supplication with thanksgiving let your requests be made known to God.
> —Philippians 4:6

How do you suppose God feels when His children approach Him with their requests?

Go away kid. You bother me!   _My child, I am so glad to see you!_

> But an hour is coming, and now is, when the true worshippers shall worship the Father in spirit and truth; for such people the Father seeks to be His worshippers.
> —John 4:23

In Step 2 we learned that many of us have a distorted concept of God. We expect God to say, "Can't you see I'm busy?" That concept of God is a product of our fearful imaginations. Our Father longs for us to spend time with Him.

Read John 4:23, printed in the margin, and the story of the father which appears on the next page. Then describe what the father in the story and the Heavenly Father in the Scripture have in common.

Don is grieving. His only son has moved away. Some call it empty-nest syndrome. Don says he's just missing someone he loves very much. He says, "I look forward to his calls and visits. I just love to hear his voice."

What do the father in the story and the Heavenly Father of whom Jesus spoke have in common?

_____

Did you note the word *seeks* in John 4:23? The Scripture says God actually seeks—goes in search of—worshippers. Both God and Don share the deep desire to spend time with their children.

Thanksgiving

Another element of prayer is thanksgiving—showing gratitude for what God does for you and others for whom you pray. Thanking God is a way of acknowledging that He is God. It also is a part of your "attitude of gratitude," which results from the new things He is making possible in your life. Gratitude is a wonderful replacement for bitterness and pride.

Gratitude is a wonderful replacement for bitterness and pride.

Practice thanksgiving by writing in the margin at least five things for which you are grateful to God. Write them in the form of a prayer of thanksgiving.

Sometimes people are puzzled when they first hear people in meetings say: "Hi, I'm _____, and I'm a grateful recovering alcoholic (addict, overeater, codependent, etc.)." Looking at all the addiction had cost them, how could they be grateful for the worst source of pain in their lives? Addictions caused enough pain to turn these addicts to Christ. Even the most painful experiences can be sources of praise when we allow them to point us to Jesus.

For which of the following can you give thanks? Check all that apply.

Spiritual blessings (such as answers to prayer, salvation, forgiveness, acceptance)
Physical blessings (such as eyes, ears, health)
Relational blessings (such as family, friends, co-workers)
Material blessings (such as home, job, money, car)
Intangible blessings (such as freedom of speech, freedom of worship)

From the list above, for what are you most thankful?

_____

Confession

Confessing our sin—so that we can experience forgiveness and a renewed fellowship with God—is another key purpose and benefit of prayer. In Step 10 you explored 1 John 1:8-9 which promises that when we confess our sin, God always forgives us and cleanses us from *all* unrighteousness.

Remember that since our forgiveness already has been paid for at the cross, confession enables us to experience what God already has granted. Confession is not a duty whereby we pay for our sin by beating ourselves. It is accepting God's gift. It frees us from the guilt that drives us to repeat the offense.

Our Father who art in heaven, Hallowed be Thy Name. Thy kingdom come. Thy will be done, On earth as it is in heaven. Give us this day our daily bread. And forgive us our debts, as we also have forgiven our debtors. And do not lead us into temptation, but deliver us from evil. [For Thine is the kingdom, and the power, and the glory, forever. Amen.]

–Matthew 6:9-13

God, grant me the serenity to accept the things I cannot change, the courage to change the things I can, and the wisdom to know the difference; living one day at a time, enjoying one moment at a time, accepting hardship as a pathway to peace; taking as Jesus did, this sinful world as it is, not as I would have it. Trusting that You will make all things right if I surrender to your will, so that I may be reasonably happy in this life and supremely happy with you in the next.

Amen[1]

Sample Prayers

Most 12-Step groups use the Lord's Prayer—sometimes called the Model Prayer.

Read the Lord's Prayer, which appears in the margin. Below write the words from the prayer that express the following elements:

praise _____

petition _____

thanksgiving _____

confession _____

Prayer is not a formula. The elements of praise, petition, thanksgiving, and confession are not always a part of every prayer. Our compulsive, addictive thinking wants a nice neat formula to "get it right." After all, we believe the things we do must be perfect. When we pray, whether our prayer is from a prayer book or from our thoughts, we need to let it be from the heart. Openness, honesty, and directness are the necessary vehicles for a meaningful relationship with God, just as they are necessary for meaningful relationships with others.

The "Serenity Prayer" summarizes the very heart of the recovery process. Usually, 12-Step groups only use the first part of the Serenity Prayer. In the margin you will find the entire prayer as Reinhold Niebuhr originally wrote it.

Explain why the Serenity Prayer is so valuable for those of us recovering from addictions.

_____

_____

_____

The prayer asks God's aid with issues related to boundaries. So much of our recovery deals with knowing and taking responsibility for things which are our business while we allow others to be responsible for their own behavior.

The AA statement of Step 11 says ". . . praying only for knowledge of His will for us and for the power to carry that out." Jesus taught us to pray, "Thy will be done." One expansion of the Steps says, "seeking His wisdom and power to live according to His will as He reveals it to us."

Why is praying for God's will so important for our continuing recovery?

_____

_____

_____

You may have answered the question in any of a number of ways because God's will is such a central issue of recovery. Since addiction grows out of self-will, we daily place our will under God's authority.

Compose a simple prayer of your own. Think about the typical elements of prayer (praise, petition, thanksgiving, confession) and use the example of the Lord's Prayer and the Serenity Prayer.

_____

_____

_____

_____

Key Concept for Lesson 1
The essence of prayer is a loving relationship with God.

> But seek first His kingdom and His righteousness; and all these things shall be added to you.
> —Matthew 6:33

The Step memory verse appears in the margin. Repeat Matthew 6:33 three times. What does God promise if we seek first His kingdom?

_____

Name at least one thing God wants you to do in response to this study. Ask Him for the grace to help you do it.

_____

_____

LESSON 2

Key Concept:
Meditation means spending time thinking about, contemplating, or pondering the things of God.

Meditation

We seek to know Christ more intimately through prayer and meditation, praying only for knowledge of His will and the power to carry that out.

> _Now we have received, not the spirit of the world, but the Spirit who is from God, that we might know the things freely given to us by God, which things we also speak, not in words taught by human wisdom, but those taught by the Spirit, combining spiritual thoughts with spiritual words._
> —1 Corinthians 2:12-13

Many Christians, concerned about current New Age practices, become suspicious at the mere mention of the word meditation. Modern Western minds may have images of a guru-like person sitting in a cross-legged lotus position and chanting in a monotone. They fail to realize that meditation is a biblical word and concept. Throughout history meditation has been important for great church leaders.

The Bible uses a number of words that mean meditation. Read the following examples. Circle the words in the verses of Scripture that express that particular form of meditation.

Consider. *And the peace of God, which surpasses all comprehension, shall guard your hearts and your minds in Christ Jesus. Finally, brethren, whatever is true, whatever is honorable, whatever is right, whatever is pure, whatever is lovely, whatever is of good repute, if there is any excellence and if anything worthy of praise, let your mind dwell on these things.*

–Philippians 4:7-8

Practice. *The things you have learned and received and heard and seen in me, practice these things; and the God of peace shall be with you.*

–Philippians 4:9

Study and Apply. *Take pains with these things; be absorbed in them, so that your progress may be evident to all.*

–1 Timothy 4:15

You may have circled the words *let your mind dwell*, *practice*, and *be absorbed in*. All of these terms are biblical expressions for meditation. Here is an extended definition for Christian meditation. Meditation is *both a mental and spiritual process of thinking, conversing, planning, anticipating, and reflecting. Meditation is for the purpose of developing and enriching one's spiritual devotion.*

A major difference

A major difference exists between Christian meditation and the meditation of the Eastern religions. Eastern religions originate from a non-personal concept of God. They rely on emptying the mind of conscious thought, because they have no personal God to get to know. In some instances, they entrust their minds to evil spirit-guide counterfeits. Christian meditation is the opposite of its Eastern counterfeit. In meditation we seek to develop a deeper understanding of and personal relationship with the true God who really exists. Don't be surprised that Satan would crudely copy and misuse God's useful, peaceful, and holy gift of meditation. Don't be discouraged from reclaiming your spiritual heritage of meditation.

Elements of Effective Meditation

Meditation will allow you to develop a clearer understanding of and deeper relationship with God. Pray before beginning any contemplative activity. Pray for guidance, wisdom, and peace as you meditate.

You will find the greatest value in meditating on Scripture. If possible, memorize the Scripture passage so you can recall it and reflect on it at any time. Focus your thoughts on certain parts of the passage as you create a mental picture. Reflect using all of your senses—seeing, hearing, tasting, smelling, and touching— as you do the activity. Ask questions about the passage, formulate answers to related problems or needs, and commit to apply or use what you have learned.

Commit to apply or use what you learn.

Using Psalm 1, try the following exercise. Use the resources of your mind and spirit in thinking, feeling, imagining, talking to others and to yourself. If as you meditate you need to complain to God, pour out your complaint to Him—with worship, spiritual insight, or solving problems as your goal.

To meditate on Psalm 1, find a quiet place to sit and relax. Begin with the following prayer.

Lord Jesus, I want to grow in my relationship with You by meditating on Your Word in these moments. As I meet with You in this way, I pray that I may receive wisdom and power to carry out Your will and plan as You reveal them to me. Help me to be nourished and refreshed by Your Spirit during this meditation. Draw me closer to Yourself. In Your Name, Lord Jesus, I pray. Amen.

Begin by slowly reading the passage aloud. Highlight or circle words which, for whatever reason, may stand out to you.

[1]Blessed is the man who does not walk in the counsel of the wicked or stand in the way of sinners or sit in the seat of mockers. [2]But his delight is in the law of the Lord, and on his law he meditates day and night. [3]He is like a tree planted by streams of water, which yields its fruit in season and whose leaf does not wither. Whatever he does prospers. [4]Not so the wicked! They are like chaff that the wind blows away.[5]Therefore the wicked will not stand in the judgment, nor sinners in the assembly of the righteous.[6]For the Lord watches over the way of the righteous, but the way of the wicked will perish.

–Psalm 1, NIV

Think about the phrase *counsel of the wicked*. Counsel means to teach by asking questions and allowing others to draw the conclusions that the counselor wants the counselee to draw.

What are you doing when you *walk in the counsel of the wicked, stand in the way of sinners*, or *sit in the seat of mockers*?

_____

_____

What are some of your feelings as you think about these things?

_____

_____

Apply the Word when you meditate. When have you found yourself *walking in the counsel of the wicked, standing in the way of sinners* or *sitting in the seat of mockers*? How did the Word affect you?

_____

_____

Delight in the Lord

Read verse 2. What would your life be like if you really delighted in the law of the Lord—if your greatest desire was to please and honor God out of a sense of love and delight?

_____

_____

Imagine yourself as a *tree planted by streams of water*. In what way will you be like that tree when your delight is in the law of the Lord?

_____

_____

In verse 4, chaff refers to unusable husks of grain, such as wheat, which are separated from usable grain during threshing and winnowing (beating the grain out of the husk, and then blowing off and scattering the unusable hulls by letting the wind carry it away). Imagine as best you can the threshing and winnowing process. Write down why you think the psalmist uses this as an illustration of what happens to the wicked.

_____

_____

Therefore the wicked will not stand in the judgment, nor sinners in the assembly of the righteous. For the Lord watches over the way of the righteous, but the way of the wicked will perish.

–Psalm 1:5-6

In your own words write verses 5 and 6. _____

_____

_____

_____

What good counsel does this passage provide as a strategy for you to use in your life?

_____

_____

_____

More about Bill

Working the Steps radically changed Bill's prayer life. Once he had difficulty praying because he felt that God was cruel and critical. By working Step 2 Bill is replacing that false concept of God with the holy yet loving God of the Bible. Before Bill worked the Steps, guilt overcame him during times when he attempted to pray. Thoughts of things he had done wrong haunted him. By working Steps 4 and 5 and Steps 8 and 9, Bill began to feel and experience the forgiveness and cleansing he previously only believed in his head.

As Bill grows in his sense of acceptance, he is growing in his ability to love and trust God. He said, "I used to think of prayer as a duty that I must perform. Now I find myself actually wanting to take time to spend with God, and that is something I thought never would happen."

Key Concept for Lesson 2
Meditation means spending time thinking about, contemplating, or pondering the things of God.

Review today's lesson. Name at least one thing God wants you to do in response to this study. Ask Him for the grace to help you do it.

_____

_____

_____

Practice Matthew 6:33—your memory verse for this Step. Use the verse as the basis of a prayer to the Father. For example, you may want to thank Him for His promise in the verse, to ask Him to help you to abide in Him, or to praise Him for His faithfulness to answer prayer.

Select two or three verses upon which to meditate this week. Commit to spend a minimum of five minutes a day in contemplation with God. Do this either after your prayer time or at some other time during the day. Keep a journal of thoughts you have as you meditate.

LESSON

3

God's Word and Obedience

We seek to know Christ more intimately through prayer and meditation, praying only for knowledge of His will and the power to carry that out.

> *I will meditate on Thy precepts, And regard Thy ways. I shall delight in Thy statutes; I shall not forget Thy word.*
> —Psalm 119:15-16

Key Concept:
Building relationships takes time, effort, and commitment.

Meditation

For the non-Christian, meditation is a human attempt to get in contact with an unknown. For the believer, meditation is a discipline of getting to know and obey the God we know and who knows us.

Christian meditation centers on God's Word. In the last lesson you studied prayer, our communication with God. We are ready to examine God's communication with us through His Word.

As you look at the verses appearing at left and find reasons to study God's Word, respond to the questions appearing in the margin.

The grass withers, the flower fades, But the word of our God stands forever.
—Isaiah 40:8

From reading in Isaiah 40:8, what can you count on to endure in your

life? _____

From reading Isaiah 40:8, what can you count on never to fail?

_____

All Scripture is inspired by God and profitable for teaching, for reproof, for correction, for training in righteousness; that the men of God may be adequate, equipped for every good work.

–2 Timothy 3:16-17

From reading 2 Timothy 3:16-17, name several things God's Word can do in your life:

_____

_____

_____

For questions 1 and 2, you may have answered God's Word or the Bible. For the last question, you may have answered teaches, trains, corrects, equips, and makes us adequate. The passage below describes a wonderful attitude we can have about studying God's Word.

O how I love Thy law! It is my meditation all the day. Thy commandments make me wiser than my enemies, For they are ever mine. I have more insight than all my teachers, For Thy testimonies are my meditation. I understand more than the aged, Because I have observed Thy precepts. I have restrained my feet from every evil way, That I may keep Thy word. I have not turned aside from Thine ordinances, For Thou Thyself hast taught me. How sweet are Thy words to my taste! Yes, sweeter than honey to my mouth! From Thy precepts I get understanding; Therefore I hate every false way. Thy word is a lamp to my feet, And a light to my path.

–Psalm 119:97-105

Does Psalm 119 describe the attitude you have about God's Word?
Yes   No

Explain _____

_____

Would you like to love God's Law in the way the psalmist describes?
Yes   No

Explain _____

_____

Remember that victorious living is largely a learned, practiced habit. We learn to exercise faith in God, to love Him, and to obey Him.

Stop and pray, asking the Spirit of God to build faith in you through His Word.

Obedience

And Samuel said, "Has the LORD as much delight in burnt offerings and sacrifices as in obeying the voice of the LORD? Behold, to obey is better than sacrifice, and to heed than the fat of rams."

–1 Samuel 15:22-23

As we mentioned earlier, we can't hope to obey God without knowing His commands. Our goal in Christian living is not perfection. We progress in our relationship with God as we practice obeying Him in our daily lives.

From the passage appearing in the margin it is better to—

do great things for God, or
obey God's words.

We can agree that Samuel would say obedience is better (answer 2). We by no means imply that we are saved or lost by whether we obey. Jesus Christ has paid for our sins, averted for us the wrath of God, and made us dear, beloved children of God. We want to grow in obedience for another reason. He is worthy of our obedience! He is Lord! He truly is excellent, and He deserves our affections and our efforts. As Christians, we have the unspeakable privilege of representing the King of kings. We can do this effectively for eternal purposes only as we allow the Holy Spirit to teach and guide us through prayer and personal Bible study. Let's look at some ways we can make learning and following a part of our daily routine.

Unspeakable privilege

Getting Started

Many of us are eager to know the Scriptures. We even may envy those who can rattle off verses at the mention of any given topic, but we often don't do anything about this desire to know. Instead, we may be intimidated by the number and complexity of the Scriptures.

Two tips for personal study are 1) get started and 2) ask the Holy Spirit to teach you and help you understand what you read. Read on a regular basis. You may start with the Book of Matthew and read one chapter each day until you get to Mark and then continue through the four Gospels and the New Testament until you finish. Then turn to Genesis and read through the Old Testament, or start again with Matthew and reread the New Testament.

Do not hurry or rush your way through. The point of reading is learning, not finishing. Why? So you can begin to apply God's truths to your life. You may want to join a Bible study so that you will have some accountability for reading and studying. Join a study such as *Step by Step Through the Old Testament* and *Step by Step Through the New Testament*. Some Bibles offer a format for reading through the Scriptures in a year. The Bible often becomes more meaningful for us when we have something for which to look. Here are some ideas for ways to study the Bible personally.

- **Attributes of God.** We have given you some of these already. Many others exist. Look for them as you read, and write them in a notebook.
- **God's commands.** Learn God's commands in order to fulfill them. As you read, you may want to ask the Holy Spirit to call your attention to His commands and then ask God's help to keep them.
- **God's promises.** The Scriptures contain thousands of God's promises for us. He is faithful to accomplish them in His time. Sometimes we want Him to fulfill a promise on our schedule and according to our wishes, but He always does what is best for us. He never breaks one of His promises. Read these and underline in your Bible those that mean the most to you. Try to memorize some so that you will know them when you need them.
- **God's warnings.** What warnings from God do you need to read and then heed? Watching for them and absorbing them is another way to study His Word effectively.
- **Word studies.** Take a word in one passage and compare it to other passages using the same word. An example of this is the word *shepherd* in Psalm 23. How does this passage use it? How do other Scripture passages use it? Does it always mean the same?
- **Character traits.** Who were the great leaders in the Bible? What were they like? What were their assets? weaknesses? What do you learn from them?

God never breaks one of His promises

- **Asking questions.** You may want to personalize your reading by asking, "In what ways has God demonstrated His love to me?" Or, in the case of a word study, "In what ways has God been a shepherd to me?" Or, "Am I acting as a shepherd to God's people?"

> **From the list you just read pick out at least three new ways you would like to study God's Word. Write them here. Add any other ideas God brings to mind.**

> _____

> _____

> _____

> **Now write on a card the methods you have chosen. Place the card in your Bible. The next time you read God's Word, use the card as a reminder to look for these things in God's Word.**

These are a few of the many possibilities for personal study. Use any method you like, but above all, get started.

Making Time for God

Earlier, we mentioned that an obstacle to our personal relationship with God is T-I-M-E. Many of us resist approaching God because we feel like we owe Him a large chunk of our time. We do owe everything to God, but truthfully, He is delighted with any effort we make to spend time with Him, especially if it means having to say no to something else to keep the appointment. These are some suggestions for pursuing time alone with God:

- **Start slowly, but be consistent.** Each day at first you may want to spend 10 minutes with God. You can read five verses of Scripture and spend the rest of your time in prayer. The point is: do it regularly.
- **Make an appointment and keep it.** Set aside a regular time reserved specifically for you and God.
- **Find a quiet place.** If necessary take the phone off the hook. Choose a time when you will be free of interruptions.
- **Ask the Holy Spirit for help and guidance.**
- **Remember that every relationship takes time.** God knows this more than anyone else. As you continue to grow in Him, you will find yourself wanting to spend more time with Him.

> ┌───┐
> **Key Concept for Lesson 4**
> Building relationships takes time, effort, and commitment.
> └───┘

> **Please pray and ask God how this concept can apply in your life. Now review this lesson. What has God shown you that can help you?**

> _____

> _____

Step Review

Please review this Step. Pray and ask God to identify the Scriptures or principles that are particularly important for your life. Underline them. Then respond to the following:

Restate the Step in your own words: _____

_____

_____

What do you have to gain by practicing this Step in your life?

_____

_____

Reword your summary into a prayer of response to God. Thank Him for this Step, and affirm your commitment to Him.

_____

_____

_____

Memorize this Step's memory verse:
But seek first His kingdom and His righteousness; and all these things shall be added to you.

–Matthew 6:33

Notes
[1]Reinhold Niebuhr, "The Serenity Prayer," (St. Meinrad, IN: Abbey Press)

STEP **12**

12. Service

We reach out to others in and with His healing love and grace.

Assisting Others

NO SECOND-CLASS BELIEVERS

When Denise first entered recovery, she heard several persons tell how God transformed their lives through a dramatic spiritual experience. As she worked her program, she kept asking, "When will my moment happen? When will God transform my life?" One night when she heard a speaker at a meeting address that very issue, she felt great relief.

The speaker explained the difference between what she called a spiritual experience and a spiritual awakening. "Some people have a dramatic experience at Step 3," she said. "Bill W., the co-founder of Alcoholics Anonymous, was like that. He had a spiritual experience that freed him from the overpowering compulsion to drink." She said that most people have a slower spiritual awakening. They work the Steps and learn to trust God one day at a time. Then one day they realize that their lives have been changed. They can't name a time, but somewhere between the decision in Step 3 and the portion of Step 12 which reads "having had a spiritual awakening," God has changed their lives. "Now here is the important part to remember," the speaker said. "One type of experience with God is not better than the other. The person who has the spiritual experience at Step 3 still needs to work the rest of the Steps. God gives to each person the type of experience he or she needs to grow."

Denise left that meeting walking on air. She always had felt like a second-class Christian, with a second-class recovery as well. Now she realized that what God was doing in her life was as valid and valuable as what He did with anybody, anywhere. (Read more about Denise on page 211).

Step 12   *Having had a spiritual awakening, we try to carry the message of Christ's grace and restoration power to others who are chemically dependent and to practice these principles in every aspect of our lives.*

Memory verse   *God was in Christ reconciling the world to Himself, not counting their trespasses against them, and He has committed to us the word of reconciliation. Therefore, we are ambassadors for Christ.*

–2 Corinthians 5:19-20

Overview for Step 12

Lesson 1: A Spiritual Awakening
    Goal: You will describe two types of spiritual transformation.
Lesson 2: Sharing the Message
    Goal: You will prepare to share your recovery testimony and your testimony of faith.
Lesson 3: Practicing the Principles
    Goal: You will practice applying the Steps to a life situation.
Lesson 4: Where Do I Go from Here?
    Goal: You will identify resources for continued growth.

A Spiritual Awakening

Having had a spiritual awakening, we try to carry the message of Christ's grace and restoration power to others who are chemically dependent and to practice these principles in every aspect of our lives.

> *Go home to your people and report to them what great things the Lord has done for you, and how He had mercy on you.*
>
> –Mark 5:19

Key Concept:
Not all spiritual transformations are alike, but a spiritual change is essential to recovery.

All of these are the work of one and the same Spirit, and he gives them to each one, just as he determines.
–1 Corinthians 12:11, NIV

You just read part of Denise's story on page 206. Her story is typical of what happens in many people's lives.

Compare the story about Denise with the message of 1 Corinthians 12:11, which appears in the margin. The Scripture passage speaks about spiritual gifts. It says that the Holy Spirit gives different individuals different gifts as He chooses. Check the best summary of Denise's story.

Everyone must have the same spiritual experience.
People who have dramatic experiences or gifts are more spiritual.
If my experience is gradual, I must be doing something wrong.
God works with every person as a unique individual.
Even those who have a dramatic experience need to mature.
Other _____

Don't attempt to have someone else's experiences.

Your spiritual awakening began when you asked Jesus Christ to be the Savior and Lord of your life—for many people this occurs in Step 3. Your experience may have been dramatic or very simple. Your experience with God may have begun long before your chemical dependency or your recovery began. In that case, you may see your recovery as God's caring for you because you are His child. On the other hand, your experience with God may have begun when you started your recovery. In that case your spiritual awakening included your new birth experience. Certainly the passage from 1 Corinthians teaches us that God works with His children as individuals. In the same way you may have chosen either of the last two summaries of the story in the exercise, or you may have written your own. The key is to reject the first three answers. Don't attempt to have someone else's experience.

Two Models: Experience and Awakening

These two models exist for our relationship with God and for our recovery. As you consider whether your recovery has been more of an experience or an awakening, remember that neither model is "best." They are different, and each model has a danger.

What might be some dangers of having the "dramatic spiritual experience" type of recovery?

_____

_____

What might be the dangers of having the "slow spiritual awakening" type of experience?

_____

_____

_____

Possible dangers

You may have additional insights into the two models. You may have answered that the dramatic experience might result in pride. It might lead you to try to force others into the same mold and to have little patience with those whose experience was different than yours. It also might lead you to think that you have arrived after Step 3 and that you have no need for the other Steps. The slow awakening model might lead you to put yourself down, to feel that you are less worthy than others, or to give up too quickly.

Has your relationship with God been more of a dramatic spiritual experience or the gradual spiritual awakening?

_____

Sharing Recovery

commission–n. authority to act for, in behalf of, or in place of another (Webster's)

ambassador–n. an authorized representative or messenger (Webster's)

God created you in His own image. God is loving and giving and reaches out in love to you without trying to control or manipulate you. It follows, then, that you will be healthiest and happiest when you are involved in reaching out in ministry to others, without trying to manipulate or control them to meet your own needs. The goal of that new beginning is to accept the **commission** of God and to become willing to care for others and reach out to them as God cares for you. Your commission is from God Himself, who gave you the ministry of reconciliation, committed to you the message of reconciliation, and appointed you as an **ambassador** of His kingdom (2 Corinthians 5:18-20).

We are not perfect, so we cannot expect to live perfectly or give infinitely to others. By now we are all too aware of our limitations and failures. Even our best efforts will save no one. We can help some people because of—and possibly in spite of—our weaknesses. Learning the delicate balance between healthy service and compulsive attempts to change others is difficult if our lives have been governed by the people-pleasing and manipulative tendencies of addiction.

Living in humility

Living in balance means learning humility by recognizing our limitations and trusting God to meet our needs. We no longer have to search for purpose, worth, meaning, and security through dependent relationships, career, performance, compulsions, addictions, or causes.

Proclaiming His Excellencies

Your past and your personality are uniquely yours and can be used for God's glory. God has called you to share Him with others. His Spirit enables you to influence those around you. Your influence can last for all eternity. You have the ability to see the world's spiritual poverty through God's eyes and to offer God's magnificent solution.

But you are a chosen people, a royal priesthood, a holy nation, a people belonging to God, that you may declare the praises of Him who has called you out of darkness into His wonderful light.
                    –1 Peter 2:9, NIV

Go therefore and make disciples of all the nations, baptizing them in the name of the Father and the Son and the Holy Spirit, teaching them to observe all that I commanded you.
                    –Matthew 28:19-20

According to 1 Peter 2:9 printed in the margin, what is the goal of being specially chosen by God?

_____

Peter said that God's purpose was that we declare God's praises. We have the privilege and the responsibility to tell others about the marvelous things God has done in our lives.

Read Matthew 28:19-20. As you yield your life to Him and to the truth of His Word, what does Christ want you to do?

_____

_____

How does your understanding about the lost condition of those who do not have Christ affect your desire to share your faith?

_____

_____

How do you feel about sharing your hope when you think about the painful slavery those with addictions experience?

_____

_____

Key Concept for Lesson 1
Not all spiritual transformations are alike, but a spiritual change is essential to recovery.

Pray and ask God how this concept can apply in your life. Now review this lesson. What has God shown you that can help you?

_____

_____

_____

Specially commissioned

By the authority of Christ Himself, you have been commissioned to carry the message of His peace to all who struggle with life's complexities. This includes those who are chemically dependent. You are one of His ambassadors.

In prayer, accept your personal commission to represent Christ among the people you know. Do not worry about how you'll do it, or even if you can do it. Leave those details to God. Tell Him you are willing. Rest in faith that He will give you the confidence you need. Thank Him for trusting you with such an awesome and wonderful responsibility.

LESSON 2

Sharing the Message

Having had a spiritual awakening, we try to carry the message of Christ's grace and restoration power to others who are chemically dependent and to practice these principles in every aspect of our lives.

> *But sanctify Christ as Lord in your hearts, always being ready to make a defense to every one who asks you to give an account for the hope that is in you, yet with gentleness and reverence.*
>
> –1 Peter 3:15

Key Concept:
I have the privilege and the responsibility to share both my recovery and my faith.

An ambassador represents his or her country. In the same way, you represent the kingdom of God and the One who called you into the freedom you now experience. You have the privilege of sharing with others how they can become free. Helping others is, in part, the telling of a story. The story tells about your progress toward health through the power of Christ.

In Step 3 we described the decision to turn our lives over to Jesus Christ as our Lord and Savior. That Step also applies to our repeated decision to turn over to Christ the details of our lives—especially our addictions. In this lesson we will examine how to share the message. Many people need the message that Jesus Christ is the answer to their drug addiction. Everyone needs the message that Jesus Christ is the answer to our sin problem. We who are in a Christ-centered recovery process have a unique opportunity to share both messages.

A unique opportunity

Your Recovery Testimony

Below you'll find an outline to help you organize your testimony to transmit effectively the message to others. Fill in the appropriate details, and use this outline as a guide to help you tell your story.

What was your life like before you began recovery? Describe how you thought, felt, and acted. You may want to use additional paper.

_____

_____

_____

_____

_____

_____

_____

_____

How did you begin to realize that you had an addiction?

_____

_____

_____

_____

Describe what made you reach out for help.

_____

_____

_____

_____

Describe how God changed your life through the recovery process.

_____

_____

_____

_____

How is your life different now than it was before you began working the Steps?

_____

_____

_____

_____

By writing down some of the many changes that have occurred in your life since you entered recovery, you are gathering some good material to share with those who are new to the program. The Scriptures give many helpful hints for successful sharing. Here are two; see if you can find others.

Brethren, even if a man is caught in any trespass, you who are spiritual, restore such a one in a spirit of gentleness; each one looking to yourself, lest you too be tempted. Bear one another's burdens, and thus fulfill the law of Christ.

–Galatians 6:1-2

Read Galatians 6:1-2. How would you try to restore in a "spirit of gentleness" another person with an addiction to alcohol or other drugs? List several different possibilities.

_____

_____

_____

Many ways exist to help restore addicts. You may have listed such actions as sharing your story with the person, taking the person to a meeting, assisting with a group or treatment center, or asking a pastor or counselor to facilitate an intervention.

Read 2 Thessalonians 3:7-9. Is your example to others as important as what you say to them? Below explain your thoughts.

_____

_____

_____

_____

For you yourselves know how you ought to follow our example; because we did not act in an undisciplined manner among you, nor did we eat anyone's bread without paying for it, but with labor and hardship we kept working night and day so that we might not be a burden to any of you; not because we do not have the right to this, but in order to offer ourselves as a model for you, that you might follow our example.

–2 Thessalonians 3:7-9

Dangers of helping

Denise had been in recovery for five months when someone asked her to visit the local high school and to speak to a support group of young people with addictions. Still unsure of her own confidence, yet wanting to help, she reluctantly agreed. As she shared her story, she felt many emotions return even though she hadn't had them for months. At first it was just annoying. Then as some of the high-school students shared their recent experiences, Denise began to feel very uncomfortable. She began to put herself into many of the experiences they shared. She secretly wished she could be the one using chemicals, while at the same time she hated the thoughts she had. She thought about times she enjoyed drinking with friends; she remembered the parties. By the time the support group session ended, Denise was visibly shaken. Yes, she'd be willing to do this again, but next time she'd arrive a little more prepared about what to expect.

What can you do to help ensure that helping another person won't cause a downfall in your recovery? List several possible safeguards.

_____

_____

_____

_____

_____

_____

Helping others without damaging our recovery is a challenge for all of us. We have to learn to care without taking away other people's responsibilities. We can ask ourselves if we are allowing others to make their own choices.
- Am I feeling their feelings for them?
- Am I continuing to work my own program?
- Am I becoming exhausted or resentful about time I spend "helping" others?
- Am I "window shopping on evil" by watching what others do—and secretly wishing I could participate?

In the margin write the names of people you would like to invite to your 12-Step group and with whom you could share your recovery testimony.

Your Christian Testimony

You have the opportunity to share your faith.

You not only can share what God has done for you in the area of addiction, you have opportunity to share your faith. To prepare to share your faith, use an outline similar to the one you used to describe your recovery. The easy-to-remember outline is: 1) what my life was like before I met Christ, 2) how I began to realize that I needed Christ, 3) how I received Christ, and 4) what my life is like now. Don't use religious or "churchy" language. Write your testimony. Then share it with your sponsor and possibly with your pastor. Enlist their aid to help you make it as clear and understandable as possible.

What my life was like before I met Christ—(Hint: think of what motivated you to trust Christ. You may write something such as "I was fearful, lonely, or lacked purpose." You may need to use additional paper.

_____

_____

_____

_____

_____

How I began to realize that I needed Christ—

_____

_____

_____

_____

How I received Christ—(Hint: People don't automatically understand what *receiving* Christ means. Explain how you prayed to ask Christ to forgive your sins and to come into your life.)

_____

_____

_____

_____

_____

Specific changes

What my life has been like since receiving Christ—(Hint: Don't paint a false picture of living "happily ever after." What are some specific changes Christ has made in your motivations, relationships, and behavior? How does He strengthen you in your troubles and encourage you in your times of depression?)

_____

_____

_____

_____

_____

_____

_____

If you were of the world, the world would love its own; but because you are not of the world, but I chose you out of the world, therefore the world hates you. Remember the word that I said to you, "A slave is not greater than his master." If they persecuted Me, they will also persecute you; if they kept My word, they will keep yours also.
–John 15:19-20

As you experience the joys of encouraging others who struggle with chemical dependency, and as you mature in your relationship with God, you will begin to feel like sharing His transforming love and power with those who are outside the program. The urge to share what you feel is the work of the Holy Spirit. Out of fear of rejection, you may shy away from this responsibility. In the Scripture appearing at left, Christ warned that just as He was rejected, you may face rejection, also. If you take a stand for Him, we assure you that at least some people will reject you and Christ.

What a comfort to know that the Father accepts you in spite of others' rejection! Jesus said that the reason others reject you is because you are His and because He chose you. Almighty God has chosen you! He has made you new, set you apart, and reconciled you to Himself. You are special to Him, even though the world may not be too thrilled with your commitment to Christ.

Sadly, we often forget that we are special and chosen. At times, we wish we belonged to the world. When we are faced with the choice of being rejected for taking a stand for Christ or going along with the world, we may feel that it is easier to choose the world.

The fear of rejection is great, but God has provided a solution to the fear of rejection! We no longer have to accept the opinions of others as the basis of our significance. Instead, the love and acceptance of the infinite, Almighty God frees us to live for Him. We can step out in faith and lovingly tell people about Christ's offer of forgiveness and healing.

Read Acts 1:8 and answer the following questions.

But you shall receive power when the Holy Spirit has come upon you; and you shall be My witnesses.

–Acts 1:8

What is your personal role in evangelism? _____

_____

What is the Holy Spirit's role in evangelism? _____

_____

God always provides the resources for the tasks He calls you to do. His Spirit will give you the power to share your testimony effectively and to overcome the fear of sharing. Your job simply is to tell the story—what you've seen, heard and experienced through His healing touch. Do not worry if others reject the message; your role is not to change other people but to share what God has done in your life. As in a courtroom, the witnesses give the testimony and the lawyers argue the case. Never confuse the two—you are His witness.

Your role is not to change other people but to share what God has done.

In the margin write the names of people with whom you could share your Christian testimony.

The following list provides some practical ways you can share the message of Christ's saving and healing power with those who are chemically dependent. Add your own ways to it. Look for opportunities to use them.

Ways to Give the Message of Hope to Those with Addictions

- Become a sponsor of someone in recovery.
- Volunteer to assist in an existing support group.
- Volunteer to start a support group at your church.
- Volunteer to help in a Christ-centered 12-Step group.
- Volunteer to help in an outpatient clinic for chemical dependency.
- Share your story with groups or individuals when they ask.
- Give your testimony in a church service.
- Provide your church staff with materials on chemical dependency.
- Encourage the distribution of information on chemical dependency through your employee benefits program at work.
- Write a book or a collection of your own experiences.
- Pray—encourage others to pray—for people in recovery or who need recovery.

Key Concept for Lesson 2
I have the privilege and the responsibility to share both my recovery and my faith.

Pray and ask God how this concept can apply in your life. Now review this lesson. What has God shown you that can help you?

_____

_____

_____

In prayer, thank God that all the struggles and pain of your past were not wasted. They can be used to instruct and encourage others. Ask Him for opportunities to share your experiences and your faith. Watch for His divine appointments to share His comfort and peace to plant the seeds of victory in the lives of others.

<table>
<tr><td>

LESSON
3

</td><td>

Practicing the Principles

</td></tr>
</table>

Having had a spiritual awakening, we try to carry the message of Christ's grace and restoration power to others who are chemically dependent and to practice these principles in every aspect of our lives.

> *So that you may walk in a manner worthy of the God who calls you into His own kingdom and glory.*
>
> *–1 Thessalonians 2:12*

Key Concept:
God continues to transform my life as I walk in His principles.

The final Step begins with the words, "Having had a spiritual awakening." Because we have followed these biblical principles, God has changed our lives. Some see a dramatic change, while others struggle with what seems only slight progress. Our experience encourages us to promise you that these Steps lead to change. The challenge is to continue in this change by practicing the Steps in all areas of our lives.

Practicing the Principles

Many times when we encounter problems, stressful situations, or painful, traumatic events, God not only helps us get through them, He often uses those circumstances to give us much better circumstances and surroundings than we had before. Unfortunately, even when the results are positive, we may remain bitter or continue to harbor resentment because the "bad guy" didn't get punished. We may continue to be angry about how the negative circumstances came about, or we may find many other ways to remain "peevish." Sometimes we feel like we're getting hit by more than we can stand and certainly by more than we deserve.

Sometimes we feel like we're getting hit by more than we can stand.

Practicing the 12-Step principles means incorporating those principles into our thoughts and behaviors every day. It means admitting our powerlessness in difficult situations. It means believing and trusting God to take care of the things we cannot. It means turning our situations and ourselves over to Him, and it means continuing to take our inventories, make our amends, and deepen our relationship with God.

> **As you read the following story, think about how you could use the Steps to deal with—or lessen the impact of—the events described.**

A very bad day

You leave the house for work in the morning, only to find that the car won't start. After multiple attempts to start the car, you finally run the battery down, so you have to call a taxi. When you arrive late at work, you discover that the boss has called an emergency meeting of all the employees. As you walk into the meeting, everyone turns to stare at you, and you wonder if you forgot to zip or button something. The boss announces that the company will lay off half of the workers at the end of the week.

When the meeting is over, you stumble to your office where you find a note from the mechanic stating that your car requires several hundred dollars in repairs. You also find a note from your child's teacher that your child has been disruptive in class. You stay very late at the office. A longtime friend who happened to be in town wanted to come by your house to see you, but you didn't have time. Then, just when you thought it couldn't get any worse, one of your old buddies from your using days stops by and invites you to party. You rush to the telephone to call your sponsor. Your sponsor answers the telephone, "Yesh? Whoosh disss?" By the slurred speech you can tell that your sponsor has been drinking.

How do you feel? And what do you do if this happened to you?

Think of the formula for the first three Steps—*I can't. God can. I think I'll let Him.* How would you apply Step 1 to the situation?

_____

_____

_____

How would you apply Step 2? _____

_____

_____

How would you apply Step 3? _____

_____

_____

Beyond your control

Apply the "Serenity Prayer" to the above situation (see page 196). What aspects of the situation are the "things you cannot change"?

_____

_____

_____

_____

You probably identified a number of things in the situation that were beyond your control—your co-workers' attitudes and actions, your boss' behavior, even whether you will continue to have a job. You now know that you have the option of believing God and turning those items over to Him.

What things can you change? _____

_____

_____

You may have identified only one thing you could change in the story. You could change your attitude toward all the horrible things that were going on.

Work the Steps

List principles from other Steps which also apply to the above situation, and describe how they might apply.

_____

_____

_____

_____

_____

_____

You could—cautiously here, without beating up on yourself—inventory your own behavior to see if you contributed to the problem. You definitely could use some prayer and meditation to cope with the situation. You might even remind yourself, "At some time in the future this is going to be a great illustration for leading a meeting on the topic of coping with stress."

Obedience As the Way of Joy

When we travel from state to state on the highway, we find different traffic laws for different types of terrain, conditions and types of roads, various sizes of towns, and many other circumstances. We follow these laws, not because we want to appease someone's need to control us, but because our safety and well-being, as well as that of all others on the road, are at stake.

He gives His commands for our good.

This illustrates the authority of Jesus. We do not earn His favor by our obedience (we already have His favor!). Rather, we submit to His authority and obey Him because He gives us His commands for our safety and sanity and for the safety of others.

The 12 Steps provide a framework—a guide—for life and health in Jesus Christ. He is the source of health. The 12 Steps point toward Him. We can help others in their spiritual awakening, but He alone is the One who saves. In our helping, we both draw the attention of others to Him and experience the strength and health God gives as we reach out in His love to others.

Pray for at least one person today who is struggling with an addiction or who is in recovery. If you haven't already done so, make yourself available to that person.

Look at the course map again and see where God is taking you in your road of recovery. Take a moment to reflect on each of the 12 Steps, and thank God for being there with you each step of the way.

Step 1: Admit powerlessness.
Step 2: Come to believe in Him.
Step 3: Turn our lives over to His management.
Step 4: Courageously make an inventory of our lives.
Step 5: Confess our sins to Him and to another person.
Step 6: Allow Him free rein in changing the patterns of our lives.

Step 7: Seek Him to renew our minds and transform us.
Step 8: Face the wrongs we have committed against others and become willing to make amends.
Step 9: Make amends.
Step 10: Continue to take inventory.
Step 11: Grow in relationship with God by prayer, meditation, and Bible study.
Step 12: Reach out to others in and with His healing love and grace.

Key Concept for Lesson 3
God continues to transform my life as I walk in His principles.

Pray and ask God how this concept can apply in your life. Now review this lesson. What has God shown you that can help you?

_____

_____

_____

_____

LESSON 4

Key Concept:
Discipleship is a lifestyle.

Where Do I Go from Here?

Having had a spiritual awakening, we try to carry the message of Christ's grace and restoration power to others who are chemically dependent and to practice these principles in every aspect of our lives.

I have no greater joy than this, to hear of my children walking in the truth.
3 John 4

Denise, the sponsor

By the time Denise completed the written work on Step 12, she understood that the Steps are a lifelong process. She learned some principles and developed disciplines that she will be practicing for the rest of her life. She knew the process was not over, but she felt a little let down and bewildered. For months she had practiced the daily discipline of writing in her 12-Step workbook. For months she had met regularly with her sponsor. Now she felt a sense of accomplishment for her efforts, but she wondered to herself, "Where do I go from here?"

Denise's feeling is common to those who complete their initial Step work. Now when Denise sponsors another person through the 12 Steps, she is sensitive to the question, "What's next?" She has begun to provide some suggestions. This final lesson in *Conquering Chemical Dependency* will share some of these resources.

Think about areas for continued growth in your life. On the list below check your top three priorities.

___ Understanding the Bible
___ Memorizing Scripture
___ Developing my prayer life
___ Building witnessing skills
___ Changing unhealthy relationships
___ Knowing God's will
___ Becoming a disciple maker
___ Caring for the physical needs of your body
___ Other _____

Remember that character development and spiritual growth are not instant. Things that are worthwhile take time.

> And do not get drunk with wine, for that is dissipation, but be filled with the Spirit.
> –Ephesians 5:18

Ephesians 5:18 reflects a helpful comparison. Getting drunk, using chemical substances to medicate our emotions, or any other addictive behavior does something for us. The immediate payoff is relief. The problem is that the benefit is temporary and destructive. Spiritual growth gives the benefits but without the destructive side effects. Spiritual growth does for us in a healthy and Christ-honoring way what our addictive behaviors did for us in an unhealthy way.

Spiritual growth

Denise has learned that she does not "complete" the 12 Steps. What she does is continue her spiritual growth. She continues to work the Steps, especially Steps 10, 11, and 12. She simply expands those Steps to include additional actions to improve her understanding of God's will, her prayer life, her discipleship. She may choose to go through the 12 Steps again, or she may want to pursue other concepts in her growth.

The following resources all are written in the interactive format you have used as you studied *Conquering Chemical Dependency* and intended for group study. They can help you to continue working Steps 11 and 12. Determine the particular area in which you need to grow, then choose one or more resources to help you. They will encourage you to continue your spiritual growth.

To build your self-worth on the forgiveness and love of Jesus Christ:
• *The Search for Significance*, by Robert S. McGee, Continues the work of replacing the four false beliefs with the principles from God's Word. *The Search for Significance* expands upon some of the work you have done in *Conquering Chemical Dependency*. (Houston: Rapha Publishing), product number 0805499903; Leader's Guide, product number 080549989X.

To identify and replace codependent behaviors:
• *Conquering Codependency: A Christ-Centered 12-Step Process*, by Pat Springle and Dale W. McCleskey. The learned perceptions and behaviors called codependency—a compulsion to rescue, help, and fix others—often add to our addictive behaviors. *Conquering Codependency* applies the 12 Steps to these habits. (Houston: Rapha Publishing), product number 080549975X; Facilitator's Guide, product number 0805499768.

To deal with painful experiences from your past:
• *Making Peace with Your Past: Help for Adult Children of Dysfunctional Families*, by Tim Sledge. This practical, biblical study guides you to identify,

understand, and come to terms with the feelings and problems of growing up in a dysfunctional family. (Nashville: LifeWay Press), product number 0805499865; Facilitator's Guide, product number 0805499873.

- *Moving Beyond Your Past*: After having come to terms with their past in the course *Making Peace with Your Past*, participants in this course focus on the present. From a biblical perspective, this course guides participants to move beyond the hurts of the past into joyful day-to-day living. (Nashville: LifeWay Press), product number 080549927X; Facilitator's Guide, product number 0805499555.

To understand God's will for your life:
- *Experiencing God: Knowing and Doing the Will of God*, by Henry Blackaby and Claude V. King. Find answers to the often-asked question, "How can I know and do the will of God?" This study helps Christians discover God's will and obediently follow it. (Nashville: LifeWay Press), product number 0805499547; Leader's Guide, product number 0805499512.

How can I know and do the will of God?

To help you grow in your prayer life:
- *Disciple's Prayer Life: Walking in Fellowship with God*, by T.W. Hunt and Catherine Walker. This course helps adults learn to pray through experiences based on prayers of the Bible. Its sessions offer practical experiences that strengthen and deepen prayer lives and help churches develop an intercessory prayer ministry. (Nashville: Convention Press), product number 0767334949.

To help you know more about the Bible:
- *Step by Step Through the Old Testament*, by Waylon Bailey and Tom Hudson. This self-instructional workbook surveys the Old Testament, provides a framework for understanding and interpreting it, and teaches Bible background. (Nashville: Convention Press), product number 0767326199; Leader's Guide, product number 0767326202.

More about the Bible

- *Step by Step Through the New Testament*, by Thomas D. Lea and Tom Hudson. This 13-unit self-instructional workbook surveys the New Testament, provides a framework for understanding and interpreting the New Testament, and teaches Bible background. (Nashville: Convention Press, product number 0805499466; Leader's Guide, product number 0767326210.

To help you learn how to disciple others:
- *MasterLife: Discipleship Training*, by Avery T. Willis, Jr. This six-month in-depth discipleship process for developing spiritual disciples and leaders trains persons to help carry out Christ's vision to make disciples of all nations. For more information contact Customer Service Center at 1-800-458-2772; FAX (615) 251-5933; email customerservice@lifeway.com or visit our Web site at www.lifeway.com/discipleplus.

To help you grow in developing a healthy lifestyle:
- *Fit 4: A LifeWay Christian Wellness Plan* addresses all four areas of life—heart, soul, mind, and strength. This wellness plan blends taking proper care of your body, being devoted to God, and maintaining healthy relationships with family, friends, and others. For more information contact Customer Service Center at 1-800-458-2772; FAX (615) 251-5933 or visit the Web site **fit4.com**.

Give Jesus first place in your life.

Step Review

Please review this Step. Pray and ask God to identify the Scriptures or principles that are particularly important for your life. Underline them. Then respond to the following:

Restate Step 12 in your own words: _____

_____

_____

What do you have to gain by practicing this Step in your life?

_____

_____

_____

_____

Reword your summary into a prayer of response to God. Thank Him for this Step, and affirm your commitment to Him.

_____

_____

_____

_____

_____

_____

_____

The Twelve Steps of Alcoholics Anonymous*

1. We admitted we were powerless over alcohol—that our lives had become unmanageable.

2. Came to believe that a Power greater than ourselves could restore us to sanity.

3. Made a decision to turn our will and our lives over to the care of God *as we understood Him.*

4. Made a searching and fearless moral inventory of ourselves.

5. Admitted to God, to ourselves, and to another human being the exact nature of our wrongs.

6. Were entirely ready to have God remove all these defects of character.

7. Humbly asked Him to remove our shortcomings.

8. Made a list of all persons we had harmed, and became willing to make amends to them all.

9. Made direct amends to such people wherever possible, except when to do so would injure them or others.

10. Continued to take personal inventory and when we were wrong promptly admitted it.

11. Sought through prayer and meditation to improve our conscious contact with God *as we understood Him*, praying only for knowledge of His will for us and the power to carry that out.

12. Having had a spiritual awakening as the result of these steps, we tried to carry this message to alcoholics, and to practice these principles in all our affairs.

*From *Alcoholics Anonymous*, 3d ed. (New York: World Services, 1976), 59-60. The Twelve Steps are reprinted here and adapted on the following pages with permission of Alcoholics Anonymous World Services, Inc. Permission to adapt the Twelve Steps does not mean that AA has revised or approved the content of this workbook, nor that AA agrees with the views expressed herein. AA is a program of recovery from alcoholism. Use of the Twelve Steps in connection with programs and activities which are patterned after AA but which address other problems does not imply otherwise.

The Christ-Centered 12 Steps for Chemical Dependency

Step 1

We admit that by ourselves we are powerless over chemical substances—that our lives have become unmanageable.

Step 2

We come to believe that God, through Jesus Christ, can restore us to sanity.

Step 3

We make a decision to turn our will and our lives over to God through Jesus Christ.

Step 4

We make a searching and fearless moral inventory of ourselves.

Step 5

We admit to God, to ourselves, and to another person the exact nature of our wrongs.

Step 6

We commit ourselves to God and desire that He remove patterns of sin from our lives.

Step 7

We humbly ask God to renew our minds so that our sinful patterns can be transformed into patterns of righteousness.

Step 8

We make a list of all persons who have hurt us and choose to forgive them. We also make a list of all persons we have harmed, and we become willing to make amends to them all.

Step 9

We make direct amends to such people where possible, except when doing so will injure them or others.

Step 10

We continue to take personal inventory, and when we are wrong, promptly admit it.

Step 11

We seek to know Christ more intimately through prayer and meditation, praying only for knowledge of His will and the power to carry that out.

Step 12

Having had a spiritual awakening, we try to carry the message of Christ's grace and restoration power to others who are chemically dependent and to practice these principles in every aspect of our lives.

CPSIA information can be obtained at www.ICGtesting.com
Printed in the USA
LVOW03s1129060214

372617LV00001B/25/P